D0205535

The Politics of a Literary Man

William Gilmore Simms
By courtesy of South Caroliniana Library
University of South Carolina—photo circa 1859

T.

The Politics of a Literary Man:
William Gilmore Simms

JON L. WAKELYN

CONTRIBUTIONS IN AMERICAN STUDIES

NUMBER 5

GREENWOOD PRESS, INC.

Westport, Connecticut   London, England

Library of Congress Cataloging in Publication Data

Wakelyn, Jon L
   The politics of a literary man.

   (Contributions to American studies, no. 5)
   Bibliography: p.
   1. Simms, William Gilmore, 1806-1870—Political and
social views. 2. Southern States—History—1775-1865.
I. Title.
PS2853.W33   818′.3′09   72-845
ISBN 0-8371-6414-1

Library of Congress Catalog Card Number: 72-845

ISBN: 0-8371-6414-1

First published in 1973

Greenwood Press, Inc., Publishing Division

51 Riverside Avenue, Westport, Connecticut 06880

Manufactured in the United States of America

For Catherine Carl Wakelyn and Thomas Stirton

Contents

Acknowledgments

THE MOST pleasant task of any author is to acknowledge the many people who have helped in his endeavor. Without the fervent eye of the librarians and archivists, most historians would flounder through their documents. My thanks go to Mrs. Clara Mae Jacobs and to Mr. Les Inabinett of the South Caroliniana Library at the University of South Carolina. The staffs of the South Carolina Historical Society, the Charleston Library Society, the Southern Historical Collection at the University of North Carolina, the Duke University Library, and the Library of Congress have been gracious and helpful.

Members of the scholarly community encouraged and at times raged at this work, but they were of great help throughout its progress. Professors John C. Guilds, Jr. and John R. Welsh, and Mrs. A. D. Oliphant shared with me their wisdom of years of acquaintance with the subject of Simms. Although they disagree with some of my views, Professors William H. Freehling and C. Hugh Holman were careful critics and perhaps saved me from some errors of declaration. Tom Stirton encouraged this work from the beginning, and Nathan Smith helped keep it going. Frank Vandiver deserves special thanks. He not only read and criticized a much earlier version of this work, but he encouraged the years of additional research and read successive versions with the eye that a great instructor

saves for his students. His confidence in the merits of Simms
and his own scholarly work and sensitivity served as inspiration
for me.

Thanks are also due to the National Endowment for the
Humanities for a generous summer stipend and to Rice University for a research grant.

Last of all and most important, in all candor, without the
sacrifice of her time and the efforts of my wife Catherine, this
work would hardly have the form it has today. Still, any errors
of omission or style belong entirely to the author.

Introduction

ON DECEMBER 20, 1860, South Carolina's political and social leaders, meeting in convention, voted unanimously to secede from the Union. Shortly thereafter, six other Southern states joined South Carolina in forming the Confederate States of America. If South Carolina was the catalyst for the other states, how it achieved such a consensus becomes an important question for those who study the causes of the Civil War.[1] Since much of the scholarly work on South Carolina's role in secession has concentrated on economic and political factors (including work on the structure of leadership), the unanimity of secessionist sentiment, particularly as it reflected the state's cultural life, has rarely been discussed. Beginning with Rush Welter's premise that "if intellectual history has meaning, it is because men acted in the light of their thoughts as well as their interests or emotions," I have sought to study the intellectual life of antebellum South Carolina in hopes of shedding some light on how that state achieved such unity of thought in the thirty vital years before secession.[2]

Pursuing the intellectual's role in political activity, I finally settled upon one representative figure who so dominated South Carolina culture that his name became synonymous with dedication and loyalty to the sectional image. The public career of William Gilmore Simms presents an excellent opportunity to study the intellectual's place in politics. As the most prolific novelist, magazine, and newspaper editor of his generation, Simms provides an extraordinary example of the uses of literature for propagandistic purposes. As a student of political theory and an active politician, Simms also demonstrates the vulnerability of a sensitive artist self-condemned to public service. His sense of public obligation grew as the South came closer to secession. Simms reflected and helped to direct the growing secessionist impulse, and at the same time was under extreme external and internal pressure, in terms of the influences of the South on his public behavior. Whether Simms was forced to conform or whether he helped to create an aura of conformity in the South is not a viable question. Simms chose to live in the South, and his career reflected the turmoils of an intellectual who had close local attachments and loyalties.

Analyzing the effect of a man of letters upon his time and his time upon his work is an unfamiliar task for a historian. Especially is it difficult in the case of Simms because of the many important, but in my opinion misleading, works on his career. Ever since the study by William P. Trent and the perceptive analysis of Vernon Louis Parrington, the puzzle of Simms' career has been why a man with such talent was unable to produce a major piece of American fiction. Trent and Parrington have judged Simms to have been the victim of an aristocratic and overbearing South Carolina intellectual elite. As a poor boy, Simms sought recognition and status. They maintain that he conformed to the outward literary norm and forever sacrificed his art to that need. Although the status question should be put to rest (Simms was obviously a respected member of the low-country aristocracy), John Higham continues to see Simms' active career as that of a political opportunist, oppressed by internal intellectual currents. Yet others, such as C. Hugh Holman and Louis Rubin, who have tried to see Simms in other guise than a victim of status, have wondered what there was in the South that kept Simms from being a great writer. Holman claims that Simms was a professional man of letters who merely happened to live in the South and that his public political life was a sideline to his vocation of writing. Holman believes that if scholars would see Simms as a public man of letters, devoted to creating an American literature, they would realize that Simms had no time to pursue carefully his own muse. Rubin, who also believes that Simms' best work was left undone, sums up the argument by saying that "the conditions of nineteenth-century Southern life did not permit him to cultivate whatever there was of talent with the intense and uninterrupted devotion that makes talent into great literature."[3]

These views that Simms' literary talents were diverted have some merit. But in my estimation a full analysis of Simms' fiction in relation to the rest of his public career should reveal that writing fiction was only part of Simms' public role. Therefore, the question of Simms' failure to become a great novelist has diverted scholars from the true merits of his fiction and the true direction of his talents. Simms was neither an original political theorist nor a first-rate social analyst, although his social and political criticism reveal much about political and social thought in the Old South. Why such a talented man was diverted from more critical writing has as little meaning as why he was diverted from fiction. His thought was part of his public service. If he was diverted from literary or theoretical greatness, it was because he understood that the artist's task was to defend his homeland. He was therefore vulnerable to a peculiar kind of insularity which may have made him feel more important politically than he actually was in fact. Therefore I shall not trouble myself with the failure of Simms' talent, for this question is as misleading today as it was in Simms' own time. Instead, I propose to examine the manner in which Simms used his talent and the motives toward which he was directed.[4]

NOTES

1. See Ralph Wooster, "Membership of the South Carolina Secession Convention," *South Carolina Historical Magazine* 55 (1954): 185-196, and "An Analysis of the Membership of Secession Conventions in the Lower South," *Journal of Southern History* 24 (1958): 360-368. Also see Robert M. Weir, "The Harmony We Were Famous For, an Interpretation of Pre-Revolutionary South Carolina Politics," *William and Mary Quarterly*, 3 Ser., 26 (Oct. 1969): 474-501 (especially 499-501).

2. Rush Welter, "The History of Ideas in America: An Essay in Redefinition," *Journal of American History* 51 (March 1965): 599-614. For the emotions, see Steven A. Channing, *Crisis of Fear* (New York, 1970), *passim*.

3. See William P. Trent, *William Gilmore Simms* (Cambridge, Mass., 1892), pp. 326-331; Vernon Louis Parrington, *Main Currents in American Thought*, 2 vols. (New York, 1954), 2: 119-130; C. Hugh Holman, "The Status of William Gilmore Simms," *American Quarterly* 10 (1958): 181-185; C. Hugh Holman, ed., *Views and Reviews in American Literature, History, and Fiction*, 1 Ser. (Cambridge, Mass., 1962), xxxv-xxxvi; Edgar T. Thompson, ed., *Perspectives on the South: Agenda for Research* (Durham, 1967), pp. 110-111.

4. I do not wish to claim that Simms was not an extremely important romantic novelist. The work of Professors John C. Guilds, Jr., and John R. Welsh on the textual editions of Simms' fiction should resurrect Simms' literary reputation. However, they will have to overcome Hawthorne's verdict that Simms did not grow as a novelist. See Randell Stewart, "Hawthorne's Contributions to the Salem Advertiser," *American Literature* 5 (1933): 330-332. For interesting but limited work on Simms' social and political views, see the essays by William R. Taylor, *Cavalier and Yankee* (New York, 1963), chap. 8, and Clement Eaton, *The Mind of the Old South* (Baton Rouge, 1964), chap. 9.

The Politics of a Literary Man

Prologue: The Formative Years

AS A YOUTH, William Gilmore Simms lived a vicarious life among his books. His father, William Gilmore Simms, Sr., had emigrated from Ireland to Charleston late in the eighteenth century. He had become a prosperous merchant and had married Harriet Singleton, a member of a respected if not affluent Charleston family. She bore her husband three sons, his namesake being born on April 17, 1806. But Harriet was sickly and unable to stand the stress of childbearing. When her first son, John, died in the autumn of 1806, she was distraught and, weakened from a winter illness, she died shortly thereafter in childbirth. The elder Simms, morose and distressed over the loss of his wife, overspeculated in business and soon went bankrupt. Unable to cope with so much personal tragedy, he left young Gilmore with the boy's Grandmother Gates and wandered into the new West, where he became a soldier of fortune and finally a well-to-do planter in Mississippi.[1]

Although his father promised to return for him, it was his grandmother who had the strongest influence on Simms' early childhood. Her first husband's family were Virginia planters who had moved to South Carolina before the Revolutionary War and had become wealthy low-country aristocrats. But the family fortune had slowly dissipated, and Mrs. Gates used what was left for Simms' upbringing. Proper Charlestonian that she was, she stressed to her grandson the importance of upholding the family's name and reputation. Often she filled young Simms' head with stories of adventure and courage from the family's past. Simms' great-great-grandfather, Thomas Singleton, had daringly defended Charleston against the British invaders during the Revolutionary War, and his great-grandfather, John Singleton, had ridden with the famous "Swamp Fox," Francis Marion, and was part of the army which had liberated Charleston.[2] But the elderly Mrs. Gates had little in common with her grandson and often seemed impatient with his lonely, melancholy nature. He would wander through the streets of Charleston and into the nearby woods, musing over the state's past deeds of conquest and settlement. Best of all, he liked to sit on the docks and listen quietly to the many tales of adventure and mystery spun by the sailors who frequented this world-famous seaport.[3]

When Simms was almost ten years old, he was involved in an incident which was to leave a lasting impression on his life. As usual, he had become so immersed in his own thoughts and so mesmerized by the sailors' stories that he forgot the time. Lengthening shadows reminded him that his grandmother would worry if he did not hurry home to supper. Running through the streets of Charleston, he was stopped abruptly by a man dressed in buckskin—quite probably his father's brother. The man told Simms that his father was expecting him in Mississippi. The frightened child screamed for his grandmother. A crowd gathered, and the stranger disappeared. Later there was a custody suit, and the judge allowed Simms to decide whether he would go to his father in the West or remain in Charleston. Simms chose to stay with his grandmother. Years later he regretted the decision, stating that his father's rights had been set aside, "I now think improperly, and as I now believe, to my irretrievable injury in many respects."[4] Charleston was to be his life. What Simms might have become had he emigrated to the Western frontier one can only speculate.

But although he was miles away, the elder Simms influenced his son's childhood. He participated in Andrew Jackson's Florida campaign and sent his son long, thrilling letters about the defense of New Orleans and the campaigns against the Creek Indians. After he had become a successful cotton planter in Mississippi, he attempted to persuade his son to move to the West. Although unwilling to settle permanently in Mississippi, young Simms visited his father. On one trip early in 1825 they traveled into the back country of Louisiana, down to New Orleans, and perhaps even as far as Texas. They hunted and fished, spent hours swapping tales with settlers, and even lived with friendly Indians for a short time. Undoubtedly many of Simms' later realistic descriptions of border existence and his veneration of Jackson resulted from these trips. His father, a poet and amateur musician, wanted his son to stay and cultivate his writing talent through capturing the thrills of the southwestward migration. He promised him a fortune from cotton, a vigorous law practice, and even a seat in Congress. But young Simms soon wearied of the frontier and longed to return to the civilization and sophistication of Charleston, his home and place of destiny.[5]

If Simms' father and grandmother both encouraged his early writing and provided many of his later literary themes, it was Charleston, together with the old-line Federalists who dominated its literary scene, that molded the young author's early views. Charleston exuded culture, tradition, snobbishness. With its old-world charm, lush gardens, and beautiful homes, its sense of its own past importance and perhaps its destiny, the city epitomized the life of culture and urbanity that Simms sought to create for himself. A center of intellectual excitement, ideal for a young man with literary ambitions, the city and its leading men of letters took Simms into their midst as a worthy successor to their conservative tradition. He was their eager pupil, joining them at the new and provocative openings of the Broad Street Theatre, reading and discussing their editorials and reviews in the city's newspapers and literary magazines, and participating in the many discussions held at the Charleston Library Society. Simms practically lived at the library, a private center of culture, with holdings of over twelve thousand volumes and subscriptions to all of the literary and political periodicals from England and the great Northern cities.[6]

Many of Charleston's writers, editors, and artists took an interest in the early literary efforts of the intense and talented young man. Long discussions with the portrait painter Charles Fraser about the details of characterization undoubtedly influenced Simms' later meticulousness in character description. He became friendly with the poets William Hayne Simmons and Henry Tudor Farmer, who criticized his work and included him in the many plans for continuing the city's high literary attainment. Simms also cultivated the acquaintance of frequent visitors and new residents of the cosmopolitan seaport, especially those interested in writing. One such visitor, the famous New England physician and man of letters James G. Percival, for a time practiced medicine in Charleston. He often discussed the nuances of style and meter with Simms, who had become a medical assistant because his grandmother felt that he should have some professional career. Both men were more interested in pursuing their muses than in seeing patients or studying medical cures. They became such good friends that when Simms started his literary career, he traveled to New Haven for Percival's advice.[7]

The young writer also knew the city's Jeffersonian liberals, including Judge William Smith and Isaac Harley. Harley, who was forced to give up his newspaper and move North in 1824, also dabbled in literature and Republican politics. An important influence on Simms' public career was the splendid craftsman and book-binder William Henry Timrod, father of the Civil War poet. Timrod, a minor poet who wrote mediocre blank verse, encouraged Simms' early efforts as Simms would later encourage the younger Timrod. A staunch Republican, the elder Timrod was a veteran of the Seminole War and, like Simms' father, talked often of his hero, Andrew Jackson. Suspicious of politicians because of the Washington politics that had almost destroyed Jackson's career, Timrod imparted his distrust of political leaders to Simms. Years later Simms wrote that, "freed from the necessity of manual labor, and with proper culture, Mr. Timrod might have taken high rank" in the field of literature.[8] Undoubtedly Timrod's lower-class status and lack of formal education had marked him in the snobbish environment of Charleston as a mechanic for life. Timrod's plight was indeed a lesson for the young and ambitious writer.

Perhaps the most important influence on Simms' early career were those Charleston intellectuals who took an active part in public life. He studied with and probably did some research for William Rivers, the early historian of South Carolina. Rivers in return instructed Simms in the political uses of history. Above all, Simms kept close watch over the editorials of the Charleston newspapers. He realized that powerful public figures like Jacob N. Cardoza, Henry Laurens Pinckney, and William Crafts were also the city's newspaper editors. Simms particularly admired Crafts, the editor of the Charleston *Courier*. This lawyer, minor poet, and frustrated Federalist office-seeker provided Simms with an excellent example of a useful literary career combined with public service, and he set out to emulate Crafts. But Simms also observed that Crafts attempted to lampoon his way into public life by poking fun at the world of Jeffersonian liberalism from an old-fashioned, anti-democratic, pro-Federalist point of view.[9] Crafts failed to gain office because he opposed the tide of change. Simms' own experience in politics would drive this lesson home.

Not all of the young writer's time was spent in the idle pleasure of learning his craft. Simms met and fell in love with the frail, blue-eyed daughter of a city clerk, Anna Malcolm Giles. Planning marriage, he severed his ties with medicine and entered professional training as an apprentice lawyer with Charles R. Carroll, a young attorney with an interest in literature. Not a serious student of the law, Simms nevertheless avidly read Blackstone, briefed cases, and generally learned the trade, yet continued to devote most of his time to writing poetry. As a matter of fact, Simms' first poem, a tribute to the late Revolutionary hero and Federalist leader Charles Cotesworth Pinckney, was published while he was working for Carroll. The privately printed poem betrayed the crude style of the young enthusiast, but it set a pattern for Simms' later work. His career had begun on a note of hero-worship and praise of the past glories of South Carolina. The poem won Simms some attention from the city's leading literary figures and certainly diverted his mind from any interest in the law.[10]

Still, after a trip to see his father in Mississippi, the young apprentice lawyer returned to Charleston determined to become a successful attorney. Having completed his studies with Carroll, Simms married Anna on October 19, 1826, seven months short of his twenty-first birthday. Since he was still too young to practice law, he returned to his writing. Schemes of an epic poem and the chance to edit his own literary journal lured Simms away from the Charleston bar. He undoubtedly would have been a good lawyer, but his true mission lay elsewhere, and he never really tried to make a living from the law.[11] Between 1827 and 1829 Simms published three volumes of poetry and two literary journals. While his work was not particularly noted for its beauty or its genius of style, it illustrated—even at this early stage—the uses to which Simms would put his literature.

Simms' early work contained a series of paradoxes which reflected why his later career has been so difficult to understand. As a nationalist he praised the South Carolina legislature for appropriating ten thousand dollars for a memorial to Thomas Jefferson as a great American, but his enthusiasm was tempered by a deep pride in Jefferson's accomplishments as a Southerner. He wrote of the national effort in defeating the British, yet he singled out the heroic Revolutionary defense of Charleston by the young women of the state. Even while dwelling on a theme of national pride, Jackson's victory at New Orleans, Simms pointed out the significance of Southerners fighting in the South under a Southern leader for a national cause.[12] Simms tried to strike a balance between nationalism and sectionalism by insisting that the South had to have freedom in order to love the nation and join in its destiny. Despite his role in secession, Simms throughout his career bore a deep love for his country; but his early poetry demonstrated that his loyalty to South Carolina and the South overrode his feelings for the nation.

For all of his attention to democratic themes and his later interest in the common folk, Simms' earliest poetry was dominated by a cult of hero worship, as he usually concentrated on men whose lives were examples of a certain aristocratic daring. Simms wished to create heroes who were both interesting and educational. In one of his poems he made a romantic martyr out of an Indian warrior, King Philip, yet he lamented the waste of this leader's energy on a lost cause. Likewise in Benedict Arnold he discovered a personality ripe for both invective and romance. Forever cursed in history for betraying his country, Arnold exemplified frustrated ambition to Simms. (He would later sympathize even more with Arnold's frustrations.) He found the life of Alexander the Great useful for romantic poetry, not for his military victories, but for his ability to unify and govern a nation. Simms was also fascinated with the early history of the American settlement and used the career of Hernando Cortes as a theme for much of his writing. Again, Cortes became the symbol, not of heroic deeds, but of the selfless, loyal sailor who was never appreciated in his native land. The young poet wrote often about Jefferson who was hardly stuff of which heroes were made. But Simms grasped the importance of Jefferson's ability to win battles and converts, not with the sword, but with the gift of literary expression.[13]

Most of all, as one who has visited Charleston might surmise, the past fascinated the young man, and historical themes dominated his poetry. Simms was a researcher who always tried to be certain about his facts, and who constantly used incidents from the past as specific examples for the present. He sketched sacred Indian customs, such as the Green Corn dance, from his own notes taken during Western travels. He wanted to preserve Indian traditions, but at the same time he was intrigued by the internal migration into the Southwest, where civilization had destroyed the beauties of unspoiled nature and necessitated the end of the proud Indian heritage. He questioned the white man's cruelty toward the Yemassee Indians and damned his people for blighting the beautiful tribe, yet he wrote in practical terms of the importance of westward settlement. Glorifying the adventure of exploration into the unknown and attempting to recreate the past deeds of Southern pioneers, he romanticized and often fantasized on the value of nature as a purifier for the white man. Yet the West had also proved to be a place for the adventurer and the speculator, a paradise for the ambitious.[14]

Simms was particularly fascinated by the distant past of his own home state. The heroics of settlement along the Ashley River and the founding of his beloved Charleston provided themes for his writing. But his glory in Charleston's past was tempered because the city had become "some Eastern city of the dead" through its inability to cope with changing times. He considered his poetry practical criticism as he wrote of past glories merely to spur a restoration of commercial power and thus restore the city's proper leadership of Southern society.[15] In his poems on Charleston's past grandeur and the history of the new West, Simms was trying to come to grips with his own heritage and to provide for his own destiny. He had the sense of wanderlust, but at an early age he realized his obligation to remain in Charleston and to devote his energy to restoring the city's splendor.

Simms' early poetry bore the stamp of an ambitious young man who was exploring the political uses of fiction and looking for a means to sustain himself through his writing. It conveyed the impression that Simms was sometimes torn over his decision to remain in Charleston, often regretting his lonely childhood, but also out for the main chance. Simms seemed to know that, for his own sins of pride and vanity, he was condemned, like Cain, to wander in search of a meaning for his own existence. His early poetry also revealed his desire to make a political and literary reputation and to rise to power in Charleston society. Thus it was not surprising that young Simms traveled in the city's elite intellectual circles and that the dedications of his poems were fraught with political significance. *The Vision of Cortes* was dedicated to his close friend, the future unionist James L. Petigru, and the *Early Lays* to the prominent young lawyer, Charles R. Carroll. Even *Lyrical and Other Poems* was initially designed as a study of Congressional politics but was later changed to sectional political themes because of Simms' growing dislike of national political corruption. Simms knew that a sectional propagandist, who instructed the state to learn from its past, could be useful to the state's leaders and thus secure a powerful position in South Carolina politics.[16]

Besides the volumes of verse, the young Simms began a career as editor which would teach him more about the importance of literary politics. His first venture into editing was the *Album*, which ran for six months in 1825. Only nineteen at the time, Simms had few backers and seemed to use the magazine mainly as a means of publishing his own poetry. Still, through twenty-six issues he managed a degree of humor, encouraged many other young Charleston writers, and began to formulate his own views on the value of sectional literature and the importance of local themes. His plan to establish a means of developing the raw literary talent of Charleston failed, since the *Album* was unable to attract enough subscribers to make it profitable. Yet he learned something about the politics of editing, as he received many primitive poems and illogical articles. Sometimes he would edit the pieces, and at other times he would completely rewrite them, but mostly Simms had to send diplomatic letters of rejection.[17]

The *Album* also revealed Simms' early feeling for politics, Charleston society, the problems of the Southern economy, and the pitfalls of trying to please each subscriber. In the first number, Simms wrote that politics, although secondary, would have an effect on his magazine. He predicted that because of the depression in cotton prices, affecting planter and merchant alike, the *Album* would never have enough paying subscribers to survive. Beyond this joke lay a sense of his section's economic plight and a deep understanding of the problems of placing so much material emphasis on the one-crop system. He accused his fellow Carolinians of misunderstanding their own political interests, while at the same time he described how all Charleston had talked learnedly of the benefits of the last presidential election. If he realized nothing else, the young editor was convinced of the need for understanding national and local politics, and he was prepared to use his journals to reflect the importance of politics for Carolinians. Simms also learned, at least temporarily, that there was a fine line between caution and pandering. By trying to please everyone, he pleased no one.[18] His next editing venture showed the search for his own style and a willingness to be frank and opinionated in his editorials and selection of materials.

In June 1828, Simms proposed another literary periodical, *The Tablet: A Weekly Literary Gazette*. With his partner, James W. Simmons, another young poet, Simms began to raise funds and solicit contributors. Planned as a vehicle for Southern writers, as the intensely chauvinistic prospectus in the Charleston *Courier* shows, *The Tablet* was never published. Instead, the magazine appeared under the title of *The Southern Literary Gazette*, a monthly publication which began in early September 1828. By March 1829, after months of frustration, Simmons was broke and sought employment elsewhere. Trying to edit the *Gazette* alone, and with a wife to support, Simms realized that there was no living then to be made in periodical literature. His second venture in editing was also a financial failure, although Simms undoubtedly learned more about the potential value of periodical literature.[19]

While it lasted, the *Gazette* was a lively magazine, intensely nationalistic and Anglophobic. Simms wanted another revolution, this time a cultural revolution which would forever separate American writers from the burden of English literature. As editor of the *Gazette* he appealed to writers to seek a national identity by creating a distinctly national literature. He urged them to use native themes, especially from the many interesting events of the past, and to record the language indigenous to the American people. As a practical man of letters he realized the importance of founding American publishing houses, even if Congress had to subsidize them. Although himself heavily under the influence of European writers, Simms sought to clarify the importance of a uniquely American literature. In his opinion, the literary character of a people "depends upon their manners and civil institutions," and for the United States to develop as a democratic society, it was necessary to overcome "those rank prejudices" which so dominated the aristocracies of Europe.[20] Early in his career, Simms was beginning to appreciate the propagandistic, if not therapeutic, qualities of literature. His fiction would always reflect society as he understood it and always help to unite a people, whether it be the nation or the South.

Even in 1828, Simms' national chauvinism was tempered with some jealousy of the North's superior position in the nation. Aware that Southern writers were neither respected nor often published in the North, he wanted the *Gazette* to publish only Southerners, writing on Southern subjects, and he called for a publishing house in Charleston. Localism was the trademark of the *Gazette*. Simms reviewed mostly Southern writers and wrote long articles on the Charleston theater. He even went so far as to praise the romantic philosophers at South Carolina College, who continued to teach metaphysics in an age which was moving toward inductive methods. Simms also turned to a study of the slave system, a volatile topic even before nullification times, as an important subject for Southern periodical literature. His *Gazette* essay on slavery betrayed the problems of an ambitious young man of principle—a loyal Southerner who was nevertheless seeking a way to support the rise of republicanism. Realizing that the slave system seemed hypocritical to a democratic society, and that most Southerners vigorously supported slavery, Simms sought a way out of the dilemma. Following the views of many objective Charlestonians, he believed that returning the Negro to Africa would provide the solution.[21] But the colonization movement was on the wane and, if Simms wished to remain useful to his section, he knew he had best avoid the subject. Thus his national feelings were compromised early in his life.

After the *Gazette* failed, a close friend, the printer and sometimes publisher James S. Burges, persuaded Simms to edit his magazine, *The Pleiades, a Weekly Literary Gazette*. But the *Pleiades* failed after only one issue, and Simms returned to his small law practice, hoping to use the legal profession as an entree into local politics. He actively supported Thomas Smith Grimké for mayor of Charleston in 1829. A member of a respected Federalist family, the Unionist Grimké was running against Henry Laurens Pinckney, the powerful editor of the Charleston *Mercury* who favored a low tariff, state rights, and nullification. Although he believed in the inevitable rise of republican government, Simms nevertheless sought to align his political future with the low-country aristocracy. He wrote speeches and actively campaigned for Grimké's election. But the mayoral election became a bitter contest as national issues, centering around a state's constitutional right to nullify a federal law, superseded local concerns. Pinckney trounced Grimké, and Simms began his political career by supporting a losing cause.[22]

Simms had ventured into politics at the expense of an already languishing law practice. He realized that writing and editing were probably better for his public career than the pursuit of the law. When E. Smith Duryea, a printer and fellow literary entrepreneur, offered to join him in purchasing the floundering Unionist newspaper, the Charleston *City and Carolina Gazette*, Simms quickly abandoned his law practice. They bought the paper on December 31, 1829, renamed it, and the first issue of the *City Gazette and Commercial Advertiser*, with Simms as editor, appeared on New Year's Day, 1830. Simms planned to continue the paper's Unionist tradition and promised to oppose the radical Pinckney and his nullificationist paper.[23] His long, varied, and active career in public life had begun.

NOTES

1. Although Simms left some autobiographical sketches in letters and manuscripts, much of his childhood is clouded by lack of documentary evidence. See Mary C. Simms Oliphant, Alfred Taylor Odell, and T. C. Duncan Eaves, eds., *The Letters of William Gilmore Simms*, 5 vols. (Columbia, S. C., 1952-1956), 1: 160-161 (hereafter cited as *Simms Letters*); *William Gilmore Simms, A Sketch, Read at a Meeting of the Alumni Society of the Memminger High School*, March 6, 1895, p. 1, MSS, Charles Carroll Simms Papers, South Caroliniana Library, University of South Carolina; William Peterfield Trent, *William Gilmore Simms* (Boston, 1892), pp. 1-5. For a view of Simms' father differing from Trent, see Joseph V. Ridgely, *William Gilmore Simms* (New York, 1962). Mrs. Oliphant believes that Simms' father and maternal grandmother had significant influence on Simms' early life. I shall attempt to sustain her view. See Mrs. A. D. Oliphant, "William Gilmore Simms —Historical Artist," *Report of the Secretary and Treasurer for 1942, University of South Caroliniana Society* (Columbia, 1943), pp. 18-19.

2. *Simms Letters*, 1: 160-161; C. Hugh Holman, "William Gilmore Simms' Picture of the Revolution as a Civil Conflict," *Journal of Southern History* 15 (February 1949): 446-447.

3. William Gilmore Simms, *Poems, Descriptive, Dramatic, Legendary and Contemplative*, 2 vols. (New York, 1853), 2: 119.

4. *Simms Letters*, 1: 161; *Simms, A Sketch*, p. 1.

5. There is some controversy as to how many times Simms traveled in the West. At least two are documented, the trips of 1825 and 1831. See Hampton M. Jarrell, "Simms's Visit to the Southwest," *American Literature* 5 (1933): 29-35; *Simms, A Sketch*, p. 2; Oliphant, "Historical Artist," p. 19.

6. Simms' relation to the South Carolina intellectual elite is best documented in his own studies of the early national literature of Charleston. See *The Nineteenth Century*, July

1869-May 1870, especially July 1869, 1, no. 2: pp. 135-136, 138-139; Aug. 1869, 1, no. 3, pp. 169, 177; Sept. 1869, 1, no. 4: 273, 275-280. Also see Trent, *Simms*, pp. 6-7.

7. *The Nineteenth Century*, Sept. 1869, 278, 279, 281; Oct. 1869, 1, no. 5: 335-338, 339; Feb. 1870, 698-700, 920-922. Trent, *Simms*, p. 13.

8. *The Nineteenth Century*, Feb. 1870, 695-696.

9. See files of Charleston *Courier* (1815-1824); *The Nineteenth Century*, Feb. 1870, 697-698; Oct. 1869, 342; May 1870, 923. For a short sketch of the Charleston intellectual circle, especially William Crafts, see Vernon Louis Parrington, *Main Currents in American Thought*, 2 vols. (New York, 1954), 2: 107-109.

10. "William Gilmore Simms' First Poem—on C. C. Pinckney," *The New York Historical Society Quarterly Bulletin* 25 (Jan. 1941): 26-27; Trent, *Simms*, p. 14. Trent mentions Anna Giles, but there is little available information on her.

11. *Simms Letters*, 1: 162; William Gilmore Simms, *Lyrical and Other Poems* (Charleston, 1827), "Letter to the Public," pp. 5-6; Oliphant, "Historical Artist," p. 20.

12. William Gilmore Simms, *Early Lays* (Charleston, 1827), pp. iii-iv, viii. In his introduction Simms gave some clues to the paradox of his love for country and loyalty to section. He was chauvinistic enough to believe that the United States could have a distinctive literature, but he also believed that a writer should develop his talents in his native section and draw on themes from his own surroundings. Obviously, this insistence upon local themes must have conditioned the young poet's future loyalties. For a different view, see John C. Guilds, "Simms' Views on National and Sectional Literature, 1825-1845," *The North Carolina Historical Review* 34 (July 1957). Simms, *Lyrical and Other Poems*, pp. 38, 91, 180-181; *Early Lays*, pp. 44-46, 73-75, 87-90.

13. Simms, *Early Lays*, pp. 46, 71-73; *Lyrical and Other Poems*, pp. 14-17, 24, 70-71, 110; William Gilmore Simms,

The Vision of Cortes, Cain, and Other Poems (Charleston, 1829), pp. 7, 8, 44.

14. Simms, *Lyrical and Other Poems*, pp. 8, 26, 43, 74, 163-166.

15. Simms, *Early Lays*, pp. 17-18, 62-64, 65-70, 80-82, 105-108. Simms gave a careful explanation of the value of historical research, pp. 107-108. Also see the poem "Carolinians! Who Inherit!" for Simms' sense of local loyalty. *The Vision of Cortes*, pp. 69-83.

16. Simms, *Early Lays*, dedication, p. iii; *Vision of Cortes*, dedication page, 45-65, 81-83, 135. Also see *Early Lays*, pp. 9-11, 80-82, 95-97; *Lyrical and Other Poems*, pp. 64, 70-71, 134, 190-191, 145-160.

17. *The Album*, 1, no. 8 (Aug. 20, 1825): 61-62, 72; 1, no. 16, (Oct. 13, 1825): 122; 1, no. 22 (Nov. 26, 1825): 177-178; 1, no. 3 (July 26, 1825): 22-23. See also John C. Guilds, "Simms's First Magazine: *The Album*," *Studies in Bibliography, Papers of the Bibliographical Society of the University of Virginia*, 8 (1956): 169-183.

18. *The Album*, 1, no. 1: iv-v; 1, no. 16: 121; Guilds, "Simms's First Magazine," p. 174. Guilds maintains that the *Album* was not political, but I have found much that was political throughout the magazine.

19. *The Southern Literary Gazette*, "Advertisement," 1, no. 1, Sept. 1828; 1, no. 12 (Nov. 1, 1829): 284-286; Trent, *Simms* pp. 49-50, 53-55; William Stanley Hoole, "William Gilmore Simms's Career as Editor," *Georgia Historical Quarterly*, 29 (March 1935), 48-49; Charleston *Courier*, June 8, 1828. If the *Gazette* has little value, its last issue at least clarifies the origin of *Martin Faber*. See "Confessions of a Murderer," *The Southern Literary Gazette*, 1, no. 12, pp. 266-269; also Trent, *Simms* pp. 67-76.

20. *The Southern Literary Gazette*, 1, no. 12: 276-278; 1, no. 1: 3, 7; Guilds, "Simms' Views," p. 395.

21. *The Southern Literary Gazette*, 1, no. 12: 272-275. Simms' own view of philosophy was developing along extremely impressionistic lines. He stated, "Gentlemen, if you have not felt in yourselves, or observed in others, what I am explaining, I cannot make you understand me." Curiously, he also praised Bacon and Locke and thought the inductive method of reasoning quite important. But his career would certainly force him to question the powers of observation. See also 1, July 1, 1829: 93-96; 1, June 1829: 33-34; 1, Aug. 1829: 127; 1, Oct. 1828: 191; 1, Jan. 1829, *passim*; Guilds, "Simms' Views," pp. 398-399.

22. Letter from Grimké to *Niles' Register*, Sept. 4, 1829, explaining his position in South Carolina politics, MSS, Thomas Smith Grimké Papers, South Caroliniana Library, University of South Carolina. See Gerda Lerner, *The Grimké Sisters from South Carolina, Rebels against Slavery* (Boston, 1967), pp. 29, 92-93; William H. Freehling, *Prelude to Civil War, the Nullification Controversy in South Carolina, 1816-1836* (New York, 1966), pp. 180-182. (Freehling is correct about Grimké's open aristocratic pose that certainly alienated many of Charleston's mechanics, but his judgment of the importance of the election as compared to the election of 1830 is not convincing.)

23. Charleston *City Gazette and Commercial Daily Advertiser*, Dec. 31, 1829 (hereafter cited as the *City Gazette*); Charleston *Courier*, Dec. 31, 1829; Hoole, "Simms as Editor," p. 49.

1 Anti-Nullification Newspaper Editor

ENTHUSIASTIC and optimistic about the opportunity to achieve some recognition and power in Charleston political circles, Simms planned to make the *City Gazette* an objective review of the important events of his day. His emphasis on a free and open press was evident in a collection of his poems called the *Tri-Color*, written in praise of the 1830 revolution in France. Simms was most impressed by the role of the Paris press in directing the move toward freedom. Despite censorship and the destruction of newspaper offices by armed militia, French editors had written articles opposing the monarchy and advocating a democratic republic. Scattered throughout the city, often forced to print their papers by hand or even to read them aloud to groups of citizens, they had insisted upon communicating their ideas. An editor was even in the vanguard of the volunteer group of citizens which had hoisted the tri-color over the Tuileries. The young, romantic Simms naively thought he could establish his own editorial position in support of a free and open exchange of ideas in Charleston.[1]

Unfortunately, when Simms became editor of the *City Gazette*, the nullification controversy, which had already been raging in South Carolina for over two years, would soon temper his enthusiasm and cause him to doubt the viability of a free press. Having grown out of a national argument over revenue and the protective tariff system, locally nullification was a squabble among a multitude of varying political factions. Emotions ran high as the opposing forces seemed to merge into two polar groups representing Union and State Rights on the one hand and Nullification on the other. Henry Laurens Pinckney, the newly elected mayor, used the *Mercury* to attack the Union group, claiming that there was a merchant conspiracy in Charleston committed to supporting a high tariff. Pinckney unjustly accused many of the city's important leaders of unequivocal nationalism, when, in reality they were neither nationalistic nor especially interested in a high tariff. Many of the Unionists whom Simms supported were the leading intellectual and political figures in the city, mainly planter-lawyers who had a stake in perpetuating their control of local politics. The Charleston *Courier* bore most of the brunt of Pinckney's attack until Simms turned the *City Gazette* into a Unionist party organ in support of the city's intellectual elite.[2]

But as Simms was soon to discover, local partisan politics were not the primary cause of the nullification controversy. The heated battle over the tariff had originated during the state's steady economic decline during the 1820s and was in part aggravated by the question of the future of slavery in the South. The Panic of 1819 and the Missouri Compromise of 1819-1821 had placed the South at an economic and political disadvantage within the Union. Although few of the nation's politicians saw any danger to the South in the protective tariff system, some of South Carolina's leaders were convinced that a slave-based agrarian economy made the growth of manufacturing almost impossible in the South. Therefore, a protective system would not only raise import prices, but would also force European nations to tax heavily Southern agricultural products. Denmark Vesey's threatened slave revolt in 1822, the growing antislavery stand of the colonization societies, and the fear of an increasingly centralized federal government which might at any time turn against slavery, all fed South Carolina's own economic discontent.[3] The local papers stated that South Carolina's white population was increasing at only one-fourth the average rate of the rest of the nation during the period from

1800 to 1830, and that from 1823 to 1828 there had been a 50 percent decrease in imports into Charleston harbor. Charleston was going broke, and many of its citizens blamed the protective system. South Carolina was losing its young people to the Southwest, and something had to be done.[4]

To add to the confusion over issues, South Carolina's most powerful national leader was put in an equivocal position on the tariff issue. Under pressure from Governor James Hamilton, George McDuffie, and Robert Y. Hayne, all nullifiers, John C. Calhoun was forced to abandon his national career and oppose the Woolens Act of 1827. After conversations with the nullifiers' intellectual leaders, President Thomas Cooper of the College at Columbia and the secessionist "Brutus," Robert Turnbull, he placated them with the anonymous publication of the "South Carolina Exposition," in the winter of 1828. Certain that he could no longer maintain the illusion of nationalism, and hated by President Andrew Jackson, Calhoun secretly began to form his own sectional political party. Although he was a moderating influence among the radicals, he became the leading theoretician and political spokesman of the nullification movement. Within a few short years, Calhoun seized almost complete political control in South Carolina, forever to the detriment of free speech in the state.[5]

Given these issues and events, how could a young and ambitious editor possibly maintain an objective view toward the nation, yet remain loyal to the interests of Charleston and the South? In order to secure a readership and perhaps head off a direct onslaught from the radical *Mercury*, Simms spent the first months of his editorship attempting to explain his political position. He planned to present the *City Gazette* as a nationalist newspaper devoted to the Union but extremely cautious of the reserved rights of states. His first obligation was to the cause of freedom of expression, and free expression meant the right to speak out against the national government's encroachment upon the constitutional rights of South Carolina. However, in 1830 Simms thought that the controversy could be solved without radical actions and that the nation had historical relevance for the South which transcended the petty squabbles over the tariff. He closed an editorial with this warning: "There are some men, who would destroy the body, to preserve a member—we are not of the class."[6]

Fully aware of Charleston's economic difficulties, Simms found the tariff oppressive to the entire state's financial growth. He debated the constitutionality of the tariff system and found it illegal, but he opposed any act by South Carolinians to nullify it. Certain that immediate tariff relief would not help the South's economy, he pointed out the more dangerous problem of the South's increasingly unequal representation in Congress. As long as the rest of the South did not understand the implications of such a weak political position, Simms knew that South Carolina could not leave the Union by itself. The nullifiers' bluster seemed merely to antagonize the other Southern states. While he readily supported "the right to Revolution—a right inherent in, and inseparable from any political society," Simms thought it inexpedient for South Carolina to act alone. The practical editor wondered who would join South Carolina in civil war over a tariff that a Northern-dominated Congress would in any case refuse to rescind.[7]

Therefore Simms began to formulate some means of making the South an equal in the nation, in hopes of moderating the radicals' secessionist plans. Prophetically he said, "There should be no minority in a nation like ours; and where there is, justice can no longer be hoped or looked for, by the body which fails any longer to oppose, by a correspondent balance, the interest which may come in collision with its own."[8] Simms' solution to the problem of balance was to have a Southerner as chief executive of the United States. Although he knew that Andrew Jackson had little sympathy for South Carolina's tariff problems, Simms thought that the "hero of New Orleans" would serve Southern interests in Washington. As a self-styled Southern aristocrat, Jackson would certainly favor the Southern position on other important issues. Settling on executive control as the best means of redress of grievances, Simms was rapidly codifying his own romantic faith in the concept of the hero.[9] He worshipped his father's hero, and throughout his life he searched for men of Jackson's aristocratic bearing to lead the South.

One can imagine Simms' surprise when Pinckney, who had been finding increasing fault with his editorials, claimed that Simms and the *City Gazette* were anti-Jackson and opposed to the democratic spirit. Obviously the *Mercury* editor, realizing that Simms' anti-tariff and practical sectionalist editorials were damaging the nullification movement, thought that an attack on Simms' view of Jackson would hurt the young editor's political position. Simms skillfully replied that the *Mercury* was calling the *City Gazette* anti-Jackson to hide its own desertion of the President. As he pointed out, Pinckney had already denounced Jackson in the South Carolina legislature. This led Simms correctly to predict that the *Mercury*, because of its radical policy, would have to oppose Jackson for reelection in 1832. Simms had also reasoned that the nullifiers believed that their support for Clay in 1832 would assure Calhoun's election to the Presidency in 1836. Positive that Jackson was best fitted to preserve the essential rights of the Southern states, he vigorously attacked Calhoun's "pious crusade." Simms' romantic attachment to Jackson, combined with his practical political knowledge, led him to defend Jackson's administration in order to save the Union. He had maneuvered the *City Gazette* into the envious political position of claiming to serve the idea of democracy while keeping the paper aligned with the aristocratic Unionist leaders of Charleston.[10]

After clarifying his positions on the tariff, the South's place in the nation, the right of nullification, and other national issues, Simms concentrated on the practical politics of the Charleston city elections. Simms' political enemy Pinckney was the mayoral candidate on the State Rights and Jackson party ticket, as the nullifier party preferred to be called. The *City Gazette* took an anti-nullifier position and supported James R. Pringle, the candidate of the State Rights and Union party. Simms claimed that the anti-nullifiers were also staunch Jackson supporters, and he realized that the mayoral election would have statewide if not national significance.[11]

The State Rights and Union party opposed nullification. It

found the tariff system in need of reform but rejected any attempt to determine the constitutionality of the tariff. Pinckney's party supported nullification as the state's only means of demonstrating the tariff's unconstitutionality, and its leaders called for a statewide convention in order to discuss their grievances.[12] The election seemed to hinge on the convention issue, and Simms wrote a scathing editorial in opposition. He was certain that a convention would cause too much excitement, and that the excitement would stampede the state into open defiance of the federal laws. He cautioned Pinckney that "nullification will compel our *Venerable Jackson*, . . . using the strong *Arm* of *Power* to reduce you and your deluded followers to submission." Also, Simms was convinced that, rather than seeking redress of Southern rights, the nullifiers planned to use the convention to create a powerful political party and to destroy any political opposition in South Carolina.[13]

There were bitter accusations on both sides. The *Mercury* launched attacks on Simms' character, branding him vulgar and ignorant, and even questioning his loyalty to South Carolina. Simms countered by calling Pinckney a shabby opportunist who would fail his state in a time of crisis. Although the election seemed secondary to the personal invective, Pringle managed to win by a vote of 838 to 754. Most of the Union candidates for warden were also victorious. Simms was elated. He was convinced that the people of Charleston had chosen wisely; they had supported the security and strength of their country. More important, Simms knew that the majority of Charlestonians had joined him in opposing a statewide convention.[14]

The *City Gazette* had taught the nullifiers that they could not yet control Charleston's politics through a nullification convention. In the fall election for state representatives and senators, the *Mercury* dropped the issue, at least openly. When Richard Cunningham, a prominent lawyer running on the nullifier ticket, defeated James Louis Petigru, the State Rights and Union party candidate for the state senate, Simms claimed that the absence of the convention issue had been the deciding factor. However, eleven out of sixteen Union party candidates won election to the state house of representatives. Also, when the state legislature met in Columbia in December, it failed to produce the two-thirds vote necessary to call a nullification convention.[15] Simms' active support of the State Rights and Union party had not been altogether in vain.

The young editor was elated over his political success, and the *Courier* praised his tenacious opposition to Pinckney. Since his party had been given a reprieve, Simms was sure that a careful reorganization drive throughout the state would give them even more political power in 1831. He hoped to convince the Charleston voters that neither the State Rights and Union party nor the *City Gazette* was submissionist; both would support South Carolina regardless of its ultimate action. But charges that he was a tool of Charleston's aristocracy and that he was himself politically ambitious were made to cast doubt on his true loyalty to the state. Simms wanted political office, but his alignment with the intellectual and aristocratic party of Petigru, Hugh Swinton Legaré, and others was the result of years of working with those men, and it was Simms' firm belief that South Carolina's best means of protecting its interests was to remain in the Union.[16]

Simms' dedication and tenacity as a newspaper editor did not leave him personally unscathed. An exchange of editorials, not political but personal slurs, with Pinckney was no help to his political and social career in status-conscious Charleston. Pinckney's vicious editorials rose above the controversy to concentrate on ruining Simms' political career. He accused Simms of belittling the Irish population of Charleston, supporting colonization for Negro slaves, advocating a high protective policy and submission to Northern aggression, and slandering South Carolina's most honored patriots. All of these allegations were untrue, and Simms correctly stated that Pinckney charged Simms with narcissism and said that Simms was his own worst enemy. "We conceive it, therefore, an essential kindness to the young man himself," said Pinckney, "by a thorough exposure . . . to confirm him, if possible, in the consciousness, he seems evidently sometimes to feel, of his own utter incompetency to political speculations." He gave the young writer "full credit for having much more rhyme than reason in his brains. Let him eschew politics and confine himself to witticisms, poetry (good luck!) and literature for ladies, (girls?) . . ."[17] As his future political behavior illustrated, Simms never completely recovered from such personal vindictiveness.

Smarting from Pinckney's vicious attacks and uncertain as to his own political future, Simms decided to take a trip into the Southwest. His father had recently died, so the young editor went to Mississippi in late winter to settle the estate. During his trip, Simms described his travels in letters which he published in the *City Gazette*. At first his columns reflected his own misfortunes. Filled with melancholy musings, they showed how deeply he resented the Pinckney men of Charleston. Soon, however, Simms began to study the society and economy of the back country. He also stored up many of his experiences and feelings about the West for his later novels. Above all, he gained new insight into the workings of newspaper politics, chronicled Western feelings toward nullification for his home audience, and began to realize just how much the new West meant to the Eastern seaboard.[18]

The young editor not only studied the West's political views toward the East and the nullification controversy, but he also began to understand more about the importance of newspapers for urban life. He went to the newspaper offices in every town that he visited. In Beaufort, South Carolina, he had long talks with John A. Stuart, editor of the *Gazette*, soon to become the influential editor of the Charleston *Mercury*. Simms argued with Stuart over the merits of holding a state convention, and he resented the power Stuart seemed to have in Beaufort with no opposition press to give the townspeople a balanced view of events. In Montgomery, Alabama, Simms saw an old friend, the Charleston nullifier Turner Bynum, who controlled both of that town's newspapers. The lack of objectivity and propagandistic value of Bynum's papers both intrigued and repulsed Simms.[19] He was not surprised to learn that a small Alabama village called Selma had a newspaper completely controlled by local politicians. His analysis of local editorials, long talks with editors, and observations of newspapers' financial difficulties, taught him many lessons about the political significance of a controlled press and the propagandistic usefulness of his own journalistic talent.[20]

Besides being interested in newspapers, Simms also learned much about the relationship of society to the economy in the new West. Visiting Savannah, he found that city's architecture more uniform and classical in style than his own Charleston. But he was more intrigued by the apparent snobbishness of its citizens and disturbed at Savannah's economic decline as a seaport, both of which were similar to Charleston. At the interior city of Augusta, Simms was shocked by the town's prosperity as compared to the east coast. Cotton, the South's staple, was abundant there, and Augusta had doubled in population since his last visit. Because of the rich soil and good river bottom land, Simms observed, there were many prosperous new towns in Alabama. He sensed a spirit of optimism, brought on by the boom times, and was impressed at the growing commercial prosperity of Mobile. He envisioned a Gulf port metropolis with economic ties to the far West luring ambitious young men from the East. Above all, New Orleans, which had grown from a town of 6,000 people in 1825 to a monstrous city of 70,000 inhabitants, both astounded and frightened Simms. He predicted that the "crescent city" would become a seaport larger than New York, and with the opening of the Yazoo purchase, would control the entire Mississippi Valley. Thus Simms chronicled the slow ebbing of his own state's economic power and predicted the shift of Southern society westward, to South Carolina's political detriment.[21]

Although he was fascinated with Western prosperity, Simms remained a Charlestonian writing for Eastern readers, and he also displayed his fears and animosity toward the implications of Western economic success and the status of its society. On his travels through the Yazoo purchase, he waxed eloquent over its untouched beauty, but the sociologist in him tempered his romantic notions. For Simms wondered just what effects so much land might have on the formation of a civilized society. His formalized, hierarchical view of society, a manifestation of his Charlestonian conservatism, balked at the hedonistic freedom of the new West. In his articles he managed to find some praise for the West's republican sentiments, but only by contrasting them with Europe's snobbish aristocracy. Yet he attacked Martin Van Buren's pandering to Western republican sentiment. The Charleston editor also found an overflow of philanthropic ventures in the West and was extremely wary of Westerners who seemed to question the slave system.[22] Throughout his life Simms retained an ambivalent attitude toward the West. He considered it a land of opportunity, yet he disliked the "boomer" mentality. He loved the raw beauty of nature but was concerned over what kind of society such freedom would produce.

Although Simms' trip was a learning experience for him, he soon tired of the West's rude lack of sophistication. After settling his father's estate, he returned to his active and hectic political career in Charleston. Simms seemed to miss the political intrigue of his native city. He had hoped that his absence would calm the arguments between the two parties. But the political struggles in South Carolina were far from over, and Simms was soon in the thick of battle over preparation for the all-important Fourth of July celebration. Pinckney was certain that the Union faction was reviving party excitement in order to divide the city further and secure political domination. Simms countered with the accusation that Pinckney was so politically ambitious that he was blind to the need for a viable two-party system to counteract radicalism. Realizing that both the *City Gazette* and the *Courier* were opposed to his nullification position, Pinckney retaliated wildly, forcing emotions on both sides to a fever pitch.[23]

With tempers flaring in the awesome summer heat, the Fourth of July celebrations were designed to mitigate violence by appealing to a common heritage. Especially did the Union and State Rights party determine to demonstrate its loyalty to the state, past and present. Hugh Swinton Legaré, Petigru, and others spoke eloquently in "the cause of Free Trade," and the unity of the "agricultural" states.[24] Simms' reputation as an editor and man of letters, plus his work in organizing the proceedings, earned him a place on the speaker's platform.

When he was called upon to enliven the festivities, the young editor humorously stated that enough prose had been spoken, and he proposed instead to read a poem. In the poem, "Our Union—a National Ode," Simms diplomatically praised the prominent Union party leaders for their loyalty to South Carolina and its heroic tradition and for their dedication to the Union. Again, maintaining his allegiance to the South, Simms called upon the nullifiers to calculate the importance of the Union. Simms was still convinced that the state would profit within the Union.[25]

Rather than healing wounds, the Fourth of July celebrations merely delayed the political split over the tariff in Charleston. Shortly after the attempt at solidarity, both the *City Gazette* and the *Courier* began to question Calhoun's outward loyalty to the Union at a time when most of South Carolina was certain of his nullification leanings, and both called for Calhoun to announce his position on nullification publicly. Simms was trying to embarrass Calhoun, but he was also preparing for the Charleston mayoral election and wanted either to claim Calhoun's aid or to turn to national politicians for local political support. Confident that the nullifier party would carry the city elections in September, Calhoun published his famous letter on the "Relations of the States and the Federal Government" on July 26, 1831, thus openly joining the nullifiers and committing himself irrevocably to sectionalism.[26] Simms was certain that Calhoun's action was detrimental to the South and to Calhoun's own political career. He was also certain that there was no support for Calhoun outside of South Carolina and that Calhoun would lose his effectiveness in countering the tariff. Simms almost seemed embarrassed that he had in any way helped to force Calhoun into the open.[27]

This sympathy for Calhoun soon passed as Simms became concerned about Calhoun's political ambitions. Under the pseudonym "Leonidas," Simms recklessly wrote that Calhoun's "vaulting ambition" had nearly caused an internal civil war in South Carolina. The *City Gazette* pointed out that the turning point in Calhoun's career had come when Jackson announced his candidacy for reelection in 1832. Driven to desperation, Calhoun openly split with Jackson, his Cabinet, and the new

Democratic party, and shifted his political support to Henry Clay. Simms closed his editorial by asking, "What could have led him to raise a whirlwind, so fearful in its howlings, and terrible in its aspects, but the hope that he would be chosen as the *master-spirit* to control and direct it?"[28] If Simms had perhaps misjudged the actions of such a complex man, there were many people in South Carolina who resented that *City Gazette* editorial and perceived Simms' intent. It clearly did not benefit Simms' own reputation.

But with the Charleston city elections in the offing, Simms had no time to worry about the political consequences of his actions. He turned the *City Gazette* into a Jackson political organ, supporting the President's bid for reelection in hopes that there was enough loyalty to Jackson left in Charleston to elect the State Rights and Union party candidate for mayor. Specifically, Simms felt that only through the use of presidential power could the tariff be lowered and the South regain its economic strength. From August on, Jackson's name was advertised on the front page of the *City Gazette* as a loyal and true Southerner. Now that the *Mercury*, under the influence of Calhoun, had turned against Jackson, Pinckney was supporting Clay for President. Simms therefore was in a position to make vigorous claims for Jackson as the only suitable man to stem the nullification tide.[29]

Continuing his attack on Calhoun, the *Mercury*, and the nullifiers, Simms sought again to clarify his position on the tariff issue, in order to help the Union party ticket and to point out the legal absurdity of nullification. He was certain that if the state legislature passed an act to nullify the nation's revenue laws (a procedure which he considered blatantly unconstitutional), it would face a united country willing to use force to keep South Carolina within the confederacy of states. He reiterated his opposition to the protective system and maintained that he would attempt any "peaceable and constitutional means" to lower the tariff. In search of a united Unionist party, Simms printed editorials which opposed the conversion of Charleston into a warlike arena and supported his own middle-ground tariff policy. The young editor was convinced that a Union and State Rights party victory in the mayoral election

would persuade the moderate powers in Washington to recon-
sider the tariff system and would ruin Pinckney's plans for a
state nullification convention. But his scheme failed, and with
Calhoun's support, Pinckney again defeated Pringle for mayor.
Charlestonians had not risen to Simms' use of Jackson as a
symbol of unity, nor had they understood his tariff position.
The city was in the hands of the nullifiers, and Simms thought
that it would probably support Pinckney's demands for a state
convention.[30]

Charleston hardly had a chance to settle down from the
election disputes when the death of William Aiken, one of its
Unionist legislators, necessitated another round of chaotic election arguments. The *City Gazette* supported John Robinson,
the Union party candidate, who opposed the tariff. Simms
wrote that Robinson was an admirer of Andrew Jackson and
the Union and that Robinson's moderate position was needed
in the legislature. Although the Union party lost again, this
time by only eight votes, Simms considered the closeness of the
election a victory for sanity. But he privately conceded that
Robinson's defeat gave the nullifiers an overwhelming majority
in the state legislature and made the calling of a state convention inevitable.[31]

With the elections over for the year, Simms began
research into another issue that would prove to be explosive.
William Lloyd Garrison had begun his anti-slavery crusade
with the *Liberator*, and many Southern editors had begun to
question what action they should take in opposition. When
North Carolina set an example by indicting Garrison, in ab-
sentia, on charges of inciting slaves to riot, Simms took the opportunity to comment on slavery and abolitionism in a long and
thoughtful editorial in the *City Gazette*. He wrote that there
was no legal way for the North Carolina courts to extradite
Garrison, let alone convict him, since he had committed no
criminal offense. As a lawyer Simms believed completely in the
sanctity of private property, and as a young Southern intellectual he supported the slave society. Therefore he called for a
revision of the Constitution in order to amend "the deficien-
cies" that allowed such abusive freedom of speech. Simms
asked all the Southern states to unite behind his amendment,

thus assuring quick national consideration through a united front. Simms closed his editorial by warning that as long as any fanatic could scatter his literature throughout the South, in defiance of state laws, South Carolina and its people would have no security or sovereignty of any kind.[32] The implications of this editorial for Simms' later views on freedom of expression were momentous.

Simms also feared Calhoun's growing power in the state and the inevitability of a state convention. He had become increasingly angry over the apparent inability of Congress to settle the tarrif issue, and he seemed to fear the worst for himself and for the future of South Carolina under radical control. But the *City Gazette*, which had lost subscribers because of its Unionist sentiments in early 1832, seemed to gain new support from the anti-nullification minority. In a long article praising its fellow-Unionist newspaper, the *Courier* shed some light on why Simms was able to pick up new subscribers. The *Courier* compared the young editor favorably to the British historian Thomas Babington Macaulay, a brilliant literary mind who committed his career to an active role in public life. Simms had also selflessly committed himself to the political arena; the *Courier*'s editors were pleased by his public role in using the *City Gazette* to attack the nullifiers. Therefore, those few new subscriptions, which turned out to be too few, were a tribute to Simms' zealous attachment to public duty.[33]

But the small triumph of Simms' success soon gave way to his renewed interest in the tariff as the central issue of South Carolina's internal controversy. Since he had previously stated that a united and moderate South could force a lower tariff without leading to nullification by a single state, he decided to concentrate on Congressional action, and he called for gradual tariff reductions over a period of years in order to placate all positions. When Jackson's Secretary of the Treasury Louis McLane introduced a compromise bill, setting up a timetable for gradual reduction, the *City Gazette* called the bill a compromise which neither party could oppose. Yet South Carolina's nullifiers in Congress opposed McLane's measure. Simms was convinced that local politics had superseded national interests. He now knew that the South Carolina nullifiers feared loss of political power in the state more than they favored tariff reductions. By keeping excitement and agitation at a fever pitch, the nullifiers could demand a convention and solidify their own power.[34]

In hopes of ending the local tariff agitation, Simms began to write again of the importance of the presidential election of 1832 to the South. When Jackson chose Martin Van Buren as his running mate, Simms, who disliked the New York politician intensely, temporarily balked at the nomination. But the young editor soon changed his mind when he discovered that Calhoun, using Pinckney's *Mercury*, was behind the stop-Van Buren group in South Carolina. Simms stressed that Van Buren was an avowed advocate of free trade who was certain to influence Jackson to lower the tariff. He also knew that the fledgling National Democrats needed support and that Southerners could offset their minority status and control a major political party if they would only jump on the bandwagon immediately. Not without ambitions for his own political career, Simms also thought that moderation would prevail if a national party were to influence South Carolina politics. So when Pinckney accused Simms of fanaticism in supporting a party that would destroy the state, Simms retaliated in kind.[35]

The wrong paper was accused of radicalism, but Jackson was no longer popular in South Carolina, and Simms needed a new position from which to offset the growing nullification sentiment. Friends were surprised when he modified his previous opposition to a state convention and favored a convention of all the Southern states. Once he had halfheartedly supported this call for sectional power, but he had become convinced that a sectional convention would be far more effective in settling the tariff problem than a single state convention in South Carolina. He thought that a cooperative venture by all of the Southern states could analyze the faults of the protective system and force Washington to act, thus stalling the growth of radical power in South Carolina. Also, he was certain that Southerners in convention would discuss the nature of the federal compact as it related to the national government's jurisdiction over the South. He foresaw controversy over the admission of new states to the Union, and he attempted to clarify this issue by advocating, in the *City Gazette*, a Southern or even a national convention to discuss the altered balance of economic and political power between North and South due to the emergence of the West.[36]

The proposal for a Southern convention was one of Simms' last services to his state and to public life as a newspaper editor. His partner, E. S. Duryea, long an invalid unable to participate in editing the *City Gazette*, died on March 25, 1832, leaving Simms the sole proprietor and sole debtor. Without funds to continue and having steadily lost most of his new subscribers, perhaps because of his perpetual political squabbles and Charleston's near-total conversion to nullification, Simms was forced to sell the paper. William Laurens Poole, a printer and minor politician, bought the paper after promising Simms to continue its Unionist sentiments. But the new editor sought no political enemies and avoided outspoken or unpopular positions in an attempt to protect his financial investment. Pinckney was pleased that a more temperate policy would appear on the *City Gazette*'s editorial page. Undoubtedly the *Courier* would miss Simms' willingness to bear the brunt of Pinckney's vicious anti-Unionist editorials.[37]

Disillusioned because of political failures, increasing financial losses, and deep personal tragedies, Simms temporarily gave up public life. With some thoughts of permanent emigration, he traveled through the Northeast in the summer of 1832, hoping to escape further involvement in South Carolina's factious battles. He visited the literary establishments in New York City, New Haven, and Boston, and met frequently with many of the North's leading men of letters. In New York he formed friendships with the poet William Cullen Bryant and the editor James Lawson, which would last his entire life. With Bryant's encouragement Simms returned to writing poetry and prose fiction and resolved to make literature a major part of his life's work. He reworked an earlier unpublished poem entitled "Atalantis," a long, meandering sea adventure, which contained much of the melancholy and tragedy of misspent youth. But even in "Atalantis," he managed to interject political commentary. Dedicating the poem to his friend Maynard D. Richardson, a fellow Unionist editor from Sumter, Simms praised Richardson's moral worth and his political struggles against adversity. The poem's themes of imprisonment, escape, and renewed loyalty betrayed Simms' personal feelings. In New York, Simms also began to revise a short story, which would soon appear as his first novel, *Martin Faber*. He also wrote for the prestigious *American Quarterly Review*, in which he published an important critique of Mrs. Frances Trollope's *Domestic Manners of the Americans*.[38]

Although Simms was immersed in Northern literary society and thoroughly enjoyed New York City's cultural benefits, his public obligations to South Carolina soon brought him back to Charleston and the fall elections. Knowing that the Charleston mayoral election would be a crucial indicator of the entire state's political direction, Simms campaigned actively for the Union and State Rights party candidate Henry DeSaussure, a Charleston lawyer. But Pinckney, who seemed to have almost a monopoly on political power, easily won reelection.[39] This loss made it more important than ever to wage a strong Union party campaign for governor in order to stem the tide of radicalism. Sure that Robert Y. Hayne, of Webster-Hayne debate fame, would be the nullifier candidate, Simms tried to rally strength for the Union party. Previously, in an editorial for the *City Gazette*, he had uncovered a corrupt political bargain between Hayne and Calhoun. Simms now revealed the details of that bargain to his Charleston friends. Hayne had agreed to trade his important Senate seat to Calhoun in exchange for nullification support for governor. In a privately printed circular Simms also attacked Hayne's shallow political philosophy. But those efforts failed, and Hayne was elected governor by a large majority. Realizing that the State Rights and Union party no longer had any power in the state, Simms interpreted Hayne's victory as a mandate for a state convention, with the nullifiers in complete control.[40]

As soon as Hayne's election was assured, Governor James Hamilton, Jr., issued an executive order for an extra session of the state legislature in order to vote on a statewide convention. The convention met on November 19 and soon adopted the Ordinance of Nullification proposed by William Harper, chancellor of the College of South Carolina. The Ordinance nullified the tariff acts of 1828 and 1832 and requested a "Test Oath" of loyalty for all persons holding office in the state of South Carolina. The proposed Test Oath required office-holders (including military) and even jurors to take an oath that they "will well and truly obey, execute, and enforce this Ordinance, and such act or acts of the Legislature as may be passed to carry the same into operation and effect, according to the true intent and meaning."[41]

Also at the nullification convention, George McDuffie, a leading party theoretician with strong political ties throughout the South, pleaded with the other Southern states to join South Carolina in opposing economic vassalage under Northern rule. Few Southern politicians found the times as serious as South Carolina's radicals described them, and no other state legislature voted any support to South Carolina.[42] Without that support nullification was doomed, but South Carolina prepared to stand alone. Governor Hayne, determined to uphold his sovereign authority in the state and committed to enforcing the convention's ordinance, issued a call for twelve thousand men to join the state militia. Out of fear of national government reprisals, if not because of the desire to control local politics, the South Carolina state government had placed itself in the precarious position of having to defend the nullification ordinance with arms if necessary.[43]

Many of Charleston's Unionists, having found that legitimate political opposition had become sedition, mostly avoided the public eye and refused to confront the nullifiers. Not so the young ex-editor who so prided himself on the right of free expression. Simms actively politicked throughout the state in early 1833, talking of his antagonism to the high tariff but urging his fellow moderates to oppose the Test Oath. He was convinced that the Unionists of Charleston who held public office would not take the oath, even if there was internal civil war. Driven to frustration, Simms declared that South Carolina should be destroyed if the state government continued to oppress its own citizens. He wrote Lawson that "a deep and deadly hostility and hate has been engendered in the bosoms of our party by the odious ordinance of that petty dictatorship, which has broken up all the bonds once sweet and sacred of our society." Simms' many weeks of trying to persuade his political allies to oppose violations of free speech made him distraught enough to contemplate vengeance against the nullifiers. As far as he was concerned, the nullifiers had ruined South Carolina's economy and destroyed free expression. He predicted that many planters who were having financial difficulties would move West to freedom and fertile fields. Tired of being called a submissionist and angry at the Union party's unwillingness to contest the nullifiers, Simms vowed to leave South Carolina.[44]

But Simms' talk of emigration was never more than a threat. His local loyalties and desire to be of public service always superseded his private ambitions. After his speaking tour Simms turned to his own form of political instrument, the power of print, to attack the nullifiers. Sorrowed over the death of his zealous young friend Maynard Davis Richardson, the Unionist editor from Sumter, Simms compiled a volume of Richardson's editorials. In his introduction to the volume he vented his anger at the nullifiers who had allowed personality to replace policy in the recent controversy. He sought to revive the dialogue of opposing views and praised the organization of debating societies in hopes of making free discussion again tolerated. Richardson's death at twenty-two had left Sumter without a Unionist paper to counteract nullification propaganda, and Simms knew that without opposition the nullifiers would never bother to question their principles. Although it was unfortunate that Richardson had postponed his career as a poet to become involved in political warfare, Simms found Richardson's "assumption of the many responsibilities" of political journalism an act of selfless dedication to the welfare of his community. He found an "immoral and diseased condition" in society and used Richardson's death to describe the dangers of an inordinate amount of power in the hands of one political faction. Richardson had to bear the scorn of one who was mistaken and misunderstood by his opposition. Simms was again attacking the dangers of nullification, but he was also describing his own plight in a state which completely misunderstood his loyalties and bitterly attacked his demands for political objectivity.[45]

The book on Richardson had little effect in arousing Simms' fellow Unionists to oppose the nullification party. For most Unionists the necessity of effective opposition had almost ended, since a worried Congress had begun debates on a compromise tariff. The nullifiers decided to postpone putting the ordinance into effect and waited for Congress to modify the tariff. On March 13, 1833, after hearing a report on Henry Clay's tariff bill, a state convention rescinded the Ordinance of Nullification. For most outside observers, nullification was a dead issue. But South Carolina still had unfinished business that would continue the personal political struggles. The nullifiers planned to obstruct free speech by demanding that the Test Oath be continued.[46]

For Simms this struggle over free speech proved that the political world of South Carolina was gloomier and more confined than ever. When Governor Hayne praised the Test Oath as an act that no man loyal to his state could find objectionable, Simms was convinced of more devious motives on the part of the nullifiers. Although he continued to oppose the Test Oath throughout 1834, Simms believed Hayne's boast that the oath of loyalty would permanently fragment the Union party. He attended a Union convention in Columbia, which met to organize opposition to the Test Oath, but he reported petty squabbling and growing political opportunism among the members of a once-united minority. After years of agitation, bitter controversies, and at times physical beatings, the Union party's spirit was broken. Simms had wanted South Carolinians to maintain an independent position of free inquiry. He was a young politician who made his living through writing what he felt, and what hurt him most was that the Test Oath forced all people to think alike. For one so sensitive to the need of protecting free inquiry, this was the final defeat.[47]

But Simms was political enough to know that harmony had to be restored to South Carolina. Thus he was not surprised when rumors spread that the legislature would soon find some compromise on the Test Oath. A bill was introduced which would allow Unionist sympathizers to take the oath, yet in no way impair the obligations which they felt toward the central government. The political sophists had found a means by which allegiance to local government could be consistent with the allegiance owed to the Constitution of the United States. Large majorities in both houses of the state legislature retained nearly the exact wording of the old oath. The Unionists were duped into believing that the state's political factions had reached an understanding.[48]

The reason for such a mild debate on the once-volatile issue of the oath was soon divulged in the gubernatorial election. George McDuffie, a loyal nullifier, was elected by a unanimous vote of the legislature. The Unionists, who had once almost totally opposed McDuffie, voted for him to a man, thereby destroying any chance for a viable two-party system in South Carolina. From 1834 on, South Carolina moved toward one political voice, one political opinion.[49]

The ramifications of the nullification controversy in South Carolina were momentous. As James L. Petigru said, "Nullification has done its work; it has prepared the minds of men for a separation of the States, and when the question is mooted again it will be distinctly union or disunion."[50] Instead of continuing the bitter squabbles among themselves, many of South Carolina's politicians found it expedient to unite under the direction of one political genius, John Caldwell Calhoun. The nullifiers had won their tariff compromise through his exercise of personal power, and Calhoun realized that political unity within South Carolina could secure a powerful role in the future of the South. These possibilities seemed to many to be worth the silencing of a few local politicians. While personal political animosities lingered for some time, the controversy had the effect of convincing South Carolina's Unionists that they could never hope to win a party struggle. They resolved never again to be found on the wrong side of political issues.[51] Nullification did incalculable damage to the hopes of any political opposition in South Carolina.

The bitter civil strife in South Carolina also affected Simms' political career. Rash, hasty, frequently violent, and sometimes unjust, he earned a reputation as a brilliant but much too emotional newspaperman. He spent the last of his inheritance and all of his earnings as a lawyer in trying to sustain the *City Gazette*. Death had deprived him of several who were close to him during those hectic nullification years—first his father and then his wife, leaving him a widower with a small child.[52]

Although he remained loyal to the Unionist cause, Simms' personal political views were in a state of transition. After watching a legitimate political faction succumb to the power of Calhoun and the nullifiers, he was cautious about joining another opposition movement. He became skeptical of any federal redress of local grievances, and he began to question the sincerity of the nationalist sentiments of Northern politicians, but he still considered the nullifiers an odious group of self-serving politicians. Much later he expressed to another young editor what must have been a growing sentiment in his mind. He said it did not pay to be outspoken in favor of free expression, since present opponents could easily become future allies. With the failure of Charleston's intellectual elite to survive politically, Simms believed that there was no longer a place in politics for one who felt as he did.[53]

In a letter to James Lawson, Simms advised his friend to avoid politics, for political life could only cause misery. On the rebound he had decided to pursue a new form of political activity and earn his living as a writer.[54] But Simms could never abandon public life or loyalty to his home state. Even as a Unionist his first obligation had been to South Carolina. As Simms turned actively to writing fiction, his political understanding of his fellow man, especially in times of crisis, was reflected in his novels and romances. As he became interested in studying society, he began to develop that critical and shrewdly calculating political mind which would serve him well in his role as a public man of letters. His career as a social critic had begun.

NOTES

1. William Gilmore Simms, *The Tri-Color; or the Three Days of Blood in Paris* (London, 1830), pp. 3, 10, 11, 14, 21.

2. Charleston *Courier*, Feb. 13, 1830. Also see Charleston *Mercury* almost every day from Nov. 1829 to Jan. 1830; Freehling, *Prelude to Civil War*, pp. 240-242, claims that a "clique of high-toned Charleston aristocrats led the unionist party." Many of those who worked on the *Southern Review* and had old, established positions in the community were unionists. No doubt their reputations as intellectuals and important men of letters held much attraction for young Simms.

3. See Freehling, *Prelude to Civil War*, pp. xii-xiii, for theory of how the necessity to protect slavery heightened the nullification conflict in South Carolina. For the Vesey plot see Richard C. Wade, "The Vesey Plot; a Reconsideration," *Journal of Southern History*, 30 (May 1964): 143-161, and John M. Lofton, *Insurrection in South Carolina; the Turbulent World of Denmark Vesey* (Yellow Springs, Ohio, 1964). For the tariff controversy see John G. Van Deusen, *The Economic Basis of Disunion in South Carolina* (New York, 1928), p. 18; Frank W. Taussig, *The Tariff History of the United States* (New York, 1931), p. 73; John L. Conger, "South Carolina and the Early Tariffs," *Mississippi Valley Historical Review* 5 (March 1919): 415-433.

4. *Fifth Census; or, Enumeration of Inhabitants of the United States 1830* (Washington, 1832), pp. 14-15; Paul Hamilton Hayne, *Lives of Robert Young Hayne and Hugh Swinton Legaré* (Charleston, 1878), pp. 34-35; *Niles' Register*, 38: 255 (*Niles'* gives the imports into and exports from Charleston for the years 1822-1829); Alfred Glaze Smith, *Economic*

Readjustment of an Old Cotton State, South Carolina 1820-1860 (Columbia, 1958), pp. 35-36.

5. Much has been written on the problem of just how much Calhoun was controlled by or controlled South Carolina politics. That his behavior during nullification had untold effect on Simms' view of political objectivity is a central point of this essay. See Calhoun to Virgil Maxcy, Sept. 11, 1830, and Calhoun to Samuel Ingham, Oct. 30, 1830, MSS, John C. Calhoun Papers, Clemson College. Most helpful to me has been the little-studied work of Gerald Capers, *John C. Calhoun Opportunist: a Reappraisal* (Gainesville, Florida, 1960); Charles M. Wiltse's *John C. Calhoun, Nullifier 1829-1839* (3 vols.; Indianapolis, 1944-1951) Vol. 2 is indispensable to any student of Calhoun. Also see Frederic Bancroft, *Calhoun and the South Carolina Nullification Movement* (Baltimore, 1928); William M. Meigs, *The Life of John Caldwell Calhoun*, 2 vols. (New York, 1917), vol. 1; Richard N. Current, *John C. Calhoun* (New York, 1963), p. 13; Chauncey S. Boucher, *The Nullification Controversy in South Carolina* (Chicago, 1916), p. 58; Charles S. Sydnor, *The Development of Southern Sectionalism, 1818-1848* (Baton Rouge, 1948), p. 186; Samuel Gaillard Stoney, ed., "The Autobiography of William John Grayson," *South Carolina Historical Magazine*, 50 (1949): 20 (hereafter cited as "Grayson"); Gerald M. Capers, "A Reconsideration of John C. Calhoun's Transition from Nationalism to Nullification," *JSH*, 14 (Feb. 1948): 34-48; *Annals of Congress*, 18 Cong., 1 sess., pp. 618, 2177, 2237, 2400; Herman V. Ames, *State Documents on Federal Relations: the States and the United States* (Philadelphia, 1902), p. 152.

6. *City Gazette*, Jan. 3, 5, 1830. There is some confusion as to Simms' position on nullification. See Freehling, *Prelude to Civil War*, p. 374. Boucher quotes heavily from the *City Gazette*, yet does not mention Simms as its editor. Hayne, p. 74; Robert Goodwyn Rhett, *Charleston; an Epic of Carolina* (Richmond, 1940), p. 193. In his article, "The Changing Loyalties of William Gilmore Simms," *JSH*, 9 (1943): 212, John Higham

claims that Simms was merely a tool of the merchant interests, whereas Trent, *Simms*, p. 60, judges that Simms had two loyalties in 1830, his country and his state. It will be evident that neither is entirely correct.

7. *City Gazette*, June 16, 30, 1830. Simms was not alone in this view; Thomas Cooper said approximately the same thing in the *City Gazette*, July 13, 1830, and the *Courier*, May 12, 1830, also took the same position; Boucher, *Nullification Controversy*, pp. 81-82.

8. *City Gazette*, June 9, 1830.

9. Ibid., July 20, 1830; *Courier*, July 28, 1830.

10. *City Gazette*, Aug. 3, 21, 1830; *Courier*, Apr. 7, 1830; *Mercury*, Jan. 12, 1830; Francis W. Pickens to James Henry Hammond, June 26, 1830, MSS, James Henry Hammond Papers, Library of Congress; Edwin P. Starr to S. Grantland, June 19, 1830, MSS, Edwin P. Starr Papers, South Caroliniana Library, University of South Carolina; Boucher, *Nullification Controversy*, p. 87.

11. *City Gazette*, Aug. 30, Sept. 7, 1830; *Mercury*, Aug. 30, 1830; *Sketch of Simms, 1895*, Charles Carroll Simms Papers; Boucher, *Nullification Controversy*, chap. 3.

12. *Mercury*, May 15, 18, 1830; Boucher, *Nullification Controversy*, pp. 88-89.

13. *City Gazette*, Aug. 27, 1830; *Courier*, Sept. 24, 1830.

14. *City Gazette*, Aug. 6, 17, 20, 24, 30, Sept. 7, Oct. 1, 1830; *Mercury*, July 30, 31, Aug. 4, 9, 17, 1830; Sydnor, p. 52; Theodore D. Jervey, *Robert Y. Hayne and His Times* (New York, 1909), p. 279. Important Unionists sought to protect Simms from Pinckney's invective; the *City Gazette* reprinted a resolution passed by a Unionist meeting concerning the *Mercury*:

> "*Resolved,* That the increasing and disgraceful attacks
> made by a portion of the Press in this city, on the princi-
> ples of those, who from conscientious motives, are ar-
> ranged against the *novel* and *dangerous doctrine of
> Nullification*, and the no less deprecated measure of a
> Convention of the People, are hostile to freedom of opin-
> ion, and groundless in fact."

15. *City Gazette*, Oct. 16, Nov. 1, 1830; *Mercury*, Sept. 11,
Dec. 4, 1830; Boucher, *Nullification Controversy*, p. 102.

16. *City Gazette*, Dec. 16, 20, 21, 30, 1830; *Mercury*, Aug. 2,
3, 1830. *Courier*, Oct. 19, 1830.

17. *Mercury*, Jan. 15, 1831; for the *Mercury*'s vicious personal attacks on Simms in 1830, see issues of May 17, June 19,
July 30, Aug. 5, 9, 13, 21, Oct. 18, 1830.

18. *Simms Letters*, 1: 16; Hoole, "A Note on Simms' Visit to
the Southwest," p. 335; Ridgely, *Simms*, pp. 11-12; Trent,
Simms, p. 67.

19. Bynum should have remained in Alabama. As editor of a
rival Greenville paper he quarrelled with the Unionist Benjamin Franklin Perry, and Perry killed Bynum in a duel.

20. *Simms Letters*, 1: 16, 25, 31, 33.

21. Ibid., pp. 17-18, 19, 32, 35, 37; Smith, *Economic Readjustment of an Old Cotton State, passim.*

22. *Simms Letters*, 1: 23, 26, 28-29, 30. Simms attacked
philanthropists "who, without knowing anything about them,
are eternally meddling with the concerns of the South." Simms'
talents as a critic of the accepted republican virtues of his country were displayed in his criticism of the large quantity of
Western lands open to settlement. He said, "I cannot but think
the possession of so much territory, greatly inimical to the well
being of this country. It not only conflicts with, and prevents

the formation of society, but it destroys that which is already well established." *Simms Letters*, 1: 37.

23. *City Gazette*, June 2, 8, 30, 1831; *Mercury*, May 31, June 7, 1831; *Courier*, June 20, 29, 1831; Boucher, *Nullification Controversy*, p. 146.

24. Hugh S. Legaré, *Writings of Hugh Swinton Legaré*, edited by his sister, 2 vols. (Charleston, 1845), Vol. 1, Speech, July 4, 1831.

25. *City Gazette*, July 8, 11, 1831; *Courier*, July 8, 13, Aug. 6, 1831; for continued *Mercury* reaction to Simms' ode see Sept. 2, 9, 1831; Bancroft, *Calhoun and the South Carolina Nullification Movement*, pp. 93-94, 99-100.

26. *Courier*, Aug. 13, 1831; Calhoun Papers, University of South Carolina, John C. Calhoun to Samuel J. Ingham, July 31, 1831; *City Gazette*, Sept. 1, 1831. The *Gazette* quoted William H. Crawford's *Georgia Journal*:

> "For about 20 years the Vice President had assumed the post and mien, and exterior of a patriot, and man of strict honor. . . . Unfortunately in the month of February last, he came out with his address to the people of the U. S. . . . That publication has produced enquiry and criticism. And enquiry and criticism cannot fail to expose the Vice President to the scorn and ridicule, . . . of the citizens of the United States."

See also Capers, *John C. Calhoun Opportunist*, pp. 146-147.

27. *City Gazette*, July 30, 1831; *Courier*, Aug. 24, 1831; Robert Campbell to Edwin P. Starr, Aug. 29, 1831, Starr Papers.

28. *City Gazette*, Nov. 29, 1831; Wiltse, *John C. Calhoun, Nullifier*, 1: 88; Bancroft, *Calhoun and the South Carolina Nullification Movement*, p. 83; J. Franklin Jameson (ed.),

"Correspondence of John C. Calhoun," *Annual Report of the American Historical Association, 1899* (Washington, 1900), II, 308 (hereinafter cited as "Calhoun Correspondence").

29. *City Gazette*, June 9, Aug. 30, 1831; *Southern Review*, 8, 39-40; Edwin P. Starr to Robert Campbell, Aug. 29, 1831, Starr Papers; *Mercury*, Apr. 28, July 7, 1831; *Courier*, Nov. 21, 1831; Arthur Styron, *The Cast-Iron Man: John C. Calhoun and American Democracy* (New York, 1935), p. 124.

30. *City Gazette*, Sept. 3, 7, 1831; *Courier*, Sept. 7, 12, 1831; *Mercury*, July 30, Sept. 7, 1831; Capers, *John C. Calhoun Opportunist*, pp. 117, 119, 136; Boucher, *Nullification Controversy*, p. 156.

31. Actually Robinson had died in May and the Unionist forces had wanted an immediate election. But Pinckney delayed, hoping the fall would bring nullifiers back to Charleston. See *Mercury*, May 16, 1831; *Courier*, May 14, 18, 1831. For the outcome of the election see *City Gazette*, Oct. 5, 11, 1831; *Courier*, Oct. 6, 13, 1831; *Southern Review* 8: 260; Starr to Campbell, Oct. 30, 1831, Starr Papers.

32. *City Gazette*, Nov. 7, 1831; Pinckney had earlier accused Simms of being anti-slavery, *Mercury*, Oct. 8, 1831.

33. *Courier*, Dec. 31, 1831; *City Gazette*, Jan. 6, 1832.

34. *City Gazette*, Jan. 30, May 8, 1832; *Mercury*, Jan. 17, 1832; Boucher, *Nullification Controversy*, p. 194.

35. *City Gazette*, Feb. 29, March 9, Apr. 5, 1832; *Mercury*, Apr. 9, 1832; Jervey, *Robert Y. Hayne*, p. 314. Simms summed up his support of Van Buren by stating, "If, in order to save the country from the contending factions who seek to make it a common spoil, if it be held necessary to take up Van Buren as combining the greater vote of the country, then let him be the man."

36. *City Gazette*, March 6, 7, Apr. 17, May 10, 1832; Boucher, *Nullification Controversy*, pp. 197-198.

37. *City Gazette*, March 31, Apr. 10, June 7, 1832; *Mercury*, May 1, 5, 1832.

38. *Simms Letters*, 1: 39, 41; William Gilmore Simms, *Atalantis: a Story of the Sea* (New York, 1832), pp. 14, 41, 75, 78, dedication; Trent, *Simms*, pp. 67-76. Although Simms' New York career was a long and rewarding one for himself, this study is concerned with Simms' career in the South. His friendships, literary quarrels, and many publishing and play-writing schemes are one part of the development of literary nationalism and have been adequately handled in Perry Miller, *The Raven and the Whale* (New York, 1956). It is hoped that C. Hugh Holman's forthcoming book will also explore this fascinating subject. Only when Simms' Northern literary career directly influences his behavior in the South will it be mentioned in this work.

39. *City Gazette*, Apr. 17, 1832; *Mercury*, Sept. 5, 1832; James Hamilton to Waddy Thompson, June 8, 1832, MSS, Waddy Thompson Papers, South Caroliniana Library, University of South Carolina; unsigned letter to Lt. Edward Rutledge, Sept. 6, 1832, MSS, Rutledge Family Papers, South Caroliniana Library, University of South Carolina; James Petigru Carson, *Life, Letters and Speeches of James Louis Petigru, the Union Man of South Carolina* (Washington, 1920), pp. 90-91.

40. *City Gazette*, Apr. 30, Oct. 1, 1832; *Mercury*, Oct. 15, 1832; Greenville *Mountaineer*, Oct. 13, 1832; Jervey, *Robert Y. Hayne*, pp. 289-290; Boucher, *Nullification Controversy*, p. 207.

41. *Courier*, Nov. 28, 1832; *Mercury*, Dec. 12, 1832; Preston to Thompson, Nov. 8, 1832, Thompson Papers; unsigned letter to Edward Rutledge, Nov. 19, 1832, Rutledge Family Papers; Ames, *State Documents on Federal Relations*, pp. 38-41. Ex-

tremely valuable, though never used in any study of Pickens is an unpublished work by Paul Hamilton Hayne, *M. M. S. of Volume First of the Work Entitled "Politics of South Carolina, . . . F. W. Pickens' Speeches, Reports, &c"* (1864[?]).

42. *Courier*, Aug. 2, 1832; Boucher, *Nullification Controversy*, pp. 216-217; Ames, *State Documents on Federal Relations*, pp. 179-180, 180-182, 183-185, 185-188.

43. Executive Department Circular signed by Gov. Hayne, Dec. 20, 1832, James Henry Hammond Papers, Library of Congress; James Henry Hammond to Robert Y. Hayne, Dec. 20, 1832, Hammond Papers; Samuel C. Jackson to Elizabeth Jackson, MSS, Samuel C. Jackson Papers, South Caroliniana Library, University of South Carolina; Hayne, *Hayne and Legaré*, pp. 67-69; *City Gazette* and *Mercury*, Dec., 1832; Wiltse, *John C. Calhoun, Nullifier*, 2, 153; Boucher, *Nullification Controversy*, p. 219.

44. *Simms Letters*, 1: 46-47, 49-50, 52; *Courier*, March 22, 1833; *Mercury*, March 6, Aug. 5, 28, 1833; Charles J. Stillé, "The Life and Services of Joel R. Poinsett," *The Pennsylvania Magazine of History and Biography*, 12 (1888): 265, 295; David Franklin Houston, *A Critical Study of Nullification in South Carolina* (New York, 1908), p. 114; Carson, *James Louis Petigru*, pp. 113-114.

45. William Gilmore Simms, *The Remains of Maynard Davis Richardson, with a Memoir of His Life* (Charleston, 1833), pp. viii, xiii, xxiii, xxix, xxx, xxxi, xxxv, xxxvi, 4-38; *Courier*, July 13, 1833. Aside from praising Simms' knowledge of the political theory of Locke and Benthem and the young author's obvious command of Jefferson's thought, the *Courier* recognized that Simms was really attacking the nullifiers' political and thought control of South Carolina.

46. Issac W. Hayne to Waddy Thompson, Jan. 1833, MSS, Waddy Thompson Papers, Southern Historical Collection, University of North Carolina; Thomas Cooper to Joseph

Priestley, Jan. 26, 1833, MSS Thomas Cooper Papers, South Caroliniana Library, University of South Carolina; unsigned letter to Edward Rutledge, Jan. 30, 1833, Rutledge Family Papers; Hammond to Hayne, Feb. 7, 1833, Hammond Papers, Library of Congress; [Robert Barnwell Rhett], *Oration of the Honorable R. Barnwell Rhett, Before the Legislature of South Carolina, November 28, 1850* (Columbia, 1850), p. 135; Henry Laurens Pinckney, *Oration on the Fourth of July, 1833* (Charleston, 1833), pp. 3, 4, 9-10; M. King to Legaré, May 5, 1833, MSS, Hugh Swinton Legaré Papers, South Caroliniana Library, University of South Carolina; *Mercury*, Jan. 23, 1833; *Simms Letters*, 1: 51. For an interesting secondary commentary see Edwin L. Green, *George McDuffie* (Columbia, 1936), pp. 118-119.

47. *Simms Letters*, 1: 54, 166; J. Franklin Jameson, ed., "Documents and Letters on Nullification in South Carolina, 1830-1834," *American Historical Review* 6 (July 1901): 117-119; Legaré, *Writings*, pp. 216-217; *Mercury*, Nov. 28, 1833, June 16, Aug. 12, 1834; *Courier*, Jan. 10, June 4, 24, July 17, 1834; Carson, *James Louis Petigru*, p. 127.

48. The vote was thirty-six to four in the Senate and ninety to twenty-eight in the House (Boucher, *Nullification Controversy*, p. 357).

49. *Niles' Register*, Dec. 20, 1834; Boucher, *Nullification Controversy*, p. 366; Freehling, *Prelude to Civil War*, pp. 318, 320.

50. Carson, *James Louis Petigru*, p. 125; Rhett, *Charleston*, p. 221; Sydnor, *Development of Southern Sectionalism*, p. 220.

51. Legaré, *Writings*, p. 217; John C. Calhoun to Samuel Ingham, Dec. 31, 1834, John C. Calhoun Papers, University of South Carolina; Stoney, "Grayson," p. 25; Wiltse, II, 154; Capers, *John C. Calhoun Opportunist*, p. 165; *Mercury*, Aug. 9, 1834.

52. *Simms Letters*, 1: 162-163; "Woodlands," p. 2, MSS, Charles Carroll Simms Papers.

53. *Simms Letters*, 5: 382-383; Samuel Albert Link, *Pioneers of Southern Literature* (Nashville, 1896), pp. 190-192; William Gilmore Simms, *Egeria* (Philadelphia, 1853), pp. 71-72. Simms said, "The mistakes and errors of youth are the evil genii which wait upon our manhood, and the ghosts that make us tremble in old age."

54. *Simms Letters*, 1: 62; see Higham, "Changing Loyalties of William Gilmore Simms," pp. 210-213.

2 Social Critic in the South

HAVING FAILED in his first political venture and having no desire to return to his moribund law practice, Simms resumed his early interests—writing fiction, editing periodical literature, and encouraging local literary talent. To clarify his own political position and to learn more about Southern society, he began to write social criticism. His fiction, often hurriedly written and poorly edited, revealed a keen interest in the South's relation to the new West and reflected the problems of the young Southern gentleman seeking fortune and position in society. His critical essays, which bore the marks of the emerging sectional conflict, were studies in the political results of nullification. They captured the growing excitement over the future of slavery and depicted a minority section, accustomed to an aristocracy of intellect, contending with a republican government. Simms presented a problem about representative government that he was never able to resolve. He realized that republicanism was the most plausible political system for his country, but he never trusted the masses. He firmly believed in the patrician system of an intellectual governing elite, yet he had little faith in the honesty and intelligence of his nation's leaders. Finally, Simms' early fiction and critical essays were greatly influenced by the political intrigue of John C. Calhoun's feud with William Campbell Preston and the Henry L. Pinckney "Gag Rule" affair.[1] During the decade he matured politically, as he began

51

to understand the political usefulness of his literary talent and became his section's most significant social critic.

During his first visit to New York, shortly after giving up the *City Gazette*, Simms wrote a lengthy review of Frances Trollope's *Domestic Manners of the Americans* for the *American Quarterly Review*. Like many European intellectuals, Mrs. Trollope, an Englishwoman, was fascinated with the new American society and its paradoxical republican government which condoned chattel slavery. She traveled through most of the United States during the years 1827-1831, keeping a critical account of the people and places she visited. She was offended by what she considered to be the almost total lack of sophistication and the filthy living conditions of most Americans. Her book, an early sociological attempt to grasp a nation's character through studying its society and customs, was also philosophical in its analysis of the "moral and religious condition" of the Americans, particularly those of the South and the Western frontier.[2]

In his review, Simms was disturbed at the flippant approach most Northerners took toward Mrs. Trollope's study. Himself concerned with the structure of American society, Simms proposed to review *Domestic Manners of the Americans* as a serious account of the American character and the nation's intellectual tastes, and he hoped to judge the work on objective grounds.[3] As a young writer his primary interest was in Mrs. Trollope's views of America's lack of cultural values. He agreed with her judgment but explained that the country was too preoccupied with taming the wilderness to have any time for great works of art and literature. Simms himself saw art and literature in the natural beauty of the Western forests and the heroic struggles to civilize the frontier. The nation owed much of its material progress to the adventurous pioneering spirit of its people. Simms knew that literary genius must await the settlement of a continent. Then Americans would chronicle the nation's great achievements and record their experiences through music, art, epic poetry, and fiction. Art would flourish, and literary genius would be recognized. If Mrs. Trollope misunderstood the genius and future of the nation, Simms did not.[4]

Mrs. Trollope's comments on America's lack of aristocratic tradition were also of some concern to the young author. The lack of refinement and respect for one's betters offended Mrs. Trollope's proper English sensibilities. She wondered at the absence of great halls and luxuries for a privileged leader class, and she was disgusted that few distinctions were made among people. The chauvinistic Simms replied that his country was without poverty and degradation and free from class conflict, since Americans never had to threaten insurrection against their government and destroy their country's traditions. He preferred coarseness and lack of breeding to a class-oriented society where initiative was stifled from infancy. Simms had countered Frances Trollope's argument for a native aristocracy with the prevailing republican political propaganda of his own generation, which he hardly believed. But he was on the attack, and the problems of Southern leadership were not really in question.[5]

Early enthusiasm for the value of free expression led Simms to defend proliferation of religious sects from Mrs. Trollope's attack. She condemned the wild antics of the camp revival and found America's lack of an accepted, established church dangerous for the country's future as a Christian nation. Reflecting the Jeffersonian deism that so heavily influenced Southern intellectuals, Simms disagreed, finding security for social and civil welfare "in the great variety and number of religious sects which inundate our country." He vehemently defended the country's support of freedom of religion, whether it meant the right to espouse atheism or the right for many different sects to preach their own version of Christianity. Simms found the Church of England odious and opposed the establishment of any church that controlled the actions of the people.[6]

Throughout most of his review Simms seemed to write as a nationalist. But when Mrs. Trollope wrote that she found nothing but contempt for the institution of domestic slavery, Simms replied as a sectionalist. Certain that her widely discussed book would add to the growing Northern abolitionist propaganda by seriously damaging the South's image as a benevolent slave society, he contended that Mrs. Trollope knew nothing about slavery. Her casual accusations, based on a short visit to the South and influenced by the radical abolitionist Frances Wright, were, in Simms' view, overly philanthropic and certainly too superficial and flippant. Simms believed that the Southern slave society was necessary to the South's economic and political existence. While he admitted that the issue was a volatile one and that the slave system had been inadequately studied, he knew its importance for "our national destinies." He closed his review with the simple but inflammatory statement that slavery could be judged and understood only by those who were intrinsically involved in the system. Like so many Southerners, Simms was already close-minded on the subject of slavery.[7]

If Simms' review of Mrs. Trollope was objectively nationalistic except for his sectional defense of slavery, his next literary venture displayed a firm loyalty to local interests of both an intellectual and a political nature. Along with two other young Charlestonians, Simms began another literary journal, *The Cosmopolitan: An Occasional*, late in the spring of 1833. The main purpose of the magazine was to publish local writers, including much of Simms' own poetry. However, Simms attempted to give the journal a national audience by writing a long article on the creation of a uniquely American literature. He praised James Fenimore Cooper for using "native materials" and cautioned the New Yorker to write only what he knew, saw, and understood. It was Cooper's work on the new West which especially interested Simms, since he too was beginning to discover many literary themes in the story of the westward migration. This dual theme of a national literature, prompted by the author's particular use of his native scenery for setting, was carried over into the second issue of *The Cosmopolitan*.[8]

The *Courier*, pleased that the young men omitted the tariff argument from the magazine, hailed the beginning of an adventure upon "which men of all parties may unite to foster" the arts. The *Mercury* made peace offerings by hoping Simms would succeed in "the comparative calm of the times." However, *The Cosmopolitan* soon became political as Simms lamented South Carolina's recent political fight over nullification. He hoped that the city's literary talents would not have to continue to make their reputations "in the turbulent and temporary notoriety of a partisan harangue, or a political and vexing controversy." South Carolina was overflowing with young artists who had neglected their craft in the frantic years of nullification. Simms seemed to want to temper his own anger and disillusion by blaming some of the city's radicalism on "restless intellects." It was time for the settlement of differences, and Charleston was prepared to show the country some of its literary and artistic talents. But all wounds were not healed, and Simms insisted upon baiting the nullifiers by dedicating the first issue of *The Cosmopolitan* to his old ally, Thomas Smith Grimké.[9]

Before Simms had time to anger many nullifiers, the magazine ceased publication. The young editors probably ran out of money and interest, and the people of Charleston seemed unaware of its passing. That was Simms' only venture into editing his own literary journal for the rest of the decade, but he did contribute much time and effort in helping other Southern editors to sustain their publications. He wrote perceptive and critical essays for the *Southern Literary Messenger*, the *Southern Rose*, and the *Southern Literary Journal*. His most important contributions were to the latter, for he sought to help Daniel K. Whitaker, an acquaintance of mediocre talent, establish periodical literature in Charleston. Simms practically supported the *Southern Literary Journal*, often writing over one hundred pages of manuscript for a single issue. Undoubtedly he sharpened some of his own social and political ideas in the magazine articles which he wrote during the 1830s.[10]

The *Courier* seemed to understand Simms' lack of interest in being limited to one literary project when it stated that the young author was a talent worthy of more ambitious endeavor. Simms had also begun to write novels, thus launching his national literary career. He was an instant success in New York literary circles. He spent at least three months out of each year there, visiting friends, attending the theater, correcting the proofs of his many hurriedly written manuscripts, and haunting Northern publishing houses. Yet while his reputation and book sales grew rapidly in the North, he chose to remain in the South and continued to use sectional themes for most of his works. Not only did he use South Carolina's past and romanticize on his trips into the Southwest; he also wrote as a social critic about the structure of society, the political drama, and the future of the South's ambitious young men. Simms seemed to be more interested in working out his own destiny and studying Southern society than he was in creating great works of literature. His early fiction appeared to answer Mrs. Trollope's criticism of the United States and the South; albeit an answer that reserved space for some cautious criticism of the society in which Simms lived.[11]

After establishing a pattern of writing successful historical and Western narratives, late in 1835 Simms tried to explain his reasons for writing novels, or epic prose, as he called his fiction. For Simms, fiction was relevant to his own volatile era only if it was useful, if it reflected a strict, personal moral code, if it served as a lesson for mankind, and if it described and analyzed the society in which he lived. He chose to write about the past, particularly the civil war in South Carolina during the American Revolution, because of his own personal bitterness and resentment over the divisions in his own day, and because the present could avoid mistakes through reading and studying the mistakes of the past. He also set novels in the Southwest in order to inform his fellow South Carolinians of the advantages and danger of the semicivilized frontiers. He constantly confronted the personal problems of loyalty to one's home, the question of free speech, and the nature of democratic versus aristocratic leadership, problems that vexed many other contemporary writers.[12]

Setting his early Revolutionary romances in the low country of South Carolina, Simms re-created actual events, used important historical figures, and traveled extensively throughout the state in order to depict plantation life of the late eighteenth century. His purposes were a blend of romantic attachment, chauvinism, and dedication to realism, and he refused to find complete fault with either side in the bloody internal war for control of South Carolina.[13] Although his description of the British occupation of Charleston was obviously a thinly veiled comparison with the nullifiers' attack on the city's Unionists, Simms still managed to find something admirable in the behavior of the infamous British officer Colonel Tarleton. A brilliant military tactician, Tarleton revealed his gentler side when he rescued young Mellichampe from the evil Bassfield. Simms took pains to point out that Tarleton was not always a bloodthirsty villain; before the war and the necessity for partisan action, he had been a peace-loving man. It was Tarleton who was allowed to make the supreme judgment about loyalty to one's beliefs as he advised that "truth and virtue no longer exist when one compromises his duty by fearing what other men may think."[14]

Although Simms found both sides guilty of excessive cruelty, a central theme of these early romances was loyalty to South Carolina. What he questioned was the meaning of this loyalty. The old patriarch Colonel Walton was loyal to England but later supported his daughter Katherine in her love of freedom and was finally executed by the British as an example for all his Whig enemies. Simms' characterization of him was compassionate, at times contemptuous, but finally sympathetic. Young Colonel Singleton accused Walton of giving his loyalty to England to protect his plantation and save his fortune. He asked how the country could be saved if its leaders were to seek personal safety above honor. But Walton proved to have a conscience. He soon found that his submission to tyranny had prolonged the civil strife in South Carolina and that perhaps the loyalty of Singleton and Katherine Walton to the new country was genuine. In *The Partisan* Walton sacrificed himself to the new cause. But Simms, perhaps re-thinking his own precarious political loyalties, later used an important scene in *Mellichampe* to re-examine the excesses of patriotism. Prophetically he commented, "The excesses of patriotism, when attaining power, have been but too frequently productive of a tyranny more dangerous in its exercise, and more lasting in its effects, than the despotism which it was invoked to overthrow."[15]

The author's seemingly ambivalent attitude toward patriotism was compounded in his study of the structure of leadership and its relationship to the republican spirit of the American Revolution. Simms was amused over the fact that every war veteran appeared to have captain's rank, and he perceptively pointed out the stupidity of General Gage, who considered Marion's troops poor soldiers merely because of their irregular dress and humble background. Lieutenant Porgy's statement, "Give me the leader that shows me the game I'm to play," revealed Simms' opinion of most men's inability to assume leadership. In *Mellichampe* he developed a theory of the natural leader and said that despite his own support of republican principles, few men were capable of leading. Simms believed that leadership required a special form of intelligence and ability both in war and in politics, which could not be trusted to the masses. Yet at the same time, Simms' early Revolutionary romances demonstrated the author's keen understanding of the class-oriented society of aristocrats and poor. He correctly showed that most of the Tories were of the lower classes, but he went on to illustrate one specific example of how a man from a poor family, Bassfield, had joined the Tories. Because Bassfield had wanted to remain neutral, a group of zealous revolutionaries had persecuted him to the point of making him seek revenge by fighting on the British side. Moreover, Bassfield thought that the British would be victorious and would give him a position in the new leadership in South Carolina. Simms had displayed some of his personal animosities of class feeling, while he realistically studied the problems of leadership in a republican society.[16]

Simms' examination of leadership took him back into the early days of South Carolina's settlement and led him to examine the westward migration. The frontier environment provided the means of finding a new life. Because it heavily influenced the behavior of its inhabitants, it became a dominant theme in much of Simms' fiction. In his earliest novel, which was really a lengthy short story, the evil Martin Faber's desire for status and wealth in a frontier community forced him to kill his mistress, and the fear of losing status finally led William Harding to expose Faber. The protagonist in Simms' earliest border romance, *Guy Rivers*, was a brilliant but evil man who had emigrated to the lawless frontier in order to gain wealth and power in the new and primitive West. Simms' portrayal of Guy was both compassionate and brutal as he systematically exposed Guy as both a victim and a potential conqueror of a weak and materialistic society. But the desire for gain and conquest could also benefit society, as Simms demonstrated in the career of Harrison in *The Yemassee*. Harrison was Simms' fictionalized version of Charles Craven, a colonial governor of South Carolina. Through his actions the audacious yet thoughtful Harrison helped to establish the permanent South Carolina colony. Simms considered Harrison a man of destiny who recognized the inability of the thoughtless masses to act without leadership. Other settlers depended on Harrison, and his ambitions became theirs as he planned their future. The governorship was his just reward. Simms did not begrudge Harrison's ambition and status-consciousness. He believed that there were natural aristocrats who had to have power, while the masses surrendered their independence in pursuing material gain.[17]

Obviously these early novels contained much of a personal political nature. None of Simms' themes was more important to him than his growing willingness to interject pro-slavery arguments into his plots. Since there had always been slaves in his household, the young writer was certainly familiar with slave behavior. In characteristic romantic terminology he gave the slaves names such as Hector and Scipio and depicted their personalities as childlike but absolutely loyal to their masters. Hector, Harrison's slave in *The Yemassee*, saved his master's life and led a slave army against an Indian attack. When offered his freedom as a reward for his devotion, he refused, claiming he would be unable to handle freedom. Mellichampe's trusted Scipio was sent on errands deep into the enemy lines to deliver messages. He outfoxed the stupid poor white Tories, and, in what must have been a fit of literary charity, was even allowed to murder Bassfield and to save Mellichampe's life. The famous comic figure Porgy owned a slave named Tom who engaged his master in long philosophical conversations about the necessity of slavery and the benefits of the system. Simms' early crude attempts at describing the happy, well-adjusted slave were his tentative response to the abolitionists. For giving the slave a fixed position in Southern society, he was early in his career hailed as an ardent defender of "an institution, much misunderstood and misrepresented by the deluded or designing professors of a false philanthropy."[18]

If Simms' defense of slavery was important to the South, of more importance was his use of fiction to persuade young Southerners to remain in and defend their native region. Simms' own definition of the romance included "placing a human agent in hitherto untried situations; it exercises its ingenuity in extricating him from them, while describing his feelings and his fortunes in their progress." In each of his early novels, either the protagonist or another important figure was taught a lesson. In *Martin Faber* it was young William Harding who had to overcome his sensitivity to public opinion and the guilt of false accusation before he could succeed in finding Faber guilty. Although Guy was the most interesting character in *Guy Rivers*, Simms seemed to have written that border romance in order to teach Ralph Colleton a lesson. Ralph, the son of a well-to-do South Carolinian, left for Tennessee to make his own fortune. After many harrowing experiences, the impetuous young man learned the value of moderation, tempered his ambition, and resolved to return to a civilized community. Even in *The Partisan*, Simms taught impetuous young Lance Frampton that loyalty to his fellow revolutionaries was more ennobling than the desire to kill Tories out of revenge. In *The Yemassee*, a secondary character, Hugh Grayson, was at first "full of high ambition." Grayson was short-tempered; "his disappointments very naturally vexed him somewhat beyond prudence, and now and then beyond the restraint of right reason." But with the help of Governor Craven, he soon assumed the duties of a loyal citizen and became an important officer in the South Carolina colonial militia. Finally, in *Mellichampe* the hero himself was too brave and headstrong to survive. The selfish young Mellichampe wanted personal revenge for his father's death and almost ruined the entire revolutionary cause in South Carolina. After a long series of episodes which illustrated the maturing process, the young man became a valuable officer, embodying the high ideals of the revolutionary cause.[19] Simms had used the German literary theme of the *Bildungsroman* in his tales and, in doing so, related man's loyalties to his local surroundings as necessary for society's survival.

Being removed from active politics and having the opportunity to work out his own political philosophy contributed to a mellowing and growth of personal 'tranquility in Simms' life. He not only had become a successful writer, but he had also met and fallen in love with Chevillette Eliza Roach, daughter of a successful planter on the Edisto River. Simms married late in 1836, after telling Lawson that *The Partisan* had made him enough money to settle down for a while. He moved to the Roach plantation "Woodlands," where he would spend many quiet, contemplative moments in his life. His literary fame was growing throughout the South, and he began

to make plans for furthering Southern letters. The earlier oppressive days of nullification had made him a wiser and more
moderate man politically, and his writing served a dual purpose
as a cathartic and a means of political self-instruction.[20]

As Simms grew more politically astute both in his fiction
and in his critical reviews, the controversy over the slave
system became increasingly volatile both in the state and in
Washington. Both of Charleston's major newspapers supported
the actions of the mob which had burned the Charleston post
office in 1835 in order to destroy abolitionist literature. The
Mercury called for a convention of slaveholding states to plan
strategy for the defense of slavery, and the once-moderate
Courier regarded censorship of the mails and the press, both
North and South, as a right of self-preservation. When the
Courier attacked all Southern moderates on the slave question
as political traitors and abolitionists, Thomas Grimké, son of
the Unionist Thomas Smith Grimké, had to explain that his
deceased father was a loyal citizen and that he, unlike his
sisters, was an active pro-slave advocate. The younger
Grimké even changed his last name to Drayton in order to
avoid the social onus placed on his family by citizens of
Charleston.[21] The state's leading politicians were making
vehement attacks on abolitionism in support of Calhoun's attempts to silence antislavery agitation. The nullifier James Henry Hammond found slavery a positive good, instrumental in
helping the South gain wealth, develop genius, and acquire
manners. Governor George McDuffie, another Calhoun
lieutenant, cautioned the state legislature to countenance no de-
viation from the growing pro-slavery argument in South
Carolina.[22]

In such an atmosphere, the slightest difference of political
opinion with Calhoun's anti-abolitionist position could damage
a political career. Simms had to have been impressed by the actions taken against his one-time enemy, Henry L. Pinckney,
who had become Charleston's Congressman as a reward for his
part in the nullification controversy. Pinckney, perhaps because
he thought there was political gain in joining the growing Clay
party or perhaps out of personal conviction, amended
Calhoun's "gag rule" bill by stating that Congress had a constitutional right to decide on slavery in the District of Colum-

bia. The reaction was immediate. Hammond damned Pinckney, and Calhoun made plans to defeat his bid for reelection
and to destroy his political career. The *Mercury*, once under
Pinckney's control, but now under the editorship of Calhoun's
ally John A. Stuart, called Pinckney's behavior shameful and
accused him of betraying Southern rights. At first the opposition nominated Isaac E. Holmes for Congress, but its support
soon shifted to Hugh S. Legaré, a Unionist during nullification times who had subsequently become a Calhoun supporter.
Pinckney campaigned vigorously in hopes of clearing his name,
but Calhoun's power and Charleston's radical anti-abolitionist
sentiment combined to elect Legaré, who had once been anathema to the nullifiers. Stuart and the *Mercury* refused to support any candidate, claiming that Legaré's election was obviously the result of Calhoun's political power because of a re-
alignment with the old Union party.[23]

The lesson left an impression on the young social critic.
The politically astute Simms may even have written his critical
review "Miss Martineau on Slavery" in hopes of furthering his
own political status in South Carolina. He had always considered himself loyal to Southern interests and had fervently
believed in the slave system. So when given the opportunity to
write a review essay of the English traveler and social critic
Harriet Martineau's *Society in America* for the young but
prestigious *Southern Literary Messenger*, Simms immediately
turned his article into a defense of the slave system.[24]

Harriet Martineau's knowledge of the slave system like
Frances Trollope's came from her abolitionist friends and was
based on little firsthand knowledge. Simms was especially
incensed that she had singled out South Carolina for special
condemnation and that she had claimed that the state's
slaveholders so feared an uprising from their ill-treated slaves
that they fabricated stories about abolitionist "incendiary
materials." Realizing that the best defense was a good offense,
Simms centered his attack on Miss Martineau's book around
her avoidance of the many Northern social problems, including
the positions of the free Negro and the white laborer in Northern society. He countered her argument that the Southern
whites despised their slaves by contending that the Negro was
hated in the North. He found the free Negro living "in a state of

continued personal insecurity," because there were few laws to protect him. Having to compete with the poor white for jobs, the free Negro, because of his physical and moral inferiority and the white man's hatred, lived in a state of chaos bordering on starvation. Attacking the factory system, Simms asked Miss Martineau to reflect on the white slavery resulting from a materialistic Northern culture. Simms found the Southern overseer much more benevolent than the Northern factory foreman, who seemed to delight in working poor whites to death. In his offensive against the corrupt manufacturing centers of the urban North, Simms answered every attack on slavery and its condition in the South by comparing it with the evils perpetrated on both black and white laborers in the North.[25]

As he attempted to analyze the social position of slaves in the South, Simms seemed most disturbed by Miss Martineau's chapter on "The Morals of Slavery," which was devoted to the abuses of slavery. Admitting that the slave system's outward freedom made brutes of some slaveholders, he also said that these men were atypical, since in his opinion the slave was as secure as any white man in the South. He maintained that the slaveholder elevated his slaves' minds and morals, in contrast to the brutal and savage life of the black man in Africa and the North. Since every primitive culture in the world's history had been subjected to long periods of bondage, slavery, Simms felt, had uplifted the slave's previous state of civilization. Simms was also a victim of his own forced defense as he rationalized that "the slaveholders of the south, having the immoral and animal and irresponsible people under their control, are the great moral conservators, in one powerful interest, of the entire world." Yet he also believed that Negro slavery was "simply a process of preparation for an improved condition, to work out their own moral deliverance." "The time will come," said Simms in a manner that belied his racism, "when the negro slave of Carolina will be raised to a condition, which will enable him to go forth out of bondage."[26] Thus he had rationalized the case for maintaining slavery in a republican society and had refuted Miss Martineau's fallacious arguments about the brutalities of the slave system to his own satisfaction.

After studying the economic structure of the United States, Miss Martineau concluded that the commercial and manufacturing North controlled the finances of the country and that the South had to rely upon the North for its economic livelihood. She was certain that the slave system caused the South's financial dependence by forcing that section to produce only raw agricultural products. Simms, a careful student of the nation's economy ever since his political arguments over the tariff system in the early 1830s, tried to counter her argument. He maintained that because Northern industry could not function without Southern cotton, slavery provided the financial strength for the entire nation. Simms was more interested in defending the social, as opposed to the material, advantages of a slave system. But he also knew that an attack on the South's economic system, especially during a period of economic chaos along the Southeastern seaboard, could have the grave social ramification of dividing the South on the subject of slavery.[27]

What also rankled Simms about *Society in America* was the author's misconception about the nation's political institutions. Miss Martineau was a feminist who supported the movement for female suffrage. A typical Southerner, Simms believed that woman's place in an ordered society was clearly in the home and that women could not function in the ruthless world of politics. But he was much more disturbed by the author's unequivocal position on majority rule in a democratic republic. Simms had doubts about giving aristocratic power to mediocre leadership, but these doubts did not make him a democrat. He thought the doctrine of majority rule was an excuse for oppression by one section over another, and called it a doctrine of physical power. "There is no abstract charm, in mere numbers, to compel obedience of those who are wronged, and who think themselves so," he warned. Worst of all, he found the idea that all men were created equal foolish and odious both to the artist and the statesman. He advised Miss Martineau to observe the "endless varieties and the boundless inequalities" of God's creation.[28] In his fear of the masses and his haughty view of the necessity for an aristocracy of talent and leadership, Simms had joined the conservative branch of both the European and the American romantic movement.

"Miss Martineau on Slavery" was an immediate success. South Carolina's leading politicians and newspapers all praised the young social critic who had so ably defended his section's slave system. The essay was reprinted often and was circulated throughout the leading cities of the South. Soon newspaper articles were quoting from Simms' review and using his examples to establish positions on slavery and to justify its benefit to Southern society. The Charleston *Courier* was pleased that a student of the South's past was assuming the role of guardian of its slave system. The novelist had found that his position in the South was enhanced by his ability to comment on the South's future in a critical fashion. Simms was to learn few more useful lessons during his public career.[29]

But other lessons, concerning the structure of politics and the nature of leadership in South Carolina, would influence Simms' fiction and help to form his own critical judgment of the democratic process. During the nullification crisis, most of South Carolina's politicians had followed Calhoun into the Clay camp in opposition to the Jackson-Van Buren group. In 1836 South Carolina, after flirting with the Harrison Whigs, supported Judge Hugh Lawson White of Virginia for President against Van Buren.[30] But by early 1837, perhaps because of a desire to consolidate his political forces in the state, Calhoun had led most of South Carolina's political leaders back into the Democratic party, ostensibly over support of the President's subtreasury plan. In a move to control the state politically, Calhoun began to use the influential Charleston *Mercury* to attack any politician who opposed the subtreasury system. Following Calhoun's abrupt shift, some of the state's politicians were left stranded as Clay Whigs. Calhoun particularly hoped to unseat three of the state's leading politicians—Congressman Waddy Thompson of Greenville; Hugh Swinton Legaré, who had previously been his nominee to oppose Pinckney; and Senator William Campbell Preston, a staunch nullifier, and second only to Calhoun in the state's political hierarchy. He accused all three men of supporting Clay's national system.[31] By late 1838, Calhoun had successfully destroyed any political opposition and had permanently ruined the Whig party in South Carolina, which assured the state's one-party rule through the Civil War. By returning to the Democratic party and ruthlessly undermining the opposition, he brought the opportunistic Unionists to his side, leaving only a handful of public figures, including Petigru, Legaré, and Thompson to challenge him. Preston's so-called Columbia Regency was replaced as the state's dominant political faction by the Charleston *Mercury* and State Bank forces led by Robert Barnwell Rhett, Franklin Harper Elmore, and their long line of relatives and political allies. Thus by the election of 1840, Calhoun was able to turn South Carolina over to Van Buren and the national Democrats with almost no political opposition.[32]

Some of the state's wiser politicians, including Simms, were skeptical about the ramifications of Calhoun's newly consolidated power. Simms, who remained devoted to Andrew Jackson, had been unsure about supporting Van Buren. He did not like Van Buren's slick Northern political tactics, but because of his admiration for Jackson, he joined many other South Carolina Unionists in supporting Van Buren in 1836. When Calhoun switched to Van Buren's position on the subtreasury, Simms was pleased, because he too was a staunch states rights man who disliked any national economic power. Thus, Simms' Unionism was permanently undermined, because he found it politically expedient to join the Calhoun camp. His new and precarious political position was tested late in 1840 when he was invited to dine with President Van Buren. He declined and asked his friend Joel R. Poinsett to convey his disappointment to the President. Perhaps this was a political refusal, since Simms realized that no South Carolina politician should be too zealous a Van Buren supporter.[33]

Simms' studies of the Pinckney and Preston affairs and the nature of political loyalty were reflected in his fiction and critical reviews in the last years of the decade. Although he complained of his own plight as a man of letters in the South, Simms had definitely committed himself and his public career to his native section. He prospered socially and politically if not financially. Knowing that a successful writer must reside in a large Eastern city, he nevertheless decided to remain in the South and settled down to a pattern of writing, editing, and politicking, spending his summers in Charleston and his winters at Woodlands, with an occasional business and editing trip to New York. As founder of the Charleston-based South Carolina Academy of Art and Design, Simms encouraged the development of a Southern literary establishment in order to create a sectional literature based on local themes, which glorified the past and defended the present South's unique social life. He wrote the rules governing the presentation of papers at the Academy and was instrumental in securing their publication. Many of the academy's discussions served as training ground for several of the state's political leaders.[34] Simms had decided on a public career based on loyalty to his own community. As with most Americans, even the transients, he desired roots. Finding his roots in Charleston, Simms sought all his life to preserve the city's romantic atmosphere.[35]

Literary life in Charleston had taught Simms the importance of the writer in public life. He elaborated upon this realization in "The Sins of Typography," one of a collection of short stories which he wrote for a second edition of *Martin Faber*. The villains of the story were strange men who had brought the pernicious influence of books into a community. At first Simms seemed to be ridiculing the reading public by poking fun at the "impetuous influence of printing" on society. But the story took a more serious turn as those who controlled the press with "their lessons and their false pictures of man and society" soon "had diseased and distracted our little community." Rumors spread that a Kentucky politician had lost an election because adverse public opinion had ruined his reputation, and that the press had fooled an undiscriminating public. Simms damned such power and the democratic community that condoned it. The only way to fight such thought control was to form an opposition press to inform the public of the truth. The writer who sought to protect his community had to become a political writer. The sensitive poet had to relinquish the idea that interfering in the affairs of "state and government" was beneath his dignity. There was immortality for the literary artist with a public mission, and it was his duty to aid his society by creating opinion favorable to the community's survival. Simms later told James Kirke Paulding, the New York novelist, that "the original literature" of a country and the writer's duty to form local opinion far exceeded the importance of mere political office-holding.[36]

Even in *Pelayo*, his little-read and seldom appreciated romance of adventure in Gothic Spain, Simms continued to in-

ject politics into his fiction. This departure from native themes
and settings, which was contrary to Simms' own literary tenets,
was probably motivated by his desire to find some new way of
attracting the depression-racked literary market. Also, many of
his contemporaries, such as Robert Montgomery Bird and Washington Irving, were succumbing to the attractions of medieval
Spain. On the surface *Pelayo* seemed to be completely outside
the mainstream of Simms' fiction. However, it dealt with a nation's loss of power due to lack of innovative leadership. Simms
wanted to understand why a once-powerful nation could decay
so rapidly. Fascinated with tales of the destruction of the
Jewish empire, he created the character of Melchior, a wise old
patriarch whose travels through medieval Spain seemed to
herald the decline of the Gothic empire. Simms postulated the
theory that there was only a certain amount of power available,
"and the loss of it from one spot simply announces its transfer
to another." He showed that historical laws were flexible except where power was concerned, and he seemed to warn his
own contemporaries of the danger of losing a sense of independence. The young and impetuous Pelayo claimed that
man's mind was free and therefore should not be controlled by
any person. Simms replied in romantic and nationalistic terms
that a nation's defense required all persons "to sacrifice friend,
self, and all."[37] His concept of national sacrifice later
influenced his own behavior toward the defense of his section.

The Charleston *Mercury* found *Pelayo* an interesting and
educational adventure but wondered why "the author has
selected a subject, having no relation to our country and
times." In his next romance, Simms compromised by returning
to a native setting but he continued the fascinating theme of
one civilization's decline and another's rise.[38] *The Damsel of
Darien* was Simms' attempt to describe the earliest European
settlement in the Western hemisphere and to explain its importance. A romance filled with many subplots and designed to
excite the reader, the *Damsel* was the story of the heroics of
one Vasco Numez, who sought to escape his past by risking his
life for the world's future. Vasco was significant because he
realized that his feeble generation would live on for posterity
because of its discovery. As in so many of his short stories,
poems, and romances, Simms himself was trying to re-create

that miracle of discovery, yet express his sadness at the destruction of the Indian tribes for the sake of civilization. For Simms, civilization brought corruption as well as order to society. Hypocrisy and political intrigue were as inevitable as the process of civilization itself.[39] Perhaps Simms was trying to describe the inevitable decline of his own generation.

Also reflected in Simms' fiction of the late 1830s was his personal rationalization for staying in South Carolina. He returned to the Germanic plot of the *Bildungsroman* in *Richard Hurdis*, one of his most interesting border tales. Young, impetuous Richard Hurdis, heartsick over the loss of his sweetheart, decided to leave his native Carolina and to strike out for the West. His homeland was too dull and too civilized. It lacked adventure, and Richard lacked dedication. His "thoughts craved freedom, . . . and the wandering spirit of our people, perpetually stimulated by the continual opening of new regions," held out the promise of great material gain. In writing of Richard Hurdis' travels into the remotest part of the frontier, Simms seemed to be re-creating the dream of all Americans and revealing his own wanderlust for the new and untamed West. But in *Richard Hurdis* Simms also condemned westward migration as an obstacle to the development of Southern civilization. The wilderness was licentious; its lack of morals and manners was a disease which made man unfit for society. Besides, Simms warned, the promise of adventure in the West lured ambitious young men to leave the South. Richard's odyssey became a chronicle of the evils of the West, and ultimately the young man returned home to Carolina, there to make a name for himself.[40] So too with Simms. His study of Western society combined with his fears for the South, and he became a wanderer only in his mind, and forever a citizen of South Carolina.

If most of Simms' fictional plots displayed a superficial analysis of society, they also contained certain elements of serious political and social criticism. Practically all of his work revealed his growing dislike of Northerners, particularly what he called their sanctimonious puritanism and their eternal lust for material possessions. His criticism of the North was also directed against the coarse "Yankee" politicians who sought to belittle Southern values.[41] In order to counteract growing

Northern power Simms again studied the qualities needed to create a successful leader for the South's defense. In *The Damsel of Darien* it was Vasco who, through his own sense of destiny and brilliant leadership, was able to overcome nature and settle a colony on the coast of Latin America. Simms, who continued to question the values of representative government, brushed aside the fact that the masses stood in Vasco's way and even demanded a democratic leadership. In "Major Rocket," a short story from *Martin Faber*, he viciously attacked the popular belief in liberty and equality. He declared that there could be "no freedom for the great mass, they were never intended to be free." As he later castigated his democratic friend William Leggett for being a Northerner with too much reform sentiment, so he allowed his characters to claim that only the ignorant were susceptible to the demagogue's shouts of reform and change.[42]

Although Simms maintained to his friend James Lawson that he was a democrat, his fiction revealed that he had no more trust in the people than he had faith in inferior leaders. His own experiences of the political chicanery in South Carolina permeated not only his fiction but his social criticism as well. His final social essay of the 1830s, "The Philosophy of the Omnibus," reflected a view of majority rule tempered by pessimism toward human nature and staunch support of state's rights. In that essay Simms depicted the rise of a mechanized society ruled by common men whose only assets were their ability to turn a profit; "it is Yankee all over." Opposed to the leveling tendencies of his own era, he accused his generation of subtracting "from man's individuality." A society which lacked discrimination and taste was not an existence which the cultured man of letters could choose. He predicted increased disagreement among the states, and he wondered how long the common politician who hankered after votes could delay "the doom of a people." Simms had cautioned against "change for change's sake," and he asked his generation to "beware what legacy is bequeathed to the next generation."[43]

With a literary following in Europe, the North, and the metropolitan South, Simms had become the South's most famous man of letters. During his development as a romanticist, he had devised a means of making himself useful to the South.

His fiction not only displayed his growth as a social and political critic, but it also came to reflect the politics of his own society. Each novel represented an attempt to clarify Simms' feelings about the serious political divisions of his times, and each reflected Simms' slowly evolving political and social beliefs. Always a loyal sectionalist, at the beginning of the decade he thought the South's future lay with the burgeoning republicanism of the North and the new West, and he expostulated staunch national sentiment in his work. At the end of the decade, after the experience of nullification and Simms' observation of local political events in their relationship to national developments, he began to question national enthusiasm. Simms came to understand why the literary artist and dedicated public servant should maintain close ties to that social structure which he knew best.[44]

When James Henry Hammond, a wealthy planter and one of South Carolina's most brilliant political leaders, invited Simms to visit him, the writer accepted. Simms had recently been elected a delegate to a state agricultural convention and had corresponded with Hammond, Barnwell County's most successful planter, on matters dealing with agricultural improvement. The two men became fast friends and developed a mutual respect for each other's intellectual and political abilities. Hammond was most impressed with Simms' literary talents, especially with the author's ability to analyze society through fiction, and he encouraged Simms to continue to write for and about the South. He also appreciated Simms' knowledge of South Carolina politics, his poise and moderation, and he encouraged Simms to seek public office. Little did Hammond know that Simms had been seeking public service for a decade. Nevertheless, a more active phase of Simms' career was soon to begin under Hammond's tutelage. The two men, one an ex-nullifier, the other an ex-Unionist, formed a political bond which would have much importance for South Carolina's future and for the future of the man of letters as active political officeholder.[45]

NOTES

1. Ridgely, *Simms* pp. 39, 61, 68, 73, 77-78. See also Guilds, "Simms's Views," and John R. Welsh, "William Gilmore Simms, Critic of the South," *JSH* 26 (1960): 201-214. For events in South Carolina during the remainder of the 1830s, Wiltse's second volume on Calhoun is still invaluable. Freehling's dissection of the Pinckney affair in his *Prelude to Civil War*, pp. 351-355, is the best treatment of that shabby intrigue, although Freehling finds more political opportunism on Pinckney's part than I am willing to recognize. Actually, Pinckney was more a victim of Calhoun's ambition and dogmatism, since he honestly never understood why he fell from favor.

2. Frances Trollope, *Domestic Manners of the Americans* 2 vols. (New York, 1894), 1: vi-vii; Trent, *Simms*, p. 73. For Mrs. Trollope see Eileen Bigland, *The Indomitable Mrs. Trollope* (New York, 1954), and Una Pope-Hennessy, *Three English Women in America* (London, 1929), pp. 23-112.

3. William Gilmore Simms, *"Domestic Manners of the Americans,* by Mrs. Trollope," *The American Quarterly Review* 12 (September 1832): 110.

4. Ibid., pp. 113-115.

5. Ibid., p. 116.

6. Ibid., pp. 122-123; for a short but incisive statement on the problems of religious diversity see Stanley M. Elkins, *Slavery: a Problem in American Institutional and Intellectual Life* (New York, 1963), pp. 27-29.

7. Ibid., pp. 112, 128; see also Trollope, *Domestic Manners of Americans*, 2: 40-57.

8. *The Cosmopolitan: An Occasional,* 1 (1833) 22-23; 2 (1834): 120-121; *Courier,* May 25, 1833; John C. Guilds, Jr., 50; Clement Eaton, *The Mind of the Old South* (Baton Rouge, 1964), p. 189.

9. *The Cosmopolitan,* 1 (1833): 5-7, 14; *Courier,* July 27, 1833; *Mercury,* May 25, 1833; Guilds, "Simms and Cosmopolitan," p. 37.

10. *Southern Literary Journal* 1 (September 1835-February 1836): 284; *Simms Letters,* 1: 131; Legaré *Writings,* p. 243; *Courier,* Oct. 1, 1838; *Mercury,* Dec. 7, 1835, May 9, 1836, May 31, 1837. Hoole, "Simms's Career," p. 50.

11. Study of Simms' early fiction reveals a nationalist literary outlook tempered with the politician's shrewd ability to seize the advantage of sectional themes as his means of expression. As a historian I am certain that I will miss much of literary significance in this early work. However, my objective is to illustrate Simms' social and political values as revealed in his fiction and to show the slow shift in the views of this young intellectual seeking literary maturity in the South.

12. That Simms was not alone in using fiction as a medium for social and political expression is evident in a slight perusal of the work of his contemporaries; see the introduction by Maude Howlett Woodfin and Carl Bridenbaugh in their edition of Nathaniel Beverly Tucker's *The Partisan Leader* (New York, 1933). Tucker, who wrote *The Partisan Leader* between 1833 and 1836, later became Simms' close friend. Simms corresponded with the Philadelphia novelist, Robert Montgomery Bird, who was writing about the problem of slavery as early as 1835; see Curtis Dahl, *Robert Montgomery Bird* (New York, 1963). For further comparison of Simms as social critic with his literary contemporaries, see Stanley T. Williams, *Life of Washington Irving* 2 vols. (New York, 1935); Joseph Ridgely, *John P. Kennedy* (New York, 1966); Dorothy Waples, *The Whig Myth of James Fenimore Cooper* (New Haven, 1938). For Simms' view of the novel's social usefulness see *The Par-*

tisan 2 vols. (New York, 1835), 1: xii: "It is in this way, only, that the novel may be made useful, when it ministers to morals, to mankind, and to society."

13. For praise of Simms' historical accuracy and realistic settings, plus Simms' own views on the importance of accuracy see *The Partisan*, 1: vi, vii, 134-135; *Mellichampe* 2 vols. (New York, 1836), 1: ix-xii; *Southern Literary Journal*, 1: 284; *Mercury*, Nov. 24, Dec. 9, 1835; *Courier*, July 28, Dec. 21, 1835.

14. *Mellichampe*, vol. 2: 51 (also see *Mellichampe* [Chicago, 1890], pp. 3, 245-246, 259); *The Partisan* (Chicago, 1890), p. 462.

15. *The Partisan* (New York, 1835), 1: 151, 160; *Mellichampe* (1836), 1: iv, v; *Courier*, Dec. 21, 1835.

16. *Mellichampe* (1836), 1: xi-xii; (1890), pp. 85, 295; *The Partisan (1890)*, pp. 52, 95, 431, 440, 445; Ridgely, *Simms*, p. 75.

17. William Gilmore Simms, *The Yemassee* 2 vols. (New York, 1835), 1: 51-52; 2: 3. Simms explicitly said, "It is fortunate, perhaps, for mankind, that there are some few minds always in advance, and forever preparing the way for society, even sacrificing themselves nobly, that the species may have victory." *Courier*, Apr. 14, 1835; see *Martin Faber* (New York, 1833), pp. 235-236; *Courier*, Oct. 12, 26, 1833; William Gilmore Simms, *Guy Rivers* (New York, 1855), pp. 279, 280, 282, 284, 365; *Courier*, July 24, 1834; *Mercury*, Aug. 13, 1834; Merle M. Hoover, *Park Banjamin* (New York, 1948), p. 61.

18. *The Yemassee* (New Haven, 1964), pp. 322, 394, 400, 405; *Courier*, May 2, 1835; *Mellichampe* (1890), pp. 235, 341, 353, 393, 424; *The Partisan* (1890), p. 110; *Courier*, May 2, 1835; Tremaine McDowell, "The Negro in the Southern Novel Prior to 1850," in Gross and Hardy, eds., *Images of the Negro in American Literature* (Chicago, 1968), pp. 63-67.

19. *The Yemassee* (1835), 1: vi; 2: 159-160; *Martin Faber*, pp. 105, 106, 114, 122, 163; *Guy Rivers*, pp. 40, 52, 56, 117, 187, 379, 395, 486, 503; *The Partisan* (1890), pp. 69, 155-157, 379; *Mellichampe* (1890), pp. 32-34, 187, 330-331, 388, 431.

20. *Mellichampe* (1890), pp. 283-284; *Simms Letters*, 1: 90-91; "Woodlands", Charles Carroll Simms Papers; Mildred L. Rutherford, *The South in History and Literature* (Athens, Ga., 1906), p. 170. The *Courier* proclaimed Simms' usefulness to the South; see issues of Dec. 7, 1833, Dec. 22, 1834, Oct. 27, 1835.

21. *Courier*, Aug. 20, Oct. 23, Nov. 17, 1835; *Mercury*, Jan. 8, Aug. 21, Sept. 28, Oct. 9, 1835.

22. John P. Richardson to James Chesnut, March 14, 1836, MSS, James Chesnut Papers, South Caroliniana Library, University of South Carolina; James Henry Hammond Diary, 1836, Hammond Papers, Library of Congress; James Henry Hammond, *Selections from the Letters and Speeches of the Honorable James Henry Hammond of South Carolina* (New York, 1866), pp. 16, 49, 50 (hereafter cited as *Letters and Speeches*); William Sumner Jenkins, *Pro-Slavery Thought in the Old South* (Chapel Hill, 1935), pp. 77-81.

23. *Mercury*, Feb. 27, March 16, 25, Apr. 12, Aug. 26, Sept. 6, Oct. 13, 1836; see the interesting letter of Edward W. Johnston to James Henry Hammond, Jan. 20, 1836, Hammond Papers, Library of Congress. For Calhoun's side see Wiltse, *John C. Calhoun* 2: 283, 284, 285, 292, 293, 294, 392; Pinckney was again able to get back into Calhoun's graces, as he joined with the ex-Union party faction to become mayor of Charleston from 1838 to 1840. See also Freehling, *Prelude to Civil War*, pp. 351-355.

24. For a sketch of Miss Martineau, see Pope-Hennessy, *Three English Women in America*, pp. 211-304: John R. Welsh, "The Mind of William Gilmore Simms" (unpublished Ph.D. dissertation, Dept. of English, Vanderbilt University,

1951), pp. 99-100, 151. For a comment on why Simms defended slavery see David Donald, "The Proslavery Argument Reconsidered," *JSH* 37 (Feb. 1971): 3-18.

25. *Simms Letters*, 1: 113-114; William Gilmore Simms, "Miss Martineau on Slavery," *Southern Literary Messenger* 3 (November 1837): 641-643, 644, 645.

26. Harriet Martineau, *Society in America* 2 vols. (New York, 1837), 2: 106-135; for a commentary on Miss Martineau's knowledge of slavery see Vera Wheatley, *The Life and Work of Harriet Martineau* (Fair Lawn, N. J., 1957); *SLM*, pp. 654, 656, 657. Also see George M. Frederickson, *The Black Image in the White Mind* (New York, 1971), pp. 52, 55.

27. *SLM*, p. 649.

28. Ibid., p. 652.

29. The republication of Simms' article in pamphlet form as *Slavery in America; Being a Brief Review of Miss Martineau on That Subject* (Richmond, 1838), reflected the immediate response to Simms' defense of slavery; see *Courier*, June 8, 1838; *Mercury*, Feb. 24, June 5, 1838; *Simms Letters*, 1: 114; Simms to Hugh S. Legaré, Jan. 29, 1838, Charles Carroll Simms Papers. A reviewer in the *Southern Literary Journal*, n.s. (Jan. 1838), p. 50, said, "We look upon it as an able and masterly vindication of the peculiar policy of the South, with especial reference to our State"; also see Frank Luther Mott, *A History of American Magazines* 4 vols. (Cambridge, 1930-1957), 1: 461. Sydnor, *Growth of Southern Sectionalism*, p. 249, points out Miss Martineau's hostility toward South Carolina.

30. The Charleston *Mercury* adopted Calhoun's political position in 1836, vehemently opposed Van Buren and even flirted with the William Henry Harrison political group; see *Mercury*, Apr. 21, July 4, 1835; Jan. 16, May 17, July 22, Nov. 3, 1836; also see Calhoun to Hammond, June 19, 1836, Francis W. Pickens to Hammond, May 9, 1835, G. B. Lamar to Ham-

mond, Dec. 11, 1836, Calhoun to Hammond, Feb. 18, 1837, Pierce Butler to Hammond, Oct. 30, 1836, Waddy Thompson to Hammond, Feb. 23, 1837, Hammond Papers, Library of Congress.

31. *Simms Letters*, 1: 77-81; George McDuffie to Richard H. Wilde, May 10, 1835, MSS, George McDuffie Papers, South Caroliniana Library, University of South Carolina; Preston to Waddy Thompson, March 29, 1835, Thompson Papers, University of North Carolina; Pickens to Hammond, Dec. 31, 1835, Hammond Papers, Library of Congress; John Richardson to James Chesnut, March 14, 1836, Chesnut Papers; Calhoun to Burt, Feb. 15, 1837, Calhoun to George McDuffie, Oct. 29, 1837, Richardson to Calhoun, Dec. 16, 1837, Thompson to Calhoun, Aug. 30, 1838, Calhoun Papers, Clemson College; Carson, *James Louis Petigru*, p. 191; Pickens to Richard C. Crallé, June 28, 1837, MSS, Francis W. Pickens Papers, Duke University; *Mercury*, March 9, 12, 20, 24, Feb. 15, 17, 23, 28, Sept. 12, 20, Oct. 2, 24, 1837, July 12, Sept. 21, 1838. Laura White, *Robert Barnwell Rhett, Father of Secession* (New York, 1931), pp. 34, 35, 41, chronicles the *Mercury's* attack on Preston as part of Calhoun's return to the Democratic party; also see Ernest M. Lander, Jr., "The Calhoun-Preston Feud, 1836-1842," *SCHM* 59 (January 1958): 24-37.

32. Calhoun to Hammond, July 4, 1836, Hammond to Pickens, May 15, 1839, Hammond to Franklin H. Elmore, March 22, 1838, Hammond Papers, Library of Congress; *Mercury*, July 25, 1838, March 2, June 8, 1840; Hayne, *Politics*, pp. 44-47, 52; Lander, "Calhoun-Preston Feud," p. 26; Jameson, "Calhoun Correspondence," pp. 374-377, 396, 454; Petigru to Legaré, Jan. 9, Feb. 26, Apr. 13, Oct. 5, 1839, Feb. 14, Apr. 6, 1838, Legaré Papers; David J. McCord to Waddy Thompson, June 19, 1838, MSS, David J. McCord Papers, South Caroliniana Library, University of South Carolina; *Courier*, Dec. 7, 1839; Meigs, *Life of John Caldwell Calhoun* II, 225; White, *Robert Barnwell Rhett*, p. 46; Lander, "Calhoun-Preston Feud," p. 37. Also see Arthur Charles Cole, *The Whig Party in the South* (New York, 1919), pp. 47-48;

Green, *Constitutional Development in South Atlantic States,* pp. 183-184.

33. *Simms Letters,* 1: 81, 159-167; 5: 338-343; also see 1: 43, 60, 75, 90, for Simms' break with his Northern Democratic reformer friend William Leggett. Hammond's correspondence reflects the fears many of Calhoun's allies had of their leader; Hammond to Marcellus Hammond, Aug. 6, 1839, E. W. Johnston to Hammond, Feb. 28, 1836; "Occasional Thoughts," Hammond's European Notebook, Paris, Apr. 30, 1837, Hammond Papers, Library of Congress.

34. *Courier,* Apr. 7, 1838; *Southern Literary Journal,* n.s. 1 (June 1837): 297-299, n.s. 2 (Jan. 1838): 7-14; *Simms Letters,* 1: 121, 144-145, 217, 319; Jay B. Hubbell, "Literary Nationalism in the Old South," in David Kelly Jackson, ed., *American Studies in Honor of William Kenneth Boyd* (Durham, N. C., 1940), pp. 177-178, 203-204.

35. *Martin Faber* 2 vols. (New York, 1837), 1: 218; William Gilmore Simms, *Carl Werner, an Imaginative Story* 2 vols. (New York, 1838), 1: 33; *Simms Letters,* 1: 219-221; Miller, *Raven and the Whale,* p. 106; Simms' national and sectional allegiances in literature are argued in Ed Winfield Parks, *William Gilmore Simms as Literary Critic* (Athens, Ga., 1961), p. 93; Guilds, "Simms's Views," p. 405; Edgar T. Thompson, ed., *Perspectives on the South; Agenda for Research* (Durham, 1967), pp. 110-111; Charles G. Sellers, ed., *The Southerner as American* (New York, 1967), pp. 180, 184.

36. *Martin Faber* (1837), 2: 7, 9, 11, 13, 172, 196; *Simms Letters,* 1: 144-145.

37. William Gilmore Simms, *Pelayo: A Story of the Goth* 2 vols. (New York, 1838), 1: 13, 14, 52, 53, 2: 123-124; *Courier,* Nov. 8, 1838; *Mercury,* June 21, 1838; *Courier,* July 4, 1837 reflects the effect of the depression on Southern letters; *Simms Letters,* 1: 138-139; Dahl, *Robert Montgomery Bird* pp. 23, 84-85. Trent, *Simms,* p. 80, says that *Pelayo* was taken from Robert Montgomery Bird's novel *Calavar.*

38. *Mercury*, Nov. 28, 1838; Trent, *Simms*, pp. 119-120; it is significant that Simms waited until 1845 to publish *Count Julian*, the sequel to *Pelayo*.

39. William Gilmore Simms, *The Damsel of Darien* 2 vols. (Philadelphia, 1839), 1: 13-14, 20, 258; 2: 109, 229; *Carl Werner*, 1: 211, 212; 2: 207-208; William Gilmore Simms, *Southern Passages and Pictures* (New York, 1839), pp. 49-52.

40. William Gilmore Simms, *Richard Hurdis* 2 vols. (Philadelphia, 1838), 1: 10-13, 15, 16, 17, 76 (Chicago, 1890), pp. 14, 37, 67, 197, 199, 300; *Southern Passages and Pictures*, pp. 16-18; *Carl Werner*, 2: 107, 110; *Mercury*, Jan. 28, 1838; *SLM*, 4: (Oct., 1838), pp. 690-691.

41. *Martin Faber* (1837), 2: 126, 183; *Richard Hurdis* (1890), pp. 121, 301, 305.

42. *Simms Letters*, 1: 99; *Martin Faber* (1837), 1: 174, II, 161; *The Damsel of Darien*, 1: 15-17, 293, 281; 2: 65, 109; *Courier*, Oct. 1, 1838.

43. *Godey's Lady's Book* (1841), pp. 104-107 (reprinted from the *Southern Literary Journal* of 1839); *Courier*, Feb. 26, 1839; *Mercury*, Feb. 7, 1839; *Simms Letters*, 5: 338-342, 1: 164-166, 166-167.

44. See *Martin Faber* (1837), 1: 153-154, 159; *Pelayo*, 1: 189.

45. *Martin Faber* (1837), 1: 231; *Simms Letters*, 1: 166; Hammond to Simms, March 9, 1841, Hammond Papers, Library of Congress.

3 Cooperationist State Legislator

IN THE EARLY 1840s Simms began a new phase of his public career. Friends attempted to persuade him to run for the state legislature, and he was more than amenable to their arguments. From his experiences during the nullification controversy he had developed a keen though cautious interest in South Carolina politics and had continued to participate actively in public affairs. That he consented to stand for election to the legislature was no surprise, although his public career adversely affected the quality and output of his fiction. Perhaps Simms ran for office because he believed that the intellectual had to court political favor in order to become a literary success, or because he was piqued at the legislature's refusal to adopt his history of the state as a public school text. Obviously, Simms' own public ambitions, which centered around a fierce loyalty to his home section and made him a powerful and respected member of one of South Carolina's leading political factions, have long been misunderstood.[1]

Simms had realized the power of a man of intellect in political life, and he firmly believed that men of letters should serve and even help to make major governmental decisions. He became a competent legislator, intricately involved in the major issues which shook and splintered but ultimately united South Carolina's political factions. His own sense of local loyalty became tempered with a shrewd understanding of political behavior, and his independence succumbed to the practical necessity for unity of purpose and thought.[2]

Many of Simms' literary contemporaries also pursued political careers. Perhaps the paltry financial rewards from trying to earn a living through fiction drove many of them into active office-seeking and, at times, rather hectic political activity. Nathaniel Hawthorne wrote a maudlin campaign biography for his Bowdoin classmate Franklin Pierce and was rewarded with the consulship at Manchester, England. He worked for the Democratic party in various local elections and obtained a job of some small significance at the Boston customs house. Never a candidate for office but always looking for a political appointment, Hawthorne was a casual student of public life who rarely allowed politics to intrude upon his fiction. He was always trying to persuade the Democrats to find jobs for other struggling authors, including his sometimes-friend, Herman Melville. But Melville, who used literature to expose politicians and to expound his own political philosophy, was never an active member of any party. An unsuccessful office-seeker, Melville only received a political appointment as district inspector of customs in New York City after the Civil War.

Simms' other Northern friends, including Walt Whitman, Washington Irving, Henry Wadsworth Longfellow, James Fenimore Cooper, and William Cullen Bryant, were all active in seeking political sinecures. Whitman ingratiated himself with the Democratic party as a reform editor in Brooklyn. Both Cooper and Irving, who were astute students of political behavior, and like Simms extremely skeptical about mass political participation, received rewards of European appointments for services rendered. But they were mostly amateurs who merely dabbled in politics at the ward level. John Greenleaf Whittier failed to persuade Longfellow to leave his chair at Harvard to run for office on the Liberty party ticket in 1844, but Longfellow wrote a few antislavery poems. The most active and successful politician among Simms' Northern friends was the historian George Bancroft. At one time the leader of the Jacksonian Democrats in New England, Bancroft served in Polk's Cabinet and was an unsuccessful candidate for governor of Massachusetts. His historical writing was decidedly political in nature. Yet Bancroft, like all the other Northern writers, never seemed to have the love of active political battle that made Simms so uncharacteristic of his generation.[3]

Southern writers had even a more difficult time earning a living through their literature, and many of them either took jobs as magazine editors or sought political appointments to supplement their incomes. Of those who tried to live by their writing alone, Edgar Allan Poe held the most intriguing political views. A lifelong antagonist of the democratic process and an intellectual snob, Poe nevertheless unsuccessfully sought a political appointment in the Philadelphia customs house. Mostly, however, Southern writers were interested only secondarily in fiction. Augustus Baldwin Longstreet, Joel R. Poinsett, Hugh Swinton Legaré, and Beverly Tucker were occasional writers who were intellectuals in politics. Only the Baltimore lawyer John Pendleton Kennedy wrote enough fiction to be classified as an active man of letters, yet even he did not attempt to earn his living as a writer. Kennedy had a much more successful career as a politician than Simms. He was one of the most powerful Whigs in the South, served in Congress, and, while Tyler's Secretary of the Navy, founded the Naval Academy. But his interest in politics could not rival Simms' and when the two writers met, it was Kennedy who was amazed at Simms' political knowledge and ability. He even accused Simms of allowing politics to interfere with his literary career.[4]

But Kennedy was mistaken. Politics was Simms' career and his writing during the early 1840s reflected his interest in public service and important political issues. Simms was fast forming a friendship with James Henry Hammond, who was seeking the author's advice on his plans to run for governor. The two men thought much along the same political lines. Both lamented the continuous growth of poor national leadership and early came to realize that the slavery issue could never be settled without bloodshed. Hammond, himself a political theorist, wanted to nourish the growing intellectual relationship; he felt that Simms' writing skills would be helpful in the years to come. When he finally began his campaign for governor, he asked Simms to file for the state legislature, in hopes of having an articulate and like-minded political lieutenant in that body.[5]

Perhaps because of his bitterness toward the political tactics of conducting a popular campaign, Simms for the time being refused Hammond's request to run for office and contented himself with giving occasional political advice. However, Simms observed Hammond's campaign and subsequent loss of the election in 1840, which no doubt affected his own political activities. At first Hammond, a staunch nullifier, seemed to be the obvious choice for governor over John P. Richardson, a rather ineffectual ex-Unionist. But reports soon appeared in the Charleston newspapers that Hammond was a member of William C. Preston's political faction and that he opposed the subtreasury plan. These reports were sheer fabrication, but even the violently anti-Unionist Charleston *Mercury*, which Robert Barnwell Rhett controlled, began to question Hammond's loyalty to South Carolina. Obviously Calhoun had decided secretly to support Richardson in order to achieve complete harmony in the state by bringing the old Unionists into his political camp. Besides, the young and talented Hammond was too popular and could someday rival Calhoun's own ambitions. But without Calhoun's backing and without any of the state's major newspapers behind him, Hammond had no chance of election.[6]

Simms observed Calhoun's power in the state as once-loyal Hammond supporters slowly drifted toward Richardson. Simms' own close friends, the Charlestonian Ker Boyce and the Carroll brothers, with whom the author had once studied law, deserted Hammond when they saw that they would gain nothing by backing a certain loser. Simms was reminded that political allegiance depended on political rewards, but despite the ostracism he had recently suffered for supporting a minority party, he continued to aid Hammond. Simms greatly admired Hammond's intellect, but he also was shrewd enough to know that Hammond's career was far from over. At any rate Simms earned Hammond's eternal gratitude for his advice and sympathy. When the legislature met to elect a governor, the outcome was a foregone conclusion, and Richardson easily defeated Hammond by a vote of 104 to 47. The Unionist-

nullification controversy was permanently buried as South
Carolina became practically a one-party state under the control
of Calhoun and his allies Rhett and Elmore.[7]

Although the election brought him no personal political
advancement, Simms seemed to relish the excitement of the
campaign. The approval he received from fellow citizens for
subverting his own ambitions to his public duty was obviously
pleasing to Simms' vanity. His patrician sense of obligation was
also manifested in his desire to keep Hammond in active
political life. He respected Hammond and hoped that his friend
would again run for governor. At first Hammond, always much
too flippant with his emotions, thought of retiring to his plantation, but Simms had nothing to fear about permanent retirement. When the Calhoun forces offered Hammond the governorship in 1842, he readily accepted. With Calhoun's support,
Hammond was easily elected, and Simms soon became a close
political adviser to the new governor.[8]

Even before Hammond was elected governor, he had
again asked Simms to seek a seat in the state legislature. In
1842, Simms' friends thought that he would become an important legislator who would serve in a strategic capacity as Hammond's spokesman in the lower house. But Simms knew that he
had many enemies in Barnwell, including Albert Rhett, and
that he would have to wage a vigorous campaign in order to
win a seat. He was not well known in the district, and he ab-
horred the thought of actually electioneering, but Simms felt a
sense of duty to run for office. Perhaps he was motivated by his
resentment toward the low quality of representation of the
district in Columbia. Nevertheless, he soon caught on to the
techniques of campaigning; he lectured widely and often attended political strategy sessions at Barnwell Courthouse. He
also began to cultivate political friends in the district such as
Samuel Wilds Trotti, a physician from Aiken, and he soon cal-
culated that he had the support of the district's most influential
politicians.[9]

Besides being a good extemporaneous speaker, Simms
wrote some articles of a distinctly political nature for Southern
magazines. He became associated with the *Magnolia* and wrote
many a politically oriented editorial for that important literary
journal. From a previous political lecture given before the

Barnwell Agricultural Society, Simms compiled articles which stressed the value of agriculture in society, a subject especially pleasing to Barnwell, an entirely agricultural district. He wrote of the farmer's innocence in the distant past and claimed that the pastoral life provided universal peace among the masses of men. But this pastoral elegance was soon ruined, as man gave up the farm to search for material wealth and destroyed the innocence of those few who remained close to nature. Those farmers who were strong escaped the evils of Europe and settled in America, a new agrarian paradise. The cycle repeated itself as cities grew and men began anew the search for gold and developed iron into weapons of destruction. Honest work had given way to Yankee cunning, and Simms was certain that he struck a chord of resentment in the citizens of Barnwell. There was a practical side to the author's political orations as he constantly stressed the value of hard work in order to compete with the North. He beseeched farmers to become more scientific in cultivating their crops and to conserve their natural resources. Although the district's farmers hardly understood his rhetoric, Simms sent copies of his articles to Barnwell's leading planters. Even the Rhett family must have understood that they could use an articulate defender of agricultural toil against the abuse by Northern manufacturers of Southern planters.[10]

Writing in the *Ladies Companion*, soon to be renamed the *Magnolia*, Simms continued to stress his views on politics and politicians, both to promote his campaign and to clarify his own views on the merits of political life. He stressed the value of education in an agrarian and republican society. Simms retained some belief in the democratic process, but he found that political leaders who followed public opinion and always adhered to majority rule often made poor decisions. Stressing the faults of an erratic and undependable politician to his future constituents, Simms called for all leaders to be judged on their character and ability. Remembering his own youthful political mistakes, he advocated thirty-five as the minimum age to hold political office. Simms seemed to ridicule his previous activities as a Unionist, and he said that he realized that there were grounds for distrust in his own career. His recantation became a patriotic call for loyalty to section above and beyond foolish personal loyalties. Vowing that he was prepared to han-

dle political responsibility, Simms promised consistent and continuous loyalty to Southern people and principles.[11]

The many lectures and political articles sharpened Simms'
views on the power of representative government and defined
his own position on Southern politics. He was well prepared to
become Hammond's political lieutenant in the state legislature,
but he would have to wait until 1844 to serve. He was chosen
to give the Fourth of July address at Aiken Courthouse, which
would have publicized his views throughout the district, but he
was forced to decline because of a death in his family. The
headstrong Simms felt that his chances for election were
ruined, and he withdrew from the campaign. Besides, in July he
had consented to assume full control of the *Magnolia*, a job he
evidently thought would be of greater service to the state.[12]

As editor of the *Magnolia*, Simms by no means abandoned
his political ambitions. He turned the magazine into a truly sectional political journal and persuaded many of his friends,
including Hammond, Poinsett, Perry, Frederick A. Porcher,
and McDuffie, to contribute articles. In the same manner
Simms made the acquaintance of David F. Jamison, an influential Barnwell politician, and he encouraged the political aspects
of agricultural reform by printing the articles of Edmund Ruffin. Simms' own popularity in Barnwell increased because of
the sectional importance of the *Magnolia*. Both the *Courier* and
the *Mercury* praised Simms for opening the magazine's pages to
the South's leading political figures.[13]

Simms again called for a better standard of literary
creativity in the South, because "the more united and
authoritative the voice that comes from the South, the farther
will it be heard, and the more difficult will it be to silence it."
His constant encouragement of Charleston's youth to write
both fiction and history was the work of a man who sought to
build personal political support among the new breed of young
and ambitious South Carolina political intellectuals. Even
Simms' own articles revealed not so much an interest in
literature as his desire to state his personal political views
before a partisan audience. Thus he often expressed his
views, attacking centralism in the United States as dangerous
to the rights of states. Although he was a bitter Anglo-
phobe, he was most disturbed, not by literary competition

with England, but by England's centralizing tendencies, which many Northern politicians emulated. Simms feared that the United States was moving toward some sort of monarchical type of government in which the North would dominate the South. He bitterly denied the claim of English critics that Jackson had wanted to be a king. He had always seen Jackson as a natural leader of men, but as a Southerner "Old Hickory" could never support a Washington-controlled government. In order to combat centralizing tendencies in the executive office, Simms advocated amending the Constitution to allow the President only one ten-year term in office. Simms' early defense of state's rights was combined with his hope that a great Southern statesman would lead the young intellectuals and teach them the necessity of protecting the South.[14]

While the *Magnolia* had established Simms in a position of political importance in South Carolina, it did not prove to be a successful financial venture. Simms, who was having financial troubles of his own, resigned as editor after one year's service. Both the *Courier* and the *Mercury* regretted Simms' departure, but they were pleased that he continued to write for the *Magnolia* and other Southern journals. The *Mercury* was especially pleased to get a semi-regular column of political and literary news from Simms. He was also free to write fiction, to engage in politics as Hammond's speech-writer and adviser, and to make the lecture rounds which so enhanced his political stature. Editing the *Magnolia* had been a good experience for Simms, and he resigned with surprisingly good will to pursue his other political interests.[15]

Simms probably found the *Magnolia* too confining to his political ambitions. Even while he edited the journal, he often lectured throughout the South in order to place his political ideas before the public. His lectures proved his claim that he had "surrendered body and soul" to politics. When he spoke before a large group of members of the Georgia Historical Society in Savannah on the use of history as art, he turned the speech into a lecture on partisan politics.[16] He accepted an invitation from Albert B. Meek, the Alabama historian, to give an anniversary lecture before the Erosophic Society of the University of Alabama, and during his visit to Alabama he gave a number of speeches on politics, the South, and the value of history. His lecture entitled *Social Principle: Or True Source of National Permanence*, delivered in December 1842, was widely discussed and reprinted, and it became the basis of an article on Simms in the *Southern Literary Messenger*. In this lecture he again attacked what he considered to be the growing materialistic culture in the South, comparing his people to the New England Puritans who had studied Milton as a politician rather than as a poet. He wondered how long the South could continue to exhaust its soil and to grow only one staple crop. He also accused Southerners of destroying their roots and traditions in their fierce desire to exploit the new lands of the West. Specifically he attacked the South's political leaders as speculators who destroyed the land. He warned that the South, being over-extended from such rapid expansion, would soon be in no position to defend itself. (Simms changed his tune when the question of Texas annexation became intricately involved in South Carolina politics.) His suggestion for curing the evils of modern society was for the youth of the South to study the past in order to understand the sense of home values and antagonism to material possessions "of our ancestors." He closed by cautioning Alabamians and South Carolinians to return to a simpler life if they hoped to defend their homeland in the coming sectional struggle.[17]

These lectures were widely discussed among South Carolina's political leaders. Many of them read the *Southern Literary Messenger*'s article on "Mr. Simms as a Political Writer." The *Messenger* conceded that many people would question that such a genius as Simms could have multiple careers as a writer of fiction, a historian, and an eminent political figure. But the magazine showed that Simms had displayed a keen knowledge of politics and politicians in the *Social Principle*, especially in his attacks on the growing materialistic nature of the South's so-called leaders. Simms' *History of South Carolina*, which had influenced the state's youth, and his brilliant essay on Miss Martineau, were mentioned as proof of his literary versatility. Not content with merely listing Simms' accomplishments, the *Messenger* sought to explain how a man of letters could also be such a brilliant politician and political analyst. It was Simms' occupation as an historical novelist that "fit him for the duties of an historian and a political writer." In accounting "for the successes of the individual mind," Simms came to understand the values of the entire Southern community. The writer in the *Messenger* claimed that by studying the lives of Southern heroes and by analyzing past political behavior through detailed fictional characterization, Simms had gained "ample preparation for the task of the political writer—the application of that knowledge to present events and the affairs of nations and society generally."[18] The *Messenger's* writer was correct. Simms did sharpen his political skills through his fiction—skills which he needed to help Governor Hammond and to prepare for his political role in the state legislature.

Simms had used his literature to develop his own political philosophy and to clarify for his personal satisfaction the important issues of his day. Also, with the aid of some of Barnwell's political leaders, Simms used the ideas and opinions expressed in his magazine and lectures to state his own beliefs to the voters of the district. The man who had considered it beneath his dignity to solicit support for office began an active campaign to assure himself a seat in the legislature. He attended the legislative session at Columbia in the fall of 1843, made many political contacts, lobbied for friends' political interests, and continued to ingratiate himself with Hammond as the governor's speech-writer and political confidant. As a campaigner he confronted the important political issues of the day, including the tariff, Texas annexation, and anti-abolitionist controversies, and he soon emerged as a thorough-going advocate of Southern unity and cooperation against the North's increasing violation of Southern rights.[19]

Although Simms claimed, and his literature demonstrated, a certain independence of behavior, and while he seemed to turn radical because he honestly believed that the South was losing its rights in the Union, political events in South Carolina and the nation heavily influenced his campaign and his subsequent role in the legislature. From the moment John Tyler became President, Calhoun began plans to run for the office in 1844. Robert Barnwell Rhett, Calhoun's campaign manager, planned to control the Democratic party's choice for President through an elaborate scheme by which each Congressional district would choose its own candidate and have one vote in

the national convention, thus circumventing the statewide convention power in the hands of Van Buren. Rhett was furious
over the lack of legislation in Congress on the volatile issues of
tariff reform and Texas annexation, but he honestly thought
that with Calhoun as President the Democratic party would
unite in favor of the South's interests.[20]

Calhoun's political supporters in South Carolina, headed
by Franklin H. Elmore and Francis W. Pickens, supported
Rhett's desire to work with the Democratic party. However,
they knew that Calhoun had to appear moderate on the issues
of Texas and the tariff in order to achieve national Democratic
support and deprive Van Buren of the nomination. To remove
Calhoun from national discussion they persuaded him to resign
from the Senate, but Calhoun's resignation created political
agitation over the senatorial succession. Rhett, among others,
wanted the seat and was not pleased with Calhoun's rather
lackadaisical support. Yet he remained Calhoun's manager and
joined others in trying to mollify the growing radical sentiment
in South Carolina under the leadership of Governor Hammond
in Columbia.[21]

Although Hammond wanted Calhoun to be President, he
believed that Calhoun was too moderate and that he lagged
behind the state's growing radical sentiment. Hammond had
conferred with Simms, who also thought that Calhoun should be
President, perhaps to rid South Carolina of his pernicious
political influence, but certainly to protect the South in the
Union. Together they decided that the tariff and Texas were
too important issues to trust to the Democratic party. They
chose Hammond's opening speech before the state legislature
as the time to call for collective action in defense of the South's
agricultural system, which was seriously endangered by the
tariff. Hammond put Calhoun in an awkward position by
claiming that Texas and Great Britain were about to sign a
treaty which would place Texas under the protection of
England and thus pose a direct threat to the future of slavery
expansion. Immediately Calhoun's supporters in the legislature
attacked Hammond's speech, but the speech had hurt
Calhoun's Presidential aspirations. Hammond was considered
a Calhoun spokesman by many national Democrats, and his
radical speech, which called for South Carolina's nullification

of the tariff of 1842 and insisted upon the protection of slave expansion into Texas, made Calhoun appear radical to the rest of the nation.[22]

Aware of Calhoun's political maneuvers in South Carolina, Simms was positive that Calhoun wanted to destroy Hammond's career. He changed his opinion of Calhoun, and he began to consider Hammond the most important political opponent in South Carolina of the federal government. Simms felt that Calhoun would sabotage any attempt at debate on the pressing issues of the time, and he hoped that Calhoun's career would be destroyed nationally. When Calhoun's hope for the Presidential nomination was damaged by the refusal of the New York convention to support Rhett's plan of county convention voting, Simms thought that the consequences would work to the political advantage of South Carolina.[23]

But Calhoun had one last plan. He had recently become Tyler's Secretary of State in order to draft the Texas statehood bill. To keep Van Buren from the nomination Calhoun agitated for the immediate annexation of Texas. Both Clay and Van Buren, mistaking public sentiment, announced their opposition to immediate annexation and ruined their chances of becoming President. But Rhett, according to his biographer Laura White, counseled Calhoun to avoid the strategy of radical agitation over Texas in hopes of throwing the election into the House of Representatives. Rhett later assumed a radical position, but in early 1844 he maintained some faith in the South's ability to control the Democratic party, and he wanted a united party to win the election. Calhoun followed Rhett's advice; knowing that he could not get the nomination, he had his name removed from the ballot at the Democratic convention in Baltimore, for the sake of party unity. Perhaps Rhett was avenging the shabby treatment he had received when he had sought Calhoun's Senate seat. At any rate, thanks to Rhett's faulty advice and the radical mood created by Hammond with the help of Simms, Calhoun was forced to wait until 1848 to try for the Presidency.[24]

In his campaign for the state legislature on the issues of Texas and the tariff, Simms moved toward an increasingly radical position. At a Barnwell meeting to discuss the future of Texas, he offered a series of resolutions to set up a district meeting and form a committee to plan strategy for informing the rest of the state of the importance of immediate action on Texas annexation. His resolutions were adopted, and Simms was named to the committee. The next day, May 23, the committee met with a large contingent of Barnwell planters at Buford's Bridge, and Simms was invited to comment on the necessity for the annexation of Texas. In a speech "of considerable length," he called on the people of the slaveholding states to force their Congressmen to agitate the Texas question. Simms asked that, in addition, Southerners withhold their support of any Presidential candidate "who is unfavorable to the annexation of Texas."[25]

Events in Washington further influenced Simms' campaign tactics. Hammond had written Calhoun that the unrest in South Carolina was caused by fear that Great Britain would annex Texas and block the extension of slavery. When the United States Senate defeated a Texas treaty on June 8, 1844, there was great agitation in the South. Rhett, who had grown completely disillusioned with Congress over Texas and the tariff situation, sent a blistering letter to his Barnwell constituents which was printed in the *Mercury* on June 27. He repudiated the Democratic party and tried to rouse the state's youth with the call for a statewide convention to be held the following April. Simms had awaited Rhett's turn to radicalism, for as a candidate in Rhett's Congressional district, he could gain much through a radical appeal. Simms also regarded the new radical movement as one last opportunity to wrest political power from Calhoun. Sensitive to prevailing public opinion, Simms prepared the most important and the most volatile speech of his political career for the Fourth of July celebration at Aiken.[26]

Directing his attack mainly toward the North, Simms began his speech with comments on South Carolina's historical struggles against outside forces. He pointed out that the Carolina settlement had always been under siege from the Spanish, the Indians, and the British. The small colony had been forced to drive out the aggressors apparently without outside help. Since there had been no unity of feeling in the past, "nay, there was a positive diversity, if not dislike" toward the colonial North, there was no basis for community of interest in contemporary times. In fact, Simms asserted the North had always trespassed upon Southern interests. But since the slave system was currently endangered by Northern attempts to deprive the South of the westward extension of slavery, the South needed additional strength and "new securities" regardless of the cost.[27]

Therefore, Simms repudiated Rhett's position on single-state action, and he called for a united South to defend its own interests and to demand the annexation of Texas as a slaveholding state. Although the speech was filled with imperialistic platitudes on expansion, Simms had some sober political reasons for demanding that Texas join the Union. Simms believed that Texas was the means by which a proper political balance of power could be maintained in Congress. Without this balance of power, he pointed out, the South had no security within the Union. The only security for the South was a show of united force, and without such unity Southerners could do nothing. Simms blamed the South's ambitious politicians, who regarded fellow Southerners as rivals, for the lack of common support. He said that the South would meet in separate convention, Texas would be recovered and sectional rights would be strengthened.[28]

Simms realized that his jeremiad was causing members of the audience to talk of war, and he promised them that Texas would defeat the Mexicans without any outside aid. But he closed his oration on a note of caution that belied his optimism. He hoped that his fellow Southerners would not fool themselves into thinking that they owed the North any moral or social obligation. Since the national union was born of necessity and common concessions, those conditions alone could preserve it. But that relationship had been transformed into the "insolence of despotism, and the unreckoning violence of a minority conscious only of injustice." Simms believed that the South had to calculate the value of such a tenuous kind of union. He warned that the Union could no longer rely on the South's conscientious willingness to continue the "noble experiment." In conclusion he stated that the failure to acquire Texas would threaten disunion and civil war, for which the North alone would be to blame.[29]

Hammond wrote that Simms had frightened the North. He agreed with Simms that Texas should be annexed at any cost.

The Charleston *Mercury*, by this time completely under radical control, praised Simms' oration. The paper was pleased with his ability to use his political powers so earnestly in defense of South Carolina. Stuart, the editor of the *Mercury*, printed the last part of Simms' speech in full, and he deemed the entire oration "worthy of study," as an example of the call for support from all Southerners. Certain that Simms was correct in predicting civil war over Texas, Stuart asked if Simms would become a leading architect of the revolution. Revolution seemed imminent, at least for South Carolina, when Rhett returned to Barnwell for a dinner in his honor at Bluffton. Simms' speech and Rhett's attempts at organizing radical sentiment formed the nucleus of the Bluffton Movement, a loosely knit group of young radicals bent on Southern unity and eventually secession.[30]

Having become a viable component of the new radical sentiment because of his speaking abilities, Simms was assured election to the legislature. But he had another means of campaigning, not open to most politicians. His poems, short stories, and novels were widely circulated in Barnwell and served not only to explain his own political sentiments, but to offer the reader some idea of how Simms himself was affected by the volatile issues of the early 1840s.[31]

Always a meticulous judge of the fallibilities of Southern society, Simms reserved his harshest judgment in the 1840s for social behavior in the North. In a mediocre and pointless short story, "The Prima Donna," he contrasted the filth and squalor of New York City's slums to the beauty of the agrarian South. He scoffed at the Yankee school teacher who could not even ride, let alone appreciate the calm and serene Southern countryside. In *Border Beagles*, a border romance, Simms' true feelings for the North became apparent. Although he gently chided Harriet Martineau in the novel, Simms vehemently demanded that an abolitionist character be lynched for his attack on slavery. In a lengthy aside, he condemned Arthur Tappan as the leading example of misguided abolitionism. His anger had overflowed, because Simms no longer regarded abolitionists as harmless cranks who could not launch a successful attack on the slave system. In his opinion, all abolitionists had become radical insurrectionists who agitated among the slaves and encouraged them to revolt against their masters.[32]

Above all, Simms' fiction of the mid-1840s reflected his changing attitudes toward westward expansion, which were in turn influenced by the question of Texas annexation. Once he had feared the prospect of Southeasterners emigrating to the West, because he felt that the West lacked civilization and that the Southeast was being dangerously depopulated. But he had come to believe that the West offered a new life, with opportunity for economic advance. It was a place where all talents were appreciated and where corrupt bankers and railroad swindlers were unwelcome. The new mecca was Texas, where land was plentiful and men were not hampered by lack of education. When a character in *Confession* talked in imperialistic tones about the conquest of all of Mexico, Simms fervently agreed that for the South to fulfill its destiny, it even ought to conquer Cuba. He believed that mongrel Spaniards and Indians were a modest price to pay for the land and water necessary to the survival of slavery. Simms was conscious of the problems which the rich Texas soil might create for the economy of South Carolina. But the South's ascendancy in the Union had to be maintained, and since Texas had become the savior of the South, Simms would become more selective when next he questioned the border's rough-and-tumble influence upon a more civilized Southeast.[33]

Although Texas was uppermost in Simms' mind, the question of political campaigning, which reflected his ambivalent views of the democratic process, also troubled him. Many of his literary figures were active candidates for their general assemblies, and they realized that political success went only to those who were dynamic speakers and "stump" politicians. Simms believed that "republicanism lacks reverence," but this premise only made his characters doubt the feasibility of popular elections; it did not keep them from feverishly campaigning for office. In *Beauchampe*, another novel of border violence and revenge, Simms centered much of the action around an election. The novel reflected his increasing interest in the manner in which politicians used their power. He devoted an entire chapter to the subject of "Stump Tactics." Simms studied the behavior of candidates as they dispensed alcohol and platitudes to the populace, telling them what they wanted to hear and following the local party line. One character discussed the way in which people shamelessly used their political leaders, and he pointed out that even the great Daniel Webster was subject to the petty whims of his constituents. A politician was "sucked, squeezed, thrown by, an atom in a dungheap." Yet one of *Beauchampe*'s heroes, the brilliant and cultivated William Calvert, was too much the aristocrat. Because he would not pander to the masses, he lost the election for Congress.[34] In this manner, politics and political issues seemed to dominate Simms' fiction of the early 1840s.

If Simms was disturbed over election tactics and what he considered to be the general low level of public responsibility and political leadership, he nevertheless was pleased that the citizens of Barnwell District had chosen him to serve in the state legislature.[35] Although he posed as an indignant writer who was forced to give up precious time to attend sessions, once Simms arrived in Columbia, even the mundane duties of helping to organize the various sessions pleased him. He lobbied behind the scenes for the appointment of his friend George Frederick Holmes to the professorship of classical languages at the College in Columbia, and he began to study the behavior of his fellow legislators. He was named chairman of the Committee on Federal Relations, perhaps the most important committee in the House, since it made policy regarding the federal government. As a member of the Joint Committee for Publications of Proceedings, Simms worked diligently to have the legislature pay the expenses for a geological survey of South Carolina. He soon became familiar with committee work, and he received praise for his conscientious participation in even the smallest of matters. Simms, who had promised to keep quiet during the session, became an active participant in the House debates on Governor Hammond's address concerning Texas, the tariff, and cooperation among the Southern states. He wrote speeches and offered resolutions in support of Hammond, and he became heatedly involved in the controversy over calling a state or Southern convention. The debate led to the organization of an anti-Calhoun political faction, the Young Carolina movement, in which Simms was deeply involved.[36]

For Simms and others of the opposition, the defense of

Governor Hammond's address to the legislature was the central issue of the entire session. Hammond had previously decided against further antagonizing the Calhoun forces and had resolved not to speak in favor of a Southern convention. But the Rhett group pursued the question of tariff reform and was becoming disenchanted with Polk, the Democratic party's Presidential candidate. They planned to push the state legislature into some sort of commitment to a separate state convention. Francis W. Pickens, Calhoun's most loyal supporter in the legislature, assisted by Christopher G. Memminger, an ex-Unionist, and Franklin Harper Elmore, the president of the Bank of South Carolina, sought to counter Rhett's radicalism and to maintain Calhoun's dominance in the state. The Calhoun forces were obviously upset over the Bluffton Movement, fearing that South Carolina's radical image would forever destroy the opportunity for Southern unity under the leadership of Calhoun.[37]

After long consultation with Simms on the subject of Hammond's future position in state politics, the governor reversed his position and delivered an argument for the immediate calling of a Southern convention. What was usually a rather dull occasion for the outgoing governor to ingratiate himself with the state's leaders by a spate of laborious platitudes, turned into a wild melee of accusations and counter-accusations. Hammond vehemently attacked the national Democratic party's equivocal position on tariff reduction, which raised the price of cotton on the European market and made the purchase of foreign goods almost prohibitive, thus causing a severe and continuing economic recession throughout the South. Turning next to slavery and Texas annexation, Hammond told the legislature that Northern Congressmen rejected the annexation treaty because they opposed any enlarging of the slave states' political power through the extension of slavery. Hammond spoke of the protection of the Southern way of life, and he proposed to hold a convention in order to unite all of the Southern states in their grievances against the North.[38]

Pickens and his aides, who knew that Henry Aiken, a Calhoun supporter, had defeated the Bluffton-Hammond candidate for governor, Whitemarsh B. Seabrook, decided to await

the public's reception of Hammond's message before announc-
ing their own reactions. When it became obvious that the
organizational ability of Simms and others was making Hammond's speech a rallying cry for radical opposition to Calhoun,
and that Hammond was gaining too much political support,
Pickens offered counterresolutions to the proposals for ac-
cepting the governor's speech. Pickens cautioned against the
feasibility of a Southern convention, and with Calhoun's
pressure he succeeded in tabling the motion to put Hammond's
speech on record. His counterproposals were mild and con-
descending, but they passed the state Senate unanimously.[39]

In the lower house, Christopher G. Memminger offered a
similar motion, and he asked that the discussion on the reception of Hammond's speech be removed from Simms' Committee on Federal Relations and placed before a committee of the
whole house. Certain that Memminger and Pickens aimed to
destroy Hammond, Simms offered counterproposals to Memminger's motion. He spoke as a strict constructionist, state's
rights supporter, who had begun to question whether the
Democratic party and President-elect Polk would defend the
South in the future. He opposed the tariff as oppressive to the
Southern economy, and he asked whether it was time for the
South to depend upon itself rather than petition the federal
government for redress of grievances. But his true interest was
Texas annexation, and he stated that the South could not survive without room to expand its economic and political power.
Bitterly attacking the growing power of abolitionism in Congress, Simms maintained that since Texas was important to the
entire slaveholding community, there should be a meeting to
decide policy. Simms had offered a resolution in the South
Carolina legislature inviting delegates from all the Southern
states to meet in Asheville, North Carolina, on March 4, 1846,
in order to discuss united Southern cooperation.[40] The
cooperation movement had begun, and Simms was in its forefront.

Although Simms' resolutions and Hammond's message
were considered too hasty, the author continued to take a
radical position on the leading issues before the legislature. He
took singular pride in leading the legislature to expel the

Massachusetts abolitionist Samuel P. Hoar, who had attempted to organize Charleston's black sailors for insurrection. When Memminger was the only member to vote against expulsion, Simms felt that the more moderate Calhoun forces had been chastised for their previous behavior. Simms also opposed Pickens' resolution against the Congressional act to rescind the unpopular "Gag" or twenty-fifth rule, partly because of dislike for Pickens' behavior toward Hammond, but more specifically because he believed that the "Gag Rule" issue was no longer important. As far as Simms was concerned, Southern cooperation would have better chance of success if abolitionism was condoned in Washington. As a member of the committee to inspect the records of the Bank of South Carolina, which was scheduled to meet the following summer, Simms opposed a resolution to reduce the Bank's annual expenses, feeling that such a measure would cut off most of its power. Simms later reversed this position when he realized how much political power Elmore wielded as president of the Bank.[41]

The Bank issue was the last of the legislature's business for that session, and many of the politicians quickly forgot the vehement battles over Hammond's message. Such was not the case with Simms. Although the Bluffton Movement for single-state action was soundly defeated and his own resolutions for united Southern action also failed, he was convinced that radical politics were in the ascendancy. Therefore he continued to agitate for the organization of a political movement to oppose what he deemed the pernicious control of the state's leadership by the Calhoun group. He hoped that his young admirers in Charleston would help to create an opposition party by spreading their ideas throughout the state. Since there was a Senate vacancy, Simms asked Hammond to run for that office and to become the leader of the new party. He also tried to persuade Alfred Proctor Aldrich, a close friend and loyal Barnwell radical, to merge his recently organized Southern League against the abolitionists with Hammond and the Charleston movement. Hammond was the key figure, because of his statewide fame, and because Simms regarded him as a proved leader who would gladly help move the South toward its future confrontation with the North. But for personal reasons Hammond decided against standing as a candidate for the Senate. Without a leader Simms' plan for an opposition party temporarily collapsed.[42]

Yet the writer was not discouraged, nor was he idle during the period between legislative terms. Aside from his heavy political correspondence and his attempts to make a living by writing fiction, he had taken on a new editorial assignment. As editor of his own magazine, the *Southern and Western Monthly Magazine*, he planned to continue his quest for Southern unity. He turned the magazine into an important organ of political propaganda in hopes of influencing his fellow Carolinians on the leading issues of the day. Simms continued to agitate for war against Mexico, and he sought maps and documents concerning the geography of Texas to prepare for the South's future control of that territory. He editorialized against war with England over Oregon and instructed Southern Congressmen to concern themselves only with Texas. To that end, he solicited articles about Texas agriculture, the Mexican army, and the economy of California from many of the South's leading intellectuals. He even asked Benjamin F. Perry, who was rapidly cooling toward Simms because of the author's blatant radicalism, to persuade General Waddy Thompson to write an article for *Southern and Western* on the political leadership of Mexico. Also, as editor of the *Charleston Book*, a collection of essays and poems by many of the state's leading politicians, Simms persuaded Henry L. Pinckney to write an article urging Southern support for war with Mexico, a theme often repeated in the *Southern and Western*.[43]

In his capacity as editor of the *Southern and Western*, Simms provided a literary platform for many Southern politicians to express their views. He wanted to clarify issues and to help budding politicians, and the magazine soon became a tool for many of the South's leading public figures. Simms also kept a sharp eye for articles which would aid his own political movement. He persuaded Hammond to publish his Clarkson letters, written to an English abolitionist minister in defense of slavery, in order to spread Hammond's reputation throughout the South. Hammond agreed, after exacting the promise that Simms would edit the manuscript. No one was more delighted with the wide acclaim Hammond received than Simms. In his critique of his friend's work for the *Southern and Western*, Simms concentrated on the merits of genius in public service, praising Hammond's contribution to the politics of slavery. Simms urged South Carolinians to force Hammond out of retirement, and the *Mercury*, in an editorial which linked the careers of Simms and Hammond, applauded both of them for defending Southern institutions.[44] No doubt Simms was elated over this publicity, which encouraged his own political ambitions.

While he was editor of the *Southern and Western*, Simms continued to take an active part in politics. Diplomatically he declined Governor Henry Aiken's offer to make him an adviser on public affairs, ostensibly because he was burdened with other duties. Actually Aiken was too moderate and too attached to Calhoun's crowd for Simms' liking. Besides, Simms was busy with a legislative committee which was examining the financial records of the Bank of South Carolina. During the examination Simms learned some lessons about political economy as he discovered that Elmore had secured Bank loans for many South Carolina politicians in the Calhoun faction. He planned to oppose the Bank's monopolistic financial power in the next legislative session.[45]

Simms slowly redefined his own views on the economy of the South as he began to question many of the methods of Southern financial self-support. In an editorial for the *Southern and Western*, Simms cautioned the South against a one-crop economy. He agitated for scientific farming and breeding and the use of fertilizers, and he called for a careful look at the feasibility of a manufacturing South. Obviously he was influenced by Edmund Ruffin's geological survey, for he advised Southerners to employ slaves in factories. He claimed that the abundant natural resources of water power, minerals, and timber, an excellent climate, and streams for transportation, could easily make the South a competitor of New England. He praised the manufacturing experiments of William Gregg and hoped that others would follow Gregg's lead. Although still philosophically an agrarian idealist, Simms found that his economic views were predicated on the critical need of a utilitarian South to protect its way of life. As he had used the magazine for political purposes, Simms also used it to instruct the South on its economic future, and he sharpened his economic knowledge to prepare himself for the upcoming session of the legislature.[46]

As Simms made plans to go to Columbia, he did some hard thinking about his magazine. It had served his political purposes, but it was a financial failure. He sold the *Southern and Western* to the *Southern Literary Messenger*, but he promised Benjamin Blake Minor to continue as book-review editor, a post which could help Simms' political career. He was unhappy to give up his magazine. As always, he was able to apply his new knowledge and to use his new associations for his own political purposes.[47]

Expecting a mild legislative session in comparison to the previous year's debate over the Southern convention, Simms wondered how he could avoid boredom and make his presence felt in Columbia. He was up for reelection and, although he claimed no interest in running again, he wanted to impress his constituents. Turning immediately to committee work, Simms soon was involved in writing legislation. He plunged the legislature into a debate on his resolution to have the people of the state elect their own Presidential electors. Simms' political bombshell would have repercussions for years to come, but his resolution, which passed the House, died in Senate committee. Speaking as a member of the Committee on Federal Relations, he proposed that the state also set up a uniform time for electing Presidential electors. In hopes of appealing to the large landholding interests in Barnwell, Simms introduced a bill to maintain the integrity of the freehold by the exemption of real estate from taxation. Also, for his constituents' convenience, Simms asked the legislature to establish a new election precinct at Silverton in Barnwell. So often did he speak that many legislators chuckled when Simms made a motion to limit the debating time of individual speakers.[48] The writer had truly become a political animal.

Simms also became deeply involved in the discussions on economic diversification. He had already made his position clear in the pages of the *Southern and Western*, and he continued to encourage manufacturing in South Carolina. Voting to charter all new commercial enterprises which came before the legislature, he also frequently spoke against the high protective tariff. When accused of self-contradiction he explained that industry could flourish in the South under free trade without restricting its growth. He even became an outspoken supporter of internal improvements, speaking favorably for chartering the Edisto and Ashley Canal Company as an asset to agricultural development. Reporting on his committee's study of the Bank of South Carolina, he diplomatically praised Elmore's honesty. But in order to counter the Bank's political influence, Simms offered a resolution to set up a state-controled government mint in Charleston to compete with Elmore's bank.[49]

When the session ended, Simms returned to Woodlands an exhausted and depressed man. But his depression soon faded as he plunged again into an active campaign for reelection. He spoke often on subjects of local interest in his district. The *Mercury* reported that he exemplified the concerned local politician who "gave earnest of his high usefulness to those whom he represents, and whom we hope he will long represent in a political station."[50]

But Simms was defeated for reelection and thus was denied the opportunity to serve Barnwell District again in the state legislature. Some friends thought that his literary career and his frequent trips to Charleston and the North had hurt his chances for reelection. There were more complicated reasons at work. Simms' political ally, Alfred P. Aldrich, head of the political opposition to Calhoun, was Commissioner in Equity for Barnwell and had strong opposition for reelection. Since Aldrich's office was chosen by the legislature, Simms faced more opposition than he otherwise would have encountered. Aldrich was unpopular in Barnwell, and Simms' active work for him made the author equally unpopular. Even so, if his constituents who felt so confident of his reelection had bothered to vote, Simms would have been returned to the legislature.[51]

Although disappointed by his defeat, Simms immediately considered running for Congress from either Barnwell or Charleston. His friends, including the ex-Blufftonite, John M. Felder, reassured Simms that his talents were much needed in active political life. Simms' political aides nominated him for lieutenant governor, a largely honorary position, but one which Simms could make politically useful. Many newspapers throughout South Carolina seconded the nomination. They said that he deserved office as a reward for past loyalty, and they claimed that his election would be a great honor for the state. Simms honestly thought he had a chance of victory. But his nomination came too late to arouse strong support, and he fell one vote short of being elected.[52]

After two quick defeats Simms should have doubted his political abilities and his popularity. But instead, he immediately went to work as chairman of the legislature-appointed Free School Commission, a position that made him many political contacts. Invited to meet with Hammond at Silver Bluffs, the two politicians planned to damage Calhoun's power in South Carolina through a direct attack on Elmore and the Bank. Simms wanted to form a new political party and, to that end, he helped to organize the Young Carolina movement and hoped to have Hammond as its leader. When McDuffie retired from the Senate, Simms attempted to force Hammond out of retirement. Hammond declined, from fear of personal embarrassment. Simms soon realized that Elmore was Calhoun's candidate for the Senate and that with Elmore in Washington, perhaps the political power of the Bank would diminish. Although he was upset when Andrew Pickens Butler, a well-meaning but rather simple Calhoun aide, was chosen Senator, Simms was pleased that Hammond had shown some interest in the office and that he had promised to help Simms in future political struggles. Thus had begun Simms' incessant activity to organize Young Carolina as a powerful political weapon to topple the Bank and perhaps even to limit Calhoun's power or to force the great man to listen to the radicals of South Carolina.[53]

Simms was a political loser, yet he emerged as a student of political behavior, a fact which was reflected in his essays, history, and fiction throughout the rest of his public career. He had learned that to represent power was almost as important as to possess it. Westward expansion for the South temporarily replaced his conservative fears of uprootedness, and he came to praise the imperialistic ambitions of Zachary Taylor. Even his aristocratic inclinations were tempered by the necessity of getting elected. As a public man of letters he promised to serve his section whenever needed. He told George Frederick Holmes that a political man must maintain his loyalty to his homeland and remain sympathetic to the efforts of his state. When Hammond told him that many believed his "excursion into politics" was for momentary pleasure, and that he had to choose between a political and a literary career, Simms felt that there was no decision to make. Literature and politics were always combined, never separated, in his devotion to South Carolina.[54] As he began to chronicle his state's past heroic deeds, the public man of letters again demonstrated that literature could be his political medium.

NOTES

1. Unfortunately the Trent-Parrington view of Simms' status in South Carolina has influenced those literary critics who have tried to explain why Simms was so active in state politics. See Bernard Smith, *Forces in American Criticism* (New York, 1939), pp. 125-126; Ridgely, *Simms*, pp. 90-91; Trent, *Simms*, pp. 128-129; Higham, "Changing Loyalties of William Gilmore Simms," pp. 215-216.

2. See Miller, *Raven and the Whale*, pp. 108-109; Benjamin T. Spencer, *The Quest for Nationality; an American Literary Campaign* (Syracuse, N. Y., 1957), pp. 116-117; Robert Edward Spiller et al, *Literary History of the United States* 4 vols. (New York, 1955-1963), 1: 608; William Gilmore Simms, *Views and Reviews in American Literature, History, and Fiction*, 1 Ser., ed. C. Hugh Holman (Cambridge, 1962), xxxvi-xxxvii; Hammond Journal, March 30, 1841, "Notes on Simms," Hammond Papers, Library of Congress.

3. Randell Stewart, *Nathaniel Hawthorne: A Biography* (New Haven, 1948), pp. 72, 75, 78, 86-89, 127, 129, 133, 136, 145; Newton Arvin, *Herman Melville* (Boston, 1921), pp. 198-199, 258-260; Henry Seidel Canby, *Walt Whitman, an American* (Boston, 1943), pp. 19, 30, 39, 42, 43-45; William L. Hedges, *Washington Irving: An American Study, 1802-1832* (Baltimore, 1965), pp. 57, 58-61, 62, 119, 190; James Grossman, *James Fenimore Cooper* (Stanford, Calif., 1949), pp. 49, 93, 95, 167; Edward Charles Wagenknecht, *Henry Wadsworth Longfellow: A Portrait of an American Humanist* (New York, 1966), pp. 54-56; Russell Blaine Nye, *George Bancroft, Brahmin Rebel* (New York, 1944), pp. 81-82, 115-118, 132-134, 135, 239-240.

4. John Pendleton Kennedy to Elizabeth Kennedy, June 28, 1840, quoted in Charles Bohner, *John Pendleton Kennedy*

(Baltimore, 1967), p. 225; also see Parrington, *Main Currents of American Thought* II, 33-37, 44-55, 109-119, 158-165; Arthur Hobson Quinn, *Edgar Allan Poe, a Critical Biography* (New York, 1941), pp. 340-341, 352-353, 360-363, 400; Eaton, *Mind of Old South*, pp. 192-193.

5. *Simms Letters*, 1: 170, 180; Simms to Hammond, Jan. 19, 1841, Hammond Papers, Library of Congress; Hammond to Francis W. Pickens, Jan. 27, 1841, MSS, Francis W. Pickens Papers, South Caroliniana Library, University of South Carolina; Simms to Israel K. Tefft, Jan. 10, 1840, Charles Carroll Simms Papers.

6. *Courier*, Jan. 13, Feb. 18, 15, Apr. 17, July 2, 1840; *Mercury*, Apr. 21, July 3, 30, 31, Oct. 5, 1840; John C. Calhoun to Franklin Harper Elmore, Nov. 24, 1840, MSS, Franklin Harper Elmore Papers, Library of Congress; Hammond Diary, June 13, 7, July 14, 1839, Diary, 1841-46, March 25, 1841, Hammond Papers, Library of Congress; Hammond Diary, Sept. 26, Oct. 6, 18, Nov. 7, 22, 29, Dec. 22, 1839, Jan. 6, 16, 29, 20, Feb. 16, March 6, July 23, Sept. 26, Dec. 26, 1840, Hammond Papers, University of South Carolina.

7. Simms to Hammond, June 15, 1840, Hammond to Magrath, Apr. 23, 1840, Hammond to Marcellus Hammond, Oct. 28, 1840, Hammond to Marcellus Hammond, Dec. 14, 1840, Sampson H. Butler to Hammond, May 29, 1840, Hammond Papers, Library of Congress; *Courier*, Dec. 11, 1840; Wiltse, *John C. Calhoun* III, 57, 59; Elizabeth Merritt, *James Henry Hammond* (Baltimore, 1923), p. 54; White, *Robert Barnwell Rhett*, p. 55. The Rhett-Elmore faction centered its power around control of the Charleston *Mercury* and the Bank of South Carolina.

8. *Courier*, March 22, Dec. 19, 1842; *Mercury*, Dec. 17, 1842; Simms to Hammond, Jan. 19, 1841, Hammond to Simms, Jan. 29, 1841, Hammond to James G. Walker, March 26, 1841, Hammond to Calhoun, July 21, 1841, Calhoun to Hammond, Aug. 1, 1841, Sept. 24, 1841, Hammond to Simms, Dec. 13, 1841, Simms to Hammond, Aug. 16, 1841,

Calhoun to Hammond, Nov. 17, 1842, Hammond Papers, Library of Congress; Hammond Diary, June 13, 1842, pp. 95-97, Hammond Papers, University of South Carolina; Hammond to Francis W. Pickens, Jan. 27, 1841, Pickens Papers, University of South Carolina; A. P. Butler to Robert Barnwell Rhett, Dec. 9, 1841, John P. Richardson to Robert B. Rhett, Jan. 21, 1842, Albert Rhett to George McDuffie, Aug. 3, 1842 [Rhett talked McDuffie out of running for governor], MSS, Robert Barnwell Rhett Papers, Southern Historical Collection, University of North Carolina.

9. *Simms Letters*, 1: 283-284, 296, 297, 299, 314, 337; Sampson H. Butler to Simms, Jan. 14, 1842, Charles Carroll Simms Papers; Hammond to Simms, Aug. 27, 1841, Simms to Hammond, Dec. 19, 1841, Jan. 29, 1842, Hammond Papers, Library of Congress.

10. *Simms Letters*, 1: 233; for Simms' *Magnolia* connection see *Courier*, Sept. 29, 1841; *Snowden's Ladies Companion*, May 1841, pp. 12-14, Aug. 1841, pp. 154-157.

11. *Snowden's Ladies Companion*, June 1841, pp. 88-91, July 1841, pp. 109-112, Oct. 1841, pp. 296-300. (Simms later collected and refined these aphorisms in his one work of political philosophy, *Egeria*. See chap. 6.)

12. Simms to Hammond, June 17, 1842, Hammond Papers, Library of Congress; *SLM* 9 (Nov. 1843): 651; *Courier*, Jan. 14, Feb. 10, 1842.

13. *Simms Letters*, 1: 318, 320, 328; 5: 367; *Magnolia*, 4 (Apr. 1842): 248-249; Hammond to Simms, Nov. 12, 1842, Hammond Papers, Library of Congress; *Mercury*, March 12, 1842; *Courier*, Nov. 24, 1842; Samuel G. Stoney, ed., "The Memoirs of Frederick Adolphus Porcher," *SCHM* 47 (1946): 95.

14. *Courier*, Aug. 19, Dec. 14, 1842; *Simms Letters*, 1: 318, 319; *Magnolia*, 1 n. s., Aug. 1842; 4 (June 1842): 377-378; 1 n. s. (July 1842), 64.

15. A. B. Meek to Simms, July 1, 1843, Charles Carroll Simms Papers; *Simms Letters*, 1: 351, 369-370 (Simms immediately began to write for the *Southern Quarterly Review*, 373-374); *Magnolia* 2 n. s., May, p. 336, June, p. 400; *Courier*, May 13, 1843; *Mercury*, Apr. 22, Aug. 4, 24, Oct. 18, Nov. 27, 1843, June 12, 1844.

16. This lecture, "The Uses of History as Art," will be discussed in the next chapter; see *Courier*, March 12, 1842.

17. A. B. Meek to Simms, Sept. 4, 1842, Miscellaneous Letters, Southern Historical Collection, University of North Carolina; William Gilmore Simms, *The Social Principle: The True Source of National Permanence* (Tuscaloosa, Ala., 1843), pp. 35-53; *Courier*, May 25, 1842, Jan. 6, 1843.

18. *SLM* 9 (Dec. 1843): 755-757; *Mercury*, Dec. 14, 1843; *Simms Letters*, 1: 400.

19. *Simms Letters*, 1: 378, 418-419, 410, 427.

20. Bluffton Committee of Invitation to Calhoun, July 13, 1842, Pickens to Calhoun, Oct. 12, 2, Nov. 6, 1841, Calhoun to Col. George F. Townes, Jan. 3, 1841, Elmore to Calhoun, May 30, 1842, Alfred Rhett to Calhoun, Sept. 18, 1842, Calhoun Papers, Clemson College; Richardson to Rhett, Jan. 21, 1841, R. M. T. Hunter to Rhett, Sept. 26, 1842, Rhett Papers, University of North Carolina; Preston to Thompson, Aug. 29, Dec. 11, 1842, Thompson to Brantz Mayer, Dec. 11, 1842, Waddy Thompson Papers, University of North Carolina; *Mercury*, Jan. 13, 24, July 27, 1843. The best work on Calhoun's try for the Presidency in 1844 is Matthew A. Fitzsimmons, "Calhoun's Bid for the Presidency, 1841-1844," *MVHR* 38 (June 1951): 39-60, especially 44-46. For Rhett's role see White, *Robert Barnwell Rhett*, pp. 55, 65.

21. Calhoun to Hammond, Sept. 24, 1841, Hammond to Calhoun, July 21, 1841, Calhoun to Hammond, Dec. 31, 1841, Hammond to Calhoun, Sept. 10, 1842, Calhoun to Hammond, Nov. 27, 1842, Jan 23, 1843, Hammond Papers,

Library of Congress; Elmore to Calhoun, May 30, 1842, Armistead Burt to Calhoun, Sept. 19, 1842, Calhoun to Burt, Sept. 29, 1842, Calhoun Papers, Clemson College; Rhett to John Stapleton, Jan. 16, 1841, Robert R. Barnwell to Rhett, Jan. 23, 1841, May 15, 1841, Albert Rhett to R. B. Rhett, June 18, 1842, Elmore to Rhett, May 4, 1843, Rhett Papers, University of North Carolina; Current, p. 25; Houston, pp. 136-137.

22. Hammond, *Letters and Speeches*, pp. 52-53, 77; Hammond to Simms, Oct. 16, 1843, McDuffie to Hammond, Feb. 24, 1844, Calhoun to Hammond, March 5, 1844, Hammond Papers, Library of Congress; Chauncey S. Boucher and Robert P. Brooks, eds., "Correspondence Addressed to John C. Calhoun, 1837-1849," *Annual Report of the American Historical Association, 1929* (Washington, 1930), pp. 181, 208-209, 210 (hereafter cited as "Correspondence to Calhoun"); Calhoun to Elmore, Jan. 16, 1844, MSS, Calhoun Papers, New York Historical Society; *Niles' Register* 46 (March 30, 1844): 66; South Carolina *Senate Journal*, 28th Legislature, 1 sess. (Columbia, 1844), pp. 436-438; Wiltse, *John C. Calhoun* II, chap. 14; Fitzsimmons, "Calhoun's Bid," p. 60; Capers, *Calhoun*, p. 209; *Mercury*, Nov. 21, 1843; *Courier*, June 27, July 3, 10, 1844; White, *Robert Barnwell Rhett*, p. 73; Chauncey S. Boucher, "The Annexation of Texas and the Bluffton Movement in South Carolina," *MVHR* 6 (June 1919): 3-33.

23. Simms to Hammond, Dec. 30, 1843, Hammond Papers, Library of Congress; Fitzsimmons, "Calhoun's Bid," p. 59.

24. See the defense of Rhett in White, *Robert Barnwell Rhett*, pp. 65-66, 67; *Mercury*, Jan. 24, Feb. 21, March 19, Apr. 30, 1844; Calhoun to Elmore, Jan. 16, 1844, James Gadsden to Calhoun, Apr. 17, 1844, Calhoun Papers, University of South Carolina; Elmore to Rhett, Feb. 24, 1844, Rhett Papers, University of North Carolina.

25. *Simms Letters* 1: 437; *Mercury*, May 25, 27, 1844; *Courier*, May 29, 31, 1844.

26. *Simms Letters*, 1: 419; Calhoun to Hammond, May 17, 1844, Hammond to Calhoun, June 7, 1844, Hammond Papers, Library of Congress; Dixon Lewis to Franklin Harper Elmore, May 9, 1844, MSS, Franklin Harper Elmore Papers, Southern Historical Collection, University of North Carolina; Calhoun to Henry W. Conner, July 3, 1844, Calhoun Papers, University of South Carolina; *Courier*, June 25, 1844.

27. William Gilmore Simms, *The Sources of American Independence* (Aiken, S. C., 1844), pp. 13-14, 19, 20, 24.

28. Ibid., pp. 25-26, 27, 28, 29; also see Henry W. Conner to Calhoun, July 24, 1844, H. Bailey to Calhoun, July 30, 1844, Calhoun Papers, University of South Carolina.

29. Simms, *Sources of American Independence*, pp. 30-31.

30. *Mercury*, Aug. 2, 8, 18, Sept. 19, 1844; *Simms Letters*, 1: 427; *Niles' Register*, Aug. 17, 1844, pp. 411-412; Hammond to Simms, June 18, 1844, Hammond Papers, Library of Congress; W. D. Porter to Calhoun, Aug. 8, 1844, James Hamilton to Calhoun, Aug. 20, 1844, Sept. 12, 1844, Calhoun Papers, Clemson College; White, *Robert Barnwell Rhett*, pp. 74-75.

31. For comments on the political nature of Simms' fiction see *Courier*, Aug. 6, 1841, June 26, July 14, 1843; also see Trent, *Simms*, pp. 127-131; Ridgely, *Simms*, p. 38; William Gilmore Simms, *Border Beagles* 2 vols. (Philadelphia, 1840), 1: 101-102, 204; 2: 240; William Gilmore Simms, *Confession: or, the Blind Heart* 2 vols. (Philadelphia, 1841), 1: 14, 112; William Gilmore Simms, *Donna Florida* (Charleston, 1843), p. 3; William Gilmore Simms, *Castle Dismal* (New York, 1844), pp. v-vi.

32. *Confession*, 1: 166; *Prima Donna*, p. 3; *Castle Dismal*, p. 109; *Border Beagles*, 2: 59, (1890), pp. 218, 248, 425, 445.

33. *Border Beagles* (1890), pp. 159, 238, 411, 493; William Gilmore Simms, *Beauchampe* 2 vols. (Philadelphia, 1842), 1: 17-18; William Gilmore Simms, *The Kinsmen* 2 vols.

(Philadelphia, 1841), 1: 233. Simms was most proud of his political insight on the Texas issue in his *Confession*, 1: 164-165; 2: 24-27; when it was reissued in the 1850s, he added a footnote, p. 209: "All these speculations were written in 1840-41. I need not remark upon those which have since been verified." For praise of Simms' comments on Texas, see *Mercury*, Oct. 11, 1844.

34. *Beauchampe*, 2: 72-77, 133, 134, 146, 147, 148, 276; also see *Castle Dismal*, p. 74; *The Kinsmen*, 1: 142, 268-269; *Confession* (1890), pp. 60, 306; William Gilmore Simms, *The Prima Donna* (Philadelphia, 1844), p. 16.

35. *Mercury*, Oct. 18, 1844.

36. *Simms Letters*, 1: 446-447, 448, 434, 440, 450; *Mercury*, Nov. 28, 1844; *Journal of the House of Representatives of South Carolina, 1844-1846* (Columbia, 1846), pp. 3, 19, 21, 70.

37. *Niles' Register*, Aug. 31, 1844, pp. 431-435; *Mercury*, Aug. 8, Sept. 19, 1844; *Courier*, Aug. 31, 1844; Pickens to Calhoun, Nov. 27, 1844, H. Bailey to Calhoun, Nov. 6, 1844, Calhoun Papers, University of South Carolina; White, *Robert Barnwell Rhett*, pp. 79-82.

38. Hammond, *Letters and Speeches*, pp. 80, 94-98, 98-100, 102; South Carolina *House Journal*, 1844, pp. 7-18; James Hamilton to Calhoun, Nov. 24, 1844, Calhoun Papers, University of South Carolina; Wiltse, *John C. Calhoun, III,* 193.

39. *Courier*, Nov. 28, 1844; Pickens to Calhoun, Nov. 2, 9, 1844, Calhoun Papers, University of South Carolina.

40. South Carolina *House Journal*, 1844, pp. 30, 41-42; clippings from Benjamin F. Perry's Greenville *Mountaineer*, Dec. 4, 1844, Charles Carroll Simms Papers; *Simms Letters*, 1: 448; 2: 9-10.

41. South Carolina *House Journal*, 1844, pp. 65-66, 70, 98-

100; *Mercury*, Dec. 9, 1844; Hammond comments on Simms, Dec. 26, 1844, Hammond Papers, Library of Congress; *Simms Letters*, 2: 5, 7, 9; Memminger to Rhett, Nov. 27, 1844, Rhett Papers, University of North Carolina; Pickens to Burt, Dec. 11, 26, 1844, Pickens Papers, University of South Carolina.

42. *Simms Letters*, 2: 6-8, 45-46, 84, 87-88; Hammond Diary, Jan. 31, July 2, Dec. 7, 1844; A. P. Aldrich to Hammond, July 1, 1845, Hammond to Simms, July 14, 1845, Hammond Papers, University of South Carolina. (There are many unexplained facts about Hammond's behavior. I am now at work on a study of Hammond's career and hope to clear up some of these issues.)

43. *The Southern and Western Monthly Magazine and Review*, 1, advertisement, p. 363; *Mercury*, Jan. 21, 1845; *Simms Letters*, 1: 446, 440-442; 2: 3-4; 5: 389-390; William Gilmore Simms, *The Charleston Book: A Miscellany in Prose and Verse* (Charleston, 1845), pp. 96-274, 275-312.

44. *Charleston Book*, pp. iii-iv, 89, 96; *Southern and Western*, 1, no. 5 (May 1845): 357; I, no. 5 (Nov. 1845): 318, 345-346; 2 (July 1845): 71-72; *Mercury*, July 18, 1845; *Simms Letters*, 2: 50-51, 60, 103; Hammond to Simms, June 18, 1845, Hammond Papers, Library of Congress.

45. *Simms Letters*, 2: 44, 65, 69; *Extract of Minutes of the Charleston Chamber of Commerce* (Charleston, 1845), July 18, 1845.

46. *Southern and Western*, 1, no. 2 (Feb. 1845): 73-84, 145-147; 2 no. 5 (Nov. 1845): 343-344; *Mercury*, Feb. 27, 1845.

47. *Simms Letters*, 2: 110, 118, 120-121, 109; *Courier*, Oct. 30, 1845; *SLM* 11 (Dec. 1845), 760-762.

48. *Simms Letters*, 2: 118, 122-123; Charleston *Southern Patriot*, Dec. 8, 1845; South Carolina *House Journal*, 1845, pp. 40, 139, 140-142, 45, 101, 75; *Mercury*, Dec. 12, 1845, Sept. 10, 15, 21, 22, 25, 26, Oct. 16, 1846; William Sloan to

Calhoun, Dec. 12, 1846, John G. Bowman to Calhoun, Nov. 19, 1846, Calhoun Papers, University of South Carolina.

49. *Simms Letters*, 2: 61; Charleston *Southern Patriot*, Dec. 13, 1845; South Carolina *Reports and Resolutions of the General Assembly* (1845), p. 54; South Carolina *House Journal*, 1845, p. 102; *Mercury*, Dec. 13, 1845.

50. *Simms Letters*, 2: 134, 148; *Mercury*, March 12, 1846.

51. *Simms Letters*, 2: 127, 191, 194, 196, 200, 203; Hammond to Simms, July 8, 1846, Oct. 15, 1846, Nov. 10, 1846, Hammond Papers, Library of Congress.

52. Greenville *Mountaineer*, Nov. 13, 1846; Columbia *South Carolinian*, Nov. 18, 28, 1846; *Simms Letters*, 2: 251, 237, 244, 196, 256-257, 214-215; John M. Felder to Simms, Oct. 22, 1846, Hammond to Simms, Dec. 18, 1846, Hammond Papers, Library of Congress.

53. *Simms Letters*, 2: 239, 240, 205, 216-218, 220, 207-209; Hammond to Simms, Oct. 6, Nov. 23, 1846, Hammond Papers, Library of Congress; Elmore to Calhoun, March 21, Dec. 26, 1846, Calhoun to James Calhoun, June 29, 1846, Pickens to Calhoun, Apr. 17, 1846, Calhoun Papers, University of South Carolina.

54. The choice of politics over literature is well illustrated in *Simms Letters*, 2: 257, 168, 242; and Hammond to Simms, Dec. 18, 1846, Hammond Papers, Library of Congress; *United States Magazine and Democratic Review*, Feb. 1846, pp. 92, 93-94. In the Charleston *Southern Patriot*, July 9, Aug. 13, 1846, Simms began to praise the exploits of Zachary Taylor; William Gilmore Simms, *Count Julian* (New York, 1845), pp. vii-viii, 68, 95; William Gilmore Simms, *The Wigwam and the Cabin* (New York, 1845), pp. 38-39, 178-179, 411.

4 Historical Propagandist

DURING HIS career in local politics Simms began a form of literary activity which brought him fame as a defender of the South's heritage. After years of research and study into the myths and realities of the South's colonial and Revolutionary past, he wrote a history and a geography of South Carolina, four biographies, many articles and historical reviews, and a number of lectures on history and historical writing. Similar to many of his contemporaries in his romantic endeavor to create a readable and usable past, Simms wrote about the most action-filled, significant moments in Southern history. Obviously under the influence of Thomas Carlyle, especially with respect to his idea of the hero in history, Simms searched for symbolic leaders like Andrew Jackson, whose lives could provide models of correct behavior for Southern politicians and educate Southern youth in this period of sectional conflict. Sensitive to his section's pride, he used events from the Revolutionary War to illustrate the need for a separate national sentiment among Southerners. While Simms followed the nineteenth century's faith in progress and republican government, his history disclosed a certain skepticism about the nature of man. In those hectic days of increasing sectional animosity, his history was almost escapist, revealing an attachment to the simpler, more ordered, and conservative past of his people.[1]

Comparison of Simms' historical writing with that of his

115

contemporaries shows that his style was in the romantic vein of
George Bancroft and Francis Parkman, yet his work was never
as polished as theirs. Although he was a tireless researcher, he
could not approach the scholarly skills of John Lothrop Motley
or William H. Prescott. They were painstakingly accurate in
their work, while Simms was usually careless and often allowed
his imagination to supersede reality. Simms' historical writing
most nearly resembled the work of George Bancroft and
Richard Hildreth in the sense that all three wrote with distinct
political bias. Bancroft sought to mold all of the nation's past
into a Jeffersonian liberal tradition; Hildreth, a skeptic about
the nation's future as a democracy, wrote from a decidedly
Federalist-Whig bias. Simms greatly respected Hildreth, although he never clarified his own philosophy of history as Hildreth did in his famous *Theory of Politics.* Among Southern
historians of his day, Simms was not as well known as Charles
Gayarré, the historian of Louisiana, although both men
generally agreed on the purpose for re-creating the past and
held similar political views. The Virginian George Tucker, who
studied the past for its present usefulness, most nearly
resembled Simms' idea of a historian. However, few of Simms'
contemporaries had as active an interest in public service, or as
zealous a view of the importance of the past. Nor did these
other historians have the lengthy literary career which certainly
influenced Simms' own idea of history.[2]

In writing historical fiction Simms was not unique in his
literary world. James Fenimore Cooper based much of his fiction on past events from the Revolution and exploration into
the Northwest frontier, but he was not interested in researching
the past. Washington Irving was especially conscious of the
legends of his own upstate New York, and he sought to give
meaning to those memories and traditions of New York's past.
Much of his literary effort centered on historical themes, and,
like Simms, he was one of the few writers of fiction who was also a historian. Although Hawthorne set at least one novel in the
past, his interest in history stopped after a campaign biography
of Franklin Pierce, which distorted the past much worse than
did historical fiction. Fellow Southerners like Charles Gayarré and John Pendleton Kennedy attempted unsuccessfully to
combine the careers of novelist and historian. But no signifi-

cant mid-nineteenth-century man of letters was able to unite the careers of novelist and historian to the extent or with the skillfulness of Simms.[3]

Simms' interest in historical fiction, mainly in South Carolina's internal struggles during the American Revolution, prompted him to write a series of Revolutionary War romances. His belief that the state was ignorant of its past resulted in a desire to enlighten the public by presenting a detailed factual account of the state's role in the Revolution. He researched every minute detail, from an actual forest scene to the furniture in a cabin, in order to make his fiction appear truthful. The *Courier* called his *Kinsmen* a realistic account of the civil strife in South Carolina and found much of Simms' fiction valuable for his own day, because Simms was "faithful to history and tradition." The *Mercury* knew "of no novelist who has dealt so faithfully with his materials."[4]

Even in his border tales Simms sought to re-create the entire struggle of westward settlement in a factual manner. It was as though he was trying to record all of the social peculiarities of the Southern people. He collected "fanciful and imaginative legends, illustrative of the traditions of the Southern States," weaving them into his earliest chronicles of settlement in the New World. Although reviewers sometimes accused him of being too explicit in his use of crude dialect, many of them appreciated his attempts to capture realistically the struggles of settling a new land. Rather than violate the past, he told Hammond, he would prefer to raise fiction to the factual tone of history. The manners, customs, and mores of the old Southwest, and the lure of the West for the half-civilized Southern frontiersmen, were his topics. His purpose was to create a fictional rendition of the ever-recurring patterns of westward migration in order to instruct Southern youth. In his historical fiction as in his history, Simms wanted to make them aware of the South's struggles for settlement and independence, so that they could uphold their tradition and discover a guide for the South's destiny.[5]

Simms also differed from his literary contemporaries in his relentless efforts to encourage Southerners to write about their past, to collect historical documents, and to organize historical associations and archives. He praised those men in public life who took time to keep memoirs, to send him records, and to sponsor historical projects. He used the many periodicals which he edited to encourage young Southern historians, to review their work, and to reprint the historical documents he had collected. He even wanted the state legislature of South Carolina to send an historiographer to Europe in order to search for documents pertaining to the American settlement. He constantly urged his friends to publish their works and to write memoirs of their own ancestors. In a short review of W. H. Trescott's *A Few Thoughts on the Foreign Policy of the United States*, Simms suggested that his fellow Charlestonians write a history of American foreign policy. A cold-hearted reviewer, particularly when a historian disagreed with his own findings on South Carolina's past, Simms quarrelled with William Bacon Stevens' *A History of Georgia*. Yet he nevertheless encouraged Stevens to bring the history of that state up to date. To Albert J. Pickett, historian of Alabama, Simms gave cautious advice on the need to distort the facts of the past for the sake of making his history more forceful for the present.[6]

Over the years Simms became a careful student of history. In his reviews of some of the leading works of his time, he sharpened his critical skills and slowly developed his own philosophy of history. He accused George Bancroft of lacking good taste and of having a faulty style. To Simms, Bancroft was a biased declaimer who defended New England's role in American history. Simms considered Thomas Babington Macaulay an excellent writer whose sources would not pass close scrutiny; but although he thought that Macaulay wrote from too narrow a point of view about events which were no longer significant, Simms praised his study of all classes of society.[7] Simms had special interest in historians who studied past institutions. In an essay on John Lord Campbell's *The Lives of the Lord Chancellors*, he praised Campbell's succinct character sketches and his knowledge of English legal history. But above all Simms was interested in how history could be used to understand a country's people and to defend a particular way of life.[8] While he commended a study of Georgia's past for its excellent commentary on political institutions, he was much more fascinated as to why Georgia first rejected slavery and later realized its necessary place in Southern society.[9] Prescott's histories of the *Conquest of Mexico* and the *Conquest of Peru* were written in a lively manner, and, like Simms' own work, centered around the lives of great men. Simms tried to understand the special chemistry which signaled the rise and fall of civilizations, and he soon perceived that internal civil war had foreshadowed the end of Peruvian civilization. But he accused Prescott of being too much the narrative historian and too little the philosopher who interpreted facts for some positive good.[10] Simms was formulating a view of history which called for the historian to be a special pleader for a cause, to write history as propaganda.

Although Simms' many review essays on historical works revealed his interest in the beauty of prose style and the importance of research, he believed that history was most valuable for the lessons which could be learned from the past. His philosophy of history was most evident in his admiration for the infamous "Parson," Mason Lock Weems. It was not Weems' scholarship but rather the moral lessons of his history which most intrigued Simms. Weems re-created the past of his native South, not in a long display of petty details, but in a vibrant manner designed to give the South's public men a guide for their present activity.[11] Recent archaeological work also influenced Simms' view of history, for like Weems, the archaeologists had chosen to excavate the past only to educate the current generation. Thus Simms' philosophy of history was a utilitarian one, based on his theory that, with the help of the historical propagandist, "each man becomes his own historian."[12] As Simms had become increasingly practical in his conservative politics, so he emerged as a historical propagandist who encouraged Southerners to use the past to defend the South's traditions and to protect those traditions from change or destruction.

Always mindful of the historian's duty to make his reader a student of the past, Simms developed the theme of the great man or hero as the proper means of communicating the past to the present. Those who had helped to settle and build the United States and others whose careers represented a turning point in history provided material for his many historical biographies, essays, and short historical sketches. Like most of his contemporaries, Simms was influenced by Carlyle, who claimed that the world's progress was the direct result of the actions of great men. Simms was not content to record the hero in action; he wanted to use the life of the hero as an example for the present. Commissioned by Everett Duyckinck to write a biography of South Carolina's great nullifier, George McDuffie, Simms interviewed McDuffie at great length and corresponded with Calhoun about McDuffie's career. He wanted to eulogize McDuffie as a courageous political leader, an early radical in the face of strong Unionist opposition. McDuffie, who had been responsible for major events in South Carolina's history, was the perfect vehicle through which Simms could instruct his fellow Southerners on their future actions.[13]

For Simms as well as for many of his fellow novelists, the model for all heroes in history was Andrew Jackson. Irving found little use for Jefferson, but Jackson appealed to something in his patrician and conservative mind. Nathaniel Hawthorne supported Jackson for President, and he invoked the hero's miraculous deeds of patriotism at New Orleans. He even patterned his biography of Franklin Pierce after Jackson, giving Pierce the sobriquet of "Young Hickory." But it was Cooper who best saw Jackson's true greatness. Cooper supported the man who stood against "agents of social and economic subversion." For Cooper as for Simms, Jackson symbolized the greatness of America's simpler past and, at the same time, the willingness of an American leader to contend with the evil forces of the future. Simms placed Jackson before Calhoun in his pantheon of heroic leaders. He believed that Jackson was the overman, "which I considered his right in the Carlyle sense."[14]

Simms boasted of Jackson as one of South Carolina's own, and, like Washington, a "hero-man, who came, when the earth had need of him." Enthralled by Jackson's deeds at New Orleans, Simms waxed eloquently over Jackson's courage and audacity. Simms stressed Jackson's role as a trainer of raw troops. Any man who could turn Southerners into disciplined fighting men could also teach them the necessity of united action, Simms said. Yet the great leader and teacher refused to accept total dictatorial powers when the opportunity presented itself during his Presidency. Although Jackson had certainly crushed the rights of South Carolina, Simms glossed over the events of nullification and recognized instead Jackson's true loyalty to state's rights. Simms chose to remember the Jackson of the Bank War and the Maysville Road veto, and he praised Jackson's opposition to those who wanted to change the tradition of local governmental autonomy and create an all-powerful central government.[15] In this way Simms slightly distorted Jackson's own achievements in order to accommodate the South's need for a hero who supported the status quo and believed in a state's rights philosophy.

Another recurrent theme in Simms' history was the lure of the West and the role of the pioneer hero in its settlement. Daniel Boone was part of that class of restless pioneers who lived a life close to nature. Boone continuously moved deeper into nature to avoid the problems of civilization, and Simms was intrigued by this example of a simple man whose mission was to open the West and to wrest a peaceful life from nature. But although he was not inclined to warfare, Boone could become a ferocious hunter of men; he had "no scruples of feeling or conscience in the moment of necessity." Proud of Boone's being a Southerner, Simms saw in his life the mysticism of nature, the frontier spirit, and the man ready for action.[16]

An example of a man on a mission was the South's first pioneer, Captain John Smith. A restless soldier of fortune, plagued with wanderlust, Smith guided a small group of Englishmen to the shores of Virginia. For Simms, Smith's settlement of Virginia represented a turning point in Western history, when the new American learned to survive in the wilderness and to build his home amid nature's abundance. In his biography of Smith, Simms described the problems of the settlement of tidewater Virginia and re-created the inevitable conquest of the Indian civilization by a superior race. Simms expressed pride in this first Southern leader, a man of vision and great power.[17]

Establishing a permanent settlement was not a simple task, and in an examination of the actual governing of the new colony Simms pointed out a lesson to his contemporaries. Smith was a warrior who did not seek political leadership, but nevertheless had leadership thrust upon him. Since the leaders of the colony were unable to provide for the new settlement, they conferred authority upon Smith. Smith was forced to become a tyrant in order to whip the soft colonists into providing for themselves, but he enabled the colony to survive. Yet when the crisis was over, the colonial politicians, acting like their latter-day counterparts, deposed Smith and forced him into obscurity. He had outlived his usefulness. That Smith was neglected after the completion of his duties, did not lessen the value of his actions for posterity, Simms insisted. Smith had learned to have confidence in his own genius, something that the neglected statesmen of Simms' own day should remember. Above all, Smith was dedicated to his own people, and he unselfishly answered his countrymen's call for help. Simms warned his readers of the public's inconstancy, and he cautioned future generations to be careful in their treatment of their truly great men.[18]

Simms, who was fascinated with the early settlement of the New World, sought to discover how the Spanish were able to conquer the great Indian civilizations of Mexico and Peru. He wanted to understand what abilities made the Spanish leaders captains of men. He learned that Francisco Pizarro, the conqueror of the Inca civilization of Peru, rose to each task as it increased in difficulty. Pizarro was an orator with enormous persuasive powers, and "his very audacity was the secret of his successes." But Simms also realized that what made Pizarro a great leader was his ability to form a government and to enforce the law.[19] The same was true of Hernando Cortes, the conqueror of Mexico, for this man of destiny could govern as well as conquer. Cortes was a great statesman who, like many of Simms' subjects for biography, was unappreciated in his native land. Both Pizarro and Cortes were deposed as soon as they had accomplished their missions, and, for Simms, this was a lesson that an unkind South could heed regarding its own great men.[20]

Simms' romantic belief in the importance of individual efforts of heroism was also revealed in his interest in early sixteenth-century France. In an age when chivalry was passing in Europe and hand-to-hand mounted combat was being replaced by cannon and footsoldiers, Simms found one Frenchman, the Chevalier Bayard, who had remained faithful to the ancient code. The classic embodiment of romantic nationalism, Bayard had selflessly served his crown and country. His interests, his rights, and his vanity had been secondary to the needs of his country. A man who refused to enter into the politics of office-seeking, Bayard never received the baton of marshall of France. Always a victim of lesser men, he nevertheless symbolized the last of the chivalric tradition. For Simms, Pierre Terrail Bayard had become an example to modern times of "all that is pure and noble in manhood."[21]

For all of his early dislike of the English, Simms was truly fascinated with the conservative nature of English statesmen in handling the law. He found many heroes in the English past, but most of them were famous legal minds or lords chancellor. His own heroes were Thomas Becket, a great talent of lofty aim, the dynamic and courageous Thomas More, and Francis Bacon, whom Simms considered the most brilliant man ever to fill the office of chancellor. Simms saved his finest praise for the Earl of Shaftesbury, not for his deeds in England, but for having the vision to promote the settlement of Carolina and to commission John Locke to write the colony's first constitution. He felt that as a politician Shaftesbury had never been surpassed, because he was an instinctive judge of human conduct. Simms was trying to understand and to communicate the character of public men—how they governed and how they inspired others.[22]

But the Englishman who most interested Simms was Oliver Cromwell. An unobtrusive hero without romance or chivalry, "he was the strict personation of that heroism which marked the Puritan fanatic, the source of our modern Yankee." As a political historian Simms was fascinated by Cromwell's messianic drive and his willingness to disrupt law and order to accomplish his ends. Believing Cromwell was sincere in his motives, Simms nevertheless considered his means of success unworthy of the ends of parliamentary government. Too ascetic for Simms, Cromwell was the anti-hero. A forerunner of the overly zealous abolitionist, the Puritan leader stood for everything Simms opposed. Simms believed that the life of Cromwell illustrated to the South the dangers of the zealot.[23]

The American Revolution was Simms' favorite historical period, and the military leaders who led America to victory over the English were essential to his use of historical biography. He wrote short biographical sketches of heroes who fought in South Carolina for Rufus Wilmot Griswold's *Washington and the Generals of the American Revolution*.[24] Characteristically, there was something in the life of each of those generals which could inspire the South to take pride in the achievements of their ancestors. Charles Cotesworth Pinckney insisted upon defending his native state and was instrumental in writing its constitution. Thomas Sumter, an early advocate of separation from Britain, independently organized a guerrilla army in the low-country swamps to fight the English. Isaac Huger, a Carolinian of French Huguenot ancestry, fought valiantly for his state. William Moultrie, who was ruined financially by the war, dedicated his life to driving the English from Charleston. Christopher Gadsden was a man of outstanding character whose loyalty to the Union took second place to his loyalty to South Carolina. Hoping the South's youth would learn from these examples of loyalty, Simms maintained that the last revolution for political rights and the representative system had not been fought, and that sectional feeling could be aroused through studying the past.[25]

By the use of documents, messages, and a vast store of personal letters, Simms pieced together a biography of Francis Marion, one of the South's greatest military heroes. Born in St. John's Parish of Huguenot parents, Marion became a hero of South Carolina during the Revolutionary War. For years his life and deeds had been almost forgotten because of South Carolina's unwillingness to keep historical records. Simms set out to restore Marion to his rightful position in history, and he claimed that not only should Southerners know of their own heroes, but the North should also have some idea of the service rendered by Southern generals in winning independence from England.[26]

Drawing a parallel with his own life, Simms said that Marion's lack of education had lessened neither his energies nor his self-confidence. Marion's mind was practical rather than intellectual. His genius prompted him to action rather than to study. He became one of the South's noblest models of the citizen soldier, assuming leadership only when called upon. Marion had elevated his native section to honor and independence, "and secured to her the blessings of liberty and peace." Reiterating that he re-created history to teach by example, Simms said that his account of Marion's actions was designed to influence the rising young generation of South Carolinians.[27] Southerners took the biography to heart. It became a best seller which influenced schoolboy and politician alike.

Simms also admired the career of Nathanael Greene. Born in New England, Greene gave up an active political career to fight for independence. A victim of inferior men who were jealous of his leadership abilities, Greene volunteered for active duty in the South. He found the South dominated by the enemy, but in two years he defeated them. Always outnumbered, Greene nevertheless managed to best the British through maneuvering and courage. His life held special meaning for Simms, not only as an example of military heroism but as an example of a Yankee who became a Southerner and proudly defended his adopted state. Simms closed his biography of Greene by saying that the South needed more such men, especially in its present time of crisis.[28]

Biography was not Simms' only historical medium. In his *History of South Carolina*, numerous articles and reviews, and historiographical essays, Simms continued to instruct those South Carolinians who were ignorant of their own past. To illustrate how past events had contributed to making present society, he devised an elaborate system of dividing American history into four distinct yet related phases. The first period dealt with the unsuccessful attempts of European nations to establish permanent colonies in the New World. The second period covered the settlement of the English people in North America. Simms was fascinated by the strength of character which allowed such a small number of people to conquer the elements and the savage natives. He maintained that there had been differences in the English colonists, for at an early period in colonial history the inflexible and hostile Puritans had denounced the love of freedom of the Southern Cavaliers. The third period, which Simms considered the most important, dealt with the causes of the American separation from England. Each of the periods influenced the fourth and last, the transition from a colonial to a republican government. To grasp this last period, to understand the moral and social characteristics and conflicts of the present American nation, Simms urged that

his readers study the American Revolution as a continuing
example of man's search for political and economic freedom.[29]

According to Simms, the events which led to the American
Revolution clearly displayed the problem of one section growing too powerful to be dominated by another. Hostility to
foreign governors and oppressive taxation had not caused
revolution, a word Simms disliked; instead, it was brought
about by the transition of moderate men to a feeling of cultural
nationalism. The growth in population, the "unfolding
resources of their territories," and the pecuniary rewards of
hard work had united the young colonies in their resentment
against England. Government from abroad "by those who were
not indigenous to the soil," was sufficient reason for the colonists to separate. Theirs was no abrupt or premature break
from England, Simms contended, because the history of
American independence dated back to the battlefield at Hast-
ings and the horrible confrontations at Marston Moor and
Naseby. Simms saw America as the appointed battlefield for
European liberty, where the common people faced their
hereditary foe, the monarch, in the cause of man. "It was really
the old spirit of the Anglo-Saxon, warring with his Norman
tyrant, that made the Revolution of America."[30]

Simms, who was upset over the attacks by Northern Congressmen and abolitionists regarding South Carolina's role in
the Revolution, wanted to make his state proud of its past, and
in his *History of South Carolina* he wrote about the Revolution
in order to depict the hardship of war on the people of South
Carolina. South Carolina was quick to oppose the Stamp Act;
its colonial legislature passed a resolution against the taxes
which were crippling its economy. England had forced South
Carolinians from command of their own militia and had even
expelled the great statesman, William Henry Drayton, from the
assembly. Although never on friendly terms with Massachusetts, South Carolina, in order to protect its own freedom,
supported the Continental Congress. South Carolina was the
first to write an independent constitution, which proclaimed the
will of the people in their desire to separate from England.
Simms then described the singular and heroic efforts of the tiny

colony to win its freedom in the face of insurmountable odds.[31]

The *History of South Carolina*, which eventually became a textbook in schools throughout the state, was written in 1840, before Simms was fully aroused by Northern attacks on the South.[32] But by 1848, in an article for the *Southern Quarterly Review* entitled "South Carolina in the Revolution," Simms had become an ardent defender of his state's role in winning the war. Commenting on Lorenzo Sabine's *Loyalists in the Revolution*, Simms asked, "If the record fails to honor the past, and cannot interest the future, why make it?" He felt that Sabine's attack on Tory families only re-opened old wounds and injured Southern character. Simms also mentioned that Sabine failed to point out that South Carolina had risen above its own internal discord. South Carolina's merits, said Simms, "consist in having been able, while contending at home against a powerful and bitter faction, to make contributions of strength, valour, wisdom and patriotism, to the common cause, which no other state in the union . . . has ever exceeded."[33]

Simms pointed out that New England had not supported the South in the Revolutionary War, although Southern troops had fought in the Northern campaigns. Sabine claimed that Northern soldiers would not fight in the South because of slavery. He insisted that the slave economy made the South militarily weak. Simms said that such an idea existed only in the twisted mind of an abolitionist. In the wake of Northern attack on slavery, Simms drew upon his knowledge of history to defend the South. He discovered that the Negro slave had remained loyal throughout the Revolutionary War.[34] Against the charge that South Carolina troops had refused to defend Charleston, Simms countered with the statement that New England troops had never ventured farther south than Virginia.[35] He desired a complete, factual, and unbiased account of the Revolution. Simms summed up his views on Northern antagonism toward the South by stating, "We do not fear but the deeds and sacrifices of Carolina, and of the whole South will bear honorable comparison with those of any part of this nation."[36]

In hopes of further countering Sabine's charges, Simms
wrote a long and detailed account of the defense of Charleston
during the Revolution. His theme was the valor of the handful
of Southerners who had defended the city with few provisions,
because the Continental Congress refused them any aid, against
an overwhelming British force. For Simms, the brilliant defense
of Charleston would forever refute "the unjust and ungenerous
insinuations that the Carolinians shrunk from the defense of
their chief city."[37] He concluded that Southern people were
slow to defend their way of life. Only after repeated disasters
had the back-country Carolinians joined their Charleston
neighbors in the war. Once aroused, however, they had fought
with great tenacity, even after being forced to leave Charleston
and to take to the forests, until they were victorious.[38]

Simms also drew parallels between the Revolutionary War
and the economic crisis of the 1840s, in order to warn the
South of its predicament. He compared Congressional in-
sistence upon a high tariff, which hurt the cotton industry, to
Charles II's restricting the tobacco trade from Virginia.[39] Also, Northern intellectuals interpreted economic measures to be
for the good of the country and falsified their dangers to the
South. Simms warned against the manipulation of both the past
and the present by the North. Much of the insolence of the
Northern attack, he said, was derived from false histories.
Therefore Southern historians must rescue and protect
Southern history from Northerners who dominated the writing
of history in America.[40]

Through the use of history as a propagandistic tool,
Simms succeeded in defending his section's honor in the
Revolution. By illustrating the growing differences between the
North and the South, he also used history in a very practical
manner. The past had taught the value of loyalty to one's native
land, and that "unanimity among our citizens" would make a
section strong. Simms' earlier speech on "The Sources of
American Independence" was not only a commitment to
radicalism but also a work of history which chronicled the
grievances of the South in the Union. Proud of South Carolina's
role as a member of the Confederacy of States, Simms pointed
out that the state gave selflessly of men and materials to the
War of 1812. He claimed that South Carolina had never
disturbed the security of its fellow states, and he wondered why

the North sought to impose such restrictions as tariffs on the South. He concluded that the common cause of the Revolution had never made a common family. Simms feared the end of the Union and wondered why South Carolina had fought so hard to uphold it. The North had violated every tenet of the Revolution, including its promise to protect the economy of the South. It had turned Congress "into an arena for most fearful conflict, and the least justifiable passions." He cautioned Northerners that the new movement toward independence would not disturb the conscience of the South, because there was no longer any reason to maintain the historic loyalty to the Union.[41]

Not only was Simms a historian, biographer, historical reviewer, and adviser to numerous young historians, but he also was regarded as one who understood the politics of historical writing. James Henry Hammond, who had previously asked Simms to write a history of the Republic, wanted him to construct an elaborate history of South Carolina. Hammond claimed that a good chapter on the politics of nullification would reinforce the Southern viewpoint. Simms considered writing that all-important history of the political transition of South Carolina to sectional independence, but he became involved in promoting another "Hickory," Zachary Taylor, for President in 1848.[42] Simms was too busy to write the systematic historical study which might have placed him among the great historians of his day.

Dedicated to public service, Simms used his historical knowledge to help in South Carolina's struggle toward sectional independence. By defending his section against unjust Northern distortion of historical fact, he became South Carolina's most famous historian. As a collector of historical documents, he helped to form the state's historical society and to develop a historical consciousness in South Carolina. William Henry Trescott, a close friend and fellow South Carolina historian, talked of Simms' historical contributions in this manner:

> I cannot refer to this glorious portion of our history [the Revolutionary War] without acknowledging the debt which, I think, the State owes to one of her most distinguished sons for the fidelity with which he has painted its most stirring scenes, and kept alive . . . the portraits of its

most famous heroes. I consider Mr. Simms's [work] . . .
as an invaluable contribution to Carolina history.[43]

The fruits of his efforts can be seen in the sensitivity with which
South Carolinians defended their past, explicitly in the
behavior of Preston Brooks.[44] But Simms was also influenced
by his personal view of history, which combined romantic and
utilitarian premises, and he came to believe his own propaganda. In the Presidential campaign of 1848, Simms supported a
Southern hero, whose life style might have been taken from one
of his own historical studies, and he joined the statewide campaign partly in pursuit of that past.

NOTES

1. Almost nothing has been written on Simms' historical and biographical studies. There are studies of Simms' use of history in his revolutionary romances, the best being C. Hugh Holman, "Revolution as Civil Conflict," *JSH* 15 (1949): 442-462; also see Eaton, *The Mind of the Old South*, p. 191; Arthur K. Moore, *The Frontier Mind* (New York, 1963), pp. 161-163; Holman, ed., *Views and Reviews*, 1: x, xi. I must apologize to the reader for the following tentative approach to the use of history as propaganda. Realizing the importance of an era's history and historians for understanding its culture, I am now at work on a much-neglected subject, the historians of the ante-bellum South. In his essay on the Louisiana historian Charles Gayarré, Clement Eaton says: "Of the many facets of Southern culture, the one that has been least studied by modern scholars—yet one that reveals much about the whole tone of Southern society is the historiography of the ante-bellum period." See Clement Eaton, *The Waning of the Old South Civilization, 1860's-1880's* (Athens, Ga., 1968), p. 54. Also see Olive Anderson, "The Political Uses of History in Mid Nineteenth-Century England," *Past and Present*, 36 (April 1967): 87-105; H. Trevor Colbourn, *The Lamp of Experience* (Chapel Hill, 1965).

2. For a study of romantic historical style, see David Levin, *History as Romantic Art* (New York, 1963). See also Robert Allen Skotheim, *American Intellectual Histories and Historians* (Princeton, 1966), pp. 15, 17-18; Harvey Wish, *The American Historian* (New York, 1960), pp. 68-69; Otis A. Pease, *Parkman's History; the Historian as Literary Artist* (New Haven, 1953), pp. 15, 84-86; John Spencer Bassett, *The Middle Group of American Historians* (New York, 1917), *passim*; Eric F. Goldman, ed., *Historiography and Urbanization* (Baltimore, 1941), pp. 145-153. For Southern historians see David Van Tassell, *Reading America's Past* (Chicago, 1960), pp. 156-157; Eaton, *Waning of the Old South Civilization*, pp. 54, 63-65, 69, 70-71, 73-74, 78; Wendell Holmes Stephenson, *The South Lives in History* (Baton Rouge, 1955);

George Brown Tindall, ed., *The Pursuit of Southern History* (Baton Rouge, 1966), pp. 3-22.

3. Hedges, *Washington Irving*, pp. 113-114, 240, 261-262; J. Franklin Jameson, *The History of Historical Writing in America* (New York, 1961), pp. 97-98, 113, 114, 117; Stewart, *Hawthorne*, pp. 127, 132, 134. George Hardy Callcott, *History in the United States 1800-1860* (Baltimore, 1970), p. 30.

4. *Mercury*, June 20, 1854, Nov. 10, 1855; *Courier*, Sept. 12, 1839, Feb. 27, 1841, March 15, 1844; *The Partisan* (1835), 1: vii, x; Oliphant, "Historical Artist," pp. 24-27; Holman, "Revolution as Civil Conflict," pp. 449, 453; Eaton, *Mind of the Old South*, p. 191.

5. William Gilmore Simms, *Grouped Thoughts and Scattered Fancies* (Richmond, 1845), pp. 58-59; William Gilmore Simms, *Helen Halsey* (New York, 1845), pp. 214-215; William Gilmore Simms, *The Lily and the Totem* (New York, 1850), pp. iv, v, vi; *Wigwam and Cabin*, p. 430; *Castle Dismal*, dedication; *Count Julian*, p. vi; Oliphant, "Historical Artist," p. 24; *Courier*, May 17, 1841, May 14, 1843; *Mercury*, Sept. 7, 1840, Sept. 9, 1841.

6. *Simms Letters*, 5: 399-400; *Southern Quarterly Review* 13: 470, 477, 488, 490-491; 16: 252-253; *Magnolia*, Oct. 1842, p. 263; *Southern and Western*, Apr. 1845, pp. 288-291; *Lily and Totem*, p. iii.

7. *Simms Letters*, 2: 510-511; *Mercury*, Apr. 6, 1855, Feb. 20, 1856.

8. *SQR*, Oct. 1847, pp. 376-377.

9. Ibid., 13: 499.

10. *SLM*, Jan. 1844, p. 61; *SQR* 13 (Jan. 1848): 136-183, (Apr. 1848): 230, 273.

11. *Southern and Western*, 1: 37-45, 47; William Gilmore

Simms, *Views and Reviews in American Literature, History and Fiction* (2 Ser.; New York, 1846), pp. 60, 124-125, 127, 134, 137, 139, 141; also see Wade Wiley Worley, "The Reflection of Ante-bellum South Carolina Culture in Simms' Magazine" (unpublished M. A. thesis, Dept. of English, Furman University, 1949), p. 44; *SLM* 9 (Dec. 1843): 755-756 and 28 (May 1859): 356.

12. Simms, *Views and Reviews* 1: 36, 38, 39, 44, 48, 50-54; William R. Taylor, *Cavalier and Yankee* (New York, 1961), pp. 240-278.

13. *Simms Letters*, 2: 57, 273, 297, 529; *SQR* 14 (July 1848): 77, 78, 79, 80-81, 510, 517-518; Hammond to Simms, June 15, 1847, Hammond Papers, Library of Congress; Hammond Diary, Jan. 23, 1847, Hammond Papers, University of South Carolina. (Simms never found time to write a biography of McDuffie.)

14. *Simms Letters*, 2: 297; Stewart, *Hawthorne*, p. 20; Hedges, *Washington Irving*, p. 190. The most essential secondary source is Marvin Meyers, *The Jacksonian Persuasion* (New York, 1960), pp. 57-100.

15. *Southern and Western* 2 (June 1845): 392, (July 1845): 58-60; *Magnolia* (Aug. 1842), pp. 90, 93-97; *Courier*, July 15, 1845.

16. Simms, *Views and Reviews* 1, 149-176.

17. William Gilmore Simms, *The Life of Captain John Smith, the Founder of Virginia* (Philadelphia, 1846), pp. 10, 11, 123, 124, 127.

18. Ibid., pp. 299, 300, 301, 349, 351, 373-374; *SQR* 12 (July 1847): 271-272, gave a favorable review.

19. *SQR* 13 (Jan. 1848): 167, (Apr. 1848): 273, 330; also see Simms' novel *Vasconselos* (New York, 1853).

20. Simms, *Views and Reviews* 1: 255-257; 2: 101-122.

21. William Gilmore Simms, *The Life of the Chevalier Bayard* (New York, 1847), pp. 1-2, 393, 395, 396, 397; *Courier*, May 31, 1847; *SQR* 14: 521; also see John S. C. Bridge, *History of France from the Death of Louis XI* 5 vols. (Oxford, Eng., 1921-1936), 1: 155; 2: 101-102; 3: 67-68, 194-199.

22. *SQR* 13: 381, 397, 405, 407-408.

23. Ibid., 14 (Oct. 1848): 517-518, 524, 525, 526-530, 534, 537. For the European romantic view of Cromwell as great man, see H. G. Schenk, *The Mind of the European Romantics* (New York, 1969), p. 187; Walter E. Houghton, *The Victorian Frame of Mind* (New Haven, 1964), pp. 122, 197, 201, 212, 215, 328-329.

24. Rufus Wilmot Griswold, *Washington and the Generals of the American Revolution* 2 vols. (Philadelphia, 1847), 1: v, vi; Joy Bayless, *Rufus Wilmot Griswold* (Nashville, Tenn., 1943).

25. Griswold, *Washington and the Generals*, 2: 313-320, 296-312, 282-290, 272-281, 57, 133-162, 258, 253-257; Simms also wrote an article on Nathanael Greene for Griswold, but much of that material was incorporated in his biography of Greene; see Griswold, 1: 61-104. For verification that Simms wrote these unsigned articles see *Simms Letters*, 2: 342-343; *Courier*, Nov. 19, 29, 1847.

26. William Gilmore Simms, *The Life of Francis Marion* (Boston, 1856), preface; David Duncan Wallace, *History of South Carolina* (Chapel Hill, 1951), pp. 300-301.

27. Simms, *Marion*, pp. 30-31, 346-347; *Courier*, Dec. 14, 1844.

28. William Gilmore Simms, *The Life of Nathanael Greene, Major-General in The Army of the Revolution* (New York, 1849), pp. 15, 26, 27, 30, 45, 47, 110, 161, 191, 282, 337, 340, 357; *Russell's Magazine* 3 (Sept. 1858): 481; Griswold, *Washington and the Generals* 1: 104.

29. *Views and Reviews* 1: 76-79, 81-84, 86; *Social Principle,* pp. 8-11; William Gilmore Simms, *The History of South Carolina* (Charleston, 1840), p. vii—Simms dedicated his history to "the youth of South Carolina." Also see pp. 69-72; *Courier,* July 27, 1840.

30. Simms, *Sources,* pp. 9, 10, 11-13; *Views and Reviews* 2: 78, 84; *Greene,* pp. 9-11; *History of South Carolina,* pp. 120-122; *Social Principle,* pp. 10-13.

31. Simms, *History of South Carolina,* pp. 123, 126, 128, 129, 136, 142, 146-147; *Social Principle,* pp. 54-55; *Marion,* pp. 12, 76, 325-326; *Simms Letters,* 2: 318-319.

32. Simms, *History of South Carolina,* pp. 160-310, especially p. 305 for Simms' early moderate view of the North's role in the American Revolution; also see *Mercury,* July 30, 1840; *Magnolia,* (July 1842), p. 59.

33. *SQR* 14 (July 1848): 39-45, 47; *Simms Letters,* 2: 511.

34. *SQR* 14 (July 1848): 61.

35. Ibid., pp. 64, 70, 77; *Views and Reviews* 1: xxxiv.

36. *SQR* 14 (July 1848): 76; Simms to Hammond, Dec. 15, 1848, Hammond to Simms, Dec. 22, 1848, Hammond Papers, Library of Congress.

37. *SQR* 14 (Oct. 1848): 264; see also 266-321.

38. Ibid., p. 335. For a somewhat different view that maintains Southern historians were never concerned with the Revolution in sectional terms, see Charles Sellers, Jr., "The American Revolution: Southern Founders of a National Tradition," in Arthur Link and Rembert Patrick, eds., *Writing Southern History* (Baton Rouge, 1966). pp. 58-60.

39. *Southern and Western* 1 (Feb. 1845): 142; *SLM* 11 (March 1845): 138.

40. *SQR*, n. s. 1 (April 1850); Hubbell, "Literary Nationalism in the Old South," p. 195.

41. Simms, *Sources*, pp. 23-24; *The Orion*, 3 (Sept. 1843): 46; *Mercury*, Aug. 18, 1844. There is also a hint of this view in Simms' *History of South Carolina*, p. 319. (In the 1850's Simms became more vehement in his denunciation of the North's past, as Southern nationalism replaced the milder sectional historical theme.)

42. A. P. Butler to Simms, Dec. 28, 1845, Lawrence Labree to Simms, Oct. 20, 1846, Charles Carroll Simms Papers; Hammond to Simms, March 2, 1845, Hammond to Simms, Jan. 14, Aug. 8, 1848, Aug. 17, 1849, Simms to Hammond, Jan. 2, Feb. 12, 1848, Hammond Papers, Library of Congress.

43. *Russell's Magazine* 5 (July 1859): 299; *SLM* 22 (April 1856): 283; *De Bow's Review*, 4: 6, n. s. (Dec. 1860): 702-712.

44. Simms' role in the Brooks-Sumner affair will be discussed in chap. 7. For the view that Brooks's actions were justified because of slander to South Carolina's Revolutionary past, see *Appendix to the Congressional Globe*, 34th Cong., 1 sess. (Washington, 1856), pp. 625-635, 702-708, 833-838. For an interpretation of Simms' importance as a sectional historian which differs from Sellers, see the interesting commentary (although by no means exhaustive analysis) by David Van Tassell, *Reading America's Past*, pp. 136-137.

5 National Political Campaigner in 1848

ALTHOUGH SIMMS continued to write fiction and history and to plan for his own political future, in the late 1840s he abandoned the idea of an elaborate history of political crises in South Carolina and entered a new phase of his public career as a campaign organizer for Zachary Taylor. Simms had previously worked for the election of local officials and had even used his newspaper to support Jackson's reelection in 1832, but he had never taken such an active part in a national election. Taylor, a Southerner, fit into Simms' plan for a Southern cooperation movement. Simms was convinced that the Young Carolina movement based in Charleston would work for Taylor, thus creating a party in opposition to the entrenched "Hunker" or Bank party. Since the South Carolina Bank party under the control of Calhoun's lieutenant, Franklin Harper Elmore, maintained direct ties to the national Democratic party and was too moderate on the question of Southern unity, Simms hoped that support of Taylor would hurt the national party system and would force Southerners to realize the necessity of a united front. To that end Simms put his enormous editorial and organizational talents to work in Taylor's behalf.[1]

Occupied with the campaign for Taylor and concerned with the future of South Carolina politics in state and nation, Simms neglected his literary career. But he understood the literary market, and he realized that with pirated European edi-

137

tions of American fiction, the low prices of books (fiction had never seemed to recover from the Panic of 1837), and the general public apathy to fiction, it was time for a self-supporting writer to find something else to do with his talent. The lecture he gave at Georgia's Oglethorpe University in the spring of 1847 provided some insight into Simms' predicament. Simms talked about the uses of intelligence and talent, and the responsibility to use them well. Ostensibly lecturing to young students on the need to study diligently and to choose their professions carefully, Simms was really explaining his own dual career. If his literary talent was not as useful as his knowledge of political campaigning, then his literature would have to wait.[2]

The direction of Simms' own career was determined by his concepts of public duty and the usefulness of talent. Once persuaded of the mission to advance and elevate his people, he realized that his intellectual faculties were no longer his private property. While he derived great personal satisfaction from writing fiction, it was not the most productive way to serve the South. Torn throughout his life between duty to his inner self and his public loyalty to his homeland, Simms chose the South, perhaps to the detriment of his literary output in the late 1840s. But he realized that he spoke for his section, that his training had been to serve; he was a poet chosen for an extraordinary mission. Part of his labor as a public man was to use his abilities to find the man who could lead the South—the individualist who could protect the South in a period of sectional struggle.[3]

But what fascination did Zachary Taylor hold for the American people? Southern novelists, such as the Whig John Pendleton Kennedy, were excited over Old Rough and Ready, and they actively campaigned for him. For Kennedy, Taylor was the man to lead the faltering Whigs to political superiority over the Democrats. Walt Whitman, a Free Soil Democrat but an ardent expansionist, cheered Taylor's candidacy. James Russell Lowell saw in Taylor the hope of a peaceful America.[4] Surprisingly, even the Charleston *Mercury* at first cheered the hero of Palo Alto and called for booming cannon to signal the fall of Vera Cruz. The *Mercury* claimed that Taylor was a Southerner who would help to expand the borders of the South.[5] Through his military feats of individual initiative, Taylor had been able to appeal to the imagination of a nation which was looking for a hero to replace the dead Jackson.

Combining his usual romantic attachments to individualism, heroism, nationalism, and westward expansion, with a practical understanding of the need for Southern growing room, Simms initially supported every action of Taylor. He told Calhoun that the South resolved to keep all of Mexico as a means of protecting slavery and adding to the slave population. The "Anglo-Norman race would never forgive the public man who should fling away territory." Besides, he said, the Mexican people needed to be uplifted, and as slaves they could help to cultivate that land. Thrilled by Taylor's victories at Buena Vista and Vera Cruz, Simms envisioned a mighty slaveholding empire covering the Tehuantepec peninsula and stretching to the Pacific. Mexico was part of the South's destiny; its annexation would assure the safety of the South and the perpetuation of slavery for a thousand years. The man of vision, the leader of this dream, was Zachary Taylor. Simms felt that Taylor would pay no attention to David Wilmot's hated proviso and that he would support Southern expansion.[6]

Taylor's military victories had stimulated the youth of South Carolina to fight for expansion. In poems and songs, Simms eulogized the role of Carolina's Palmetto Regiment in the Mexican War. He sought to express a feeling of triumph in these often crude but proud poems. He felt that this was the opportunity for young Carolina to demonstrate the glory of its heritage, to realize that it too could achieve the rights its fathers had fought for. He depicted the Mexicans as mongrels who were unfit to do battle with the Carolinians. If they were not redcoats or Yankees, they were the only enemy Simms could find. The sons of Sumter and Marion, children of the noblest of military warriors, had a chance to display their valor. Above all, Simms knew that they were fighting for Carolina's fame and future.[7]

There were other reasons why Simms found Taylor politically interesting, even before the military hero allowed his name to be mentioned as a Presidential candidate. Taylor belonged to no political party and was not a politician. At a

time when many Southerners were becoming antagonistic
toward both major parties and were increasingly suspicious of
politicians, a non-politician appealed to Simms. During 1847
Taylor said that he would accept no party nomination, that he
opposed national nominating conventions, and that under no
circumstances would he be a convention candidate. If he was a
Whig, he was a moderate one who would be the tool of no party.[8] Simms deplored political parties because they demanded
national patriotism above loyalty to the South. He thought that
Taylor, a man free from political ties, would be instrumental in
breaking down the political system and the Democratic hold on
South Carolina politics.[9]

Simms also hoped that a Taylor campaign in South
Carolina would depose the entrenched power of the Elmore-
Bank machine to make room for a young, vigorous party.
Meeting with Hammond early in January 1847, he attempted
to persuade the governor to return to politics and to support a
pro-Taylor movement in the state. He also told the up-country
politician, James L. Orr, that an organized party which appealed to young people and rallied behind Taylor's candidacy
could depose the old "Hunkers." Simms envisioned himself as
the leader of this new party, plotted its successes, and
organized secret meetings in Charleston to promote Taylor's
candidacy. He planned a campaign, chose candidates, and propa-
gandized against entrenched power throughout the state. He
was not perturbed by the challenge of having to depose
Calhoun.[10]

Simms was motivated by more than mere desire for personal political power and the creation of a healthy political opposition in South Carolina. As a Southerner, Taylor could lead
a cooperationist movement of Southern states toward a united
destiny. The author believed that by breaking down the party
system, the South would have to form a Southern Rights party.
Simms' dream of a Southern convention to weld a powerful
defense of the South could be achieved if the South united
around Taylor and if South Carolina would choose Hammond
as its leader. Simms was convinced that Taylor would pursue a
vigorous foreign policy against England and even the North if
necessary. Also, Simms believed that Taylor would help to
bring Texas into the Southern union, while his military heroics

and his expansionist views made him the rallying point for Southern politicians in the national movement.[11]

Although he had been organizing support for Taylor, Simms would not openly announce his position until Calhoun dropped out of the race, for his first loyalty belonged to South Carolina's native son. He was no confidant of Calhoun's and although the two men corresponded, Simms never advised Calhoun that his candidacy was impossible. Calhoun had an almost pathological desire to be President, and Simms was certain that he would blunder into inconsistencies which would ruin his chances for the office. Although he disagreed with Calhoun's conservative national politics and his political domination of South Carolina, Simms admired his reputation as the most respected mind in Congress. Yet Simms did not support Calhoun's candidacy out of personal devotion, for he actually hoped his fellow Carolinian would lose his bid for the Presidency. He thought that another national political loss would force Calhoun to retire permanently and thus free South Carolina politics from his control.[12]

Immediately following the election of James K. Polk, many of Calhoun's friends urged him to seize power in the Democratic party, to move to end the national nominating convention, and to consider running for the Presidency in 1848.[13] Since he knew that he could never be elected by a national nominating convention, Calhoun acted to head off any use of the convention system in South Carolina.[14] He followed the advice of his close friend, Alabama's Senator Dixon Lewis, by outwardly supporting Polk, but he did not heed Simms' counsel regarding expansion. Simms believed that war with Mexico was necessary to protect slavery. Calhoun, however, kept silent on the war issue during most of Polk's administration, because he thought that the annexation of additional land would only inspire increased sectional agitation.[15]

Calhoun's reconciliatory attitude toward Polk and the Southern Democrats did not last. In February 1847, he disregarded Simms' advice and attacked the administration's Ten Regiment Bill, which increased American arms and manpower in Mexico.[16] Perhaps because of his faltering candidacy or because he had finally realized that only a powerful sectional political front could elect him, Calhoun made pro-slavery resolutions in the Senate which many Northern Demo-crats could not support.[17] He then returned to South Carolina and on March 9, 1847, in Charleston, he committed himself to a Southern convention and called for a third party, ostensibly a Southern Rights party, to promote his candidacy. He sought the abandonment of the old two-party system in the South, and he reiterated his opposition to a national party con-vention.[18] Simms joined many politicians throughout the South who followed Calhoun's advice and agitated for a Southern party to support not Calhoun but the hero of the Mex-ican War, Zachary Taylor. Calhoun knew that without united Southern support his chances for the Presidency were dead. Even so, when Taylor emerged as the South's candidate, Calhoun remained neutral in the Presidential contest.[19]

With Calhoun out of the campaign and many South Carolina Democrats leaning toward Taylor, Simms felt free to bring his campaign into the open. In this latest venture he was assisted by Young Charleston, a group of Whigs, Independents, and Taylor Democrats. Young Charleston first defined its reasons for supporting Taylor through letters to the editors of Charleston's newspapers. When the group failed to persuade either the *Mercury* or the *Courier* to support Taylor, it founded its own newspaper, the *Palo Alto*. Simms served as an editor and critic on the paper, which published many of his articles and speeches. The Taylor movement also needed the support of the state's leading politicians, and through Simms they hoped to receive Hammond's open commitment to Taylor. By his speech-es and at meetings, both public and private, Simms helped to organize the campaign, which peaked in August when in-dependent Democrats openly nominated Taylor.[20]

Early in 1848, before the national conventions, many of Calhoun's allies among the entrenched powers in South Carolina leaned toward Taylor. Even the Rhett-controlled Charleston *Mercury* published articles favorable to his candidacy. Franklin H. Elmore, director of the Bank of South Carolina, also flirted with the rapidly organized Taylor Clubs in Charleston, but he hesitated to lend them his support until he knew Calhoun's position. A number of loyal Whigs who cared little for Taylor nevertheless boosted his campaign because they were confident of his nomination. Simms wrote occasional comments and letters to friends about the South's need for Taylor, and he sought to associate the all-Mexico Carolinians (ardent expansionists), regardless of party, with the Taylor campaign.[21]

The dream of united support for Taylor in South Carolina ended when the national conventions met in the late spring. Calhoun opposed any South Carolinians' going to Baltimore for the Democratic convention. But since Robert Barnwell Rhett was certain that the Democrats would not nominate Taylor, he sent lieutenants to observe the party's convention in hopes of some political gain for South Carolina.[22] Rhett had been leaning toward Taylor, but when the Democrats nominated Cass and the Whigs followed in June by nominating Taylor, Rhett agreed to direct the Cass campaign in South Carolina. Vowing to carry the state without Calhoun's help, Rhett announced the *Mercury*'s full support of the Democratic ticket, and he refused to print any more letters concerning Taylor's candidacy. James Hamilton, Franklin Harper Elmore, and Armistead Burt lent their prestigious names to the Cass campaign, and Francis W. Pickens spoke throughout the up-country for the Democratic party.[23]

Simms and his fellow Taylorites realized that Taylor had little chance of carrying the state without the support of the Democratic party. In two articles published in the Charleston *Courier*, Simms set down the principles of a new party of independent Democrats. He claimed that the ancient political powers of the state had no loyalty to the Democratic party, and that they used the party only to continue their ascendancy in South Carolina. The proposed new party, it was hoped, would destroy the older leaders to make way for a Young Carolina, dedicated to the unity of the South and opposed to formal parties. Simms said that the Baltimore Convention was a fraud and that the true Democrats of Charleston would rally around the hero of Buena Vista as they had years earlier for Jackson. As an independent, Taylor was the candidate of the people, not of the Whigs.[24] Simms was elected a vice president of the Democracy of Charleston for Taylor movement, along with Ker Boyce, Henry A. DeSaussure, James Burges, James Gadsden, and others. The new party nominated William C. Butler from Kentucky as Taylor's running mate. At the July 31

meeting of the Taylor Democrats, Simms spoke on the urgency
of the campaign, and he supported the party's resolutions on
the importance of Taylor's candidacy to the future of the
South. The audience applauded his jibes at the "Hunkers" and
agreed with his demand for hard work and rapid organization
of the new party.[25]

Proud of his speech and his place in the party, Simms
solicited Hammond's formal endorsement of Taylor. He told
Hammond that the party needed a newspaper since neither the
Mercury nor the *Courier* would print their articles. Selecting
certain Cass supporters for special condemnation, Simms told
Hammond that Elmore, one of Hammond's political foes, was
an ardent Cass Democrat. He said that Cass had backing in the
interior of the state, but that many politicians, including the
young people of Charleston, were alert to the political domination of Rhett and Elmore. He asked Hammond to influence Samuel W. Trotti and Alfred P. Aldrich, two important Barnwell
politicians, to organize support for Taylor in the area around
Columbia as well as the low country southwest of
Charleston.[26]

In his attempt to bring Hammond out of retirement and
into the forefront of the Taylor movement, Simms promised to
work against the Bank of South Carolina. Simms, who knew
that Hammond had written the damaging "Anti-Debt" articles
in the *Mercury* and that he would do almost anything to ensure
the failure of the Bank, promised to uncover information
against the Bank and to edit Hammond's articles on the subject. Simms was himself convinced that the powers of the Bank
were not limited to economic matters. The Bank, presided over
by Elmore with assistance from Rhett and Calhoun, also
financed the "Hunker" politics in the state.[27] Simms told
Hammond that the people clamored for him to lead the Taylor
party and to become a candidate for Congress. If Hammond
would accept the challenge, Simms said, he could become a
political power in the state second only to Calhoun. He urged
Hammond to write a letter in support of Taylor and to publish
it in all the newspapers of the state. After lengthy conversations
with his political allies, Simms offered Hammond a formal
speaking engagement before the Charleston Democrats for
Taylor.[28] But Hammond refused to make any statement

other than an early letter, which Simms had carefully edited, in praise of Taylor. Perhaps Calhoun's neutrality influenced Hammond's own reluctance to give Taylor his formal endorsement. Without Hammond, the Taylor movement was deprived of the political leadership and dignity needed to promote the campaign throughout the state.[29]

Hammond's equivocation was a blow to Simms' hopes. But Simms enjoyed his political role too much to let Hammond disturb him, and he turned instead to an all-too-familiar problem. He knew that without some means of communicating the views of the Taylor Democrats, the Taylor supporters would have no chance against Cass. The entrenched "Hunkers" controlled the Charleston newspapers and distorted Taylor's position, especially regarding slavery. The *Palo Alto* was founded as a Taylor newspaper. It was printed only during the election campaign, and its avowed purposes were to announce Taylor meetings and to present the general's political views. Although Simms was not the editor of the *Palo Alto*, he did write for it, and he edited many feeble attempts by Young Charleston at political propaganda. Many of his views regarding the importance of Taylor's candidacy to the South and the need to destroy Charleston's political power base were aired in the *Palo Alto*. Despite the *Mercury*'s vicious attacks on the paper, it managed to survive the campaign, and it served a useful purpose in bringing many of Charleston's young intellectuals under the influence of the South's leading man of letters.[30]

Early in September, Simms gave two lectures which were widely applauded and reprinted in the *Palo Alto*, before the Taylor Independents and Democrats. After he had made his old stock phrases about Taylor's honesty and independence, Simms attacked Cass as a Free Soiler. His position had been formulated in the *Palo Alto* as that paper grew increasingly suspicious of the Northern Democratic party and began to claim that Taylor was the only man who could protect slavery. Tired of Northern men with Southern principles, Simms declared that the South had to unite behind a Southern candidate who could control the nation and ensure the preservation and expansion of slavery. Since Cass opposed the extension of slavery and was unsound with regard to the tariff and internal improvements, Simms said that Southerners should not support him. Simms wanted a Southern Democratic party to splinter from the national party and to form its own faction, within or without the Union. Since 1844 Simms had searched for a cause around which all Southerners could rally. The Taylor campaign in South Carolina filled this need, and it marked the true beginning of the cooperationist movement in the South.[31]

Furious at Calhoun's neutrality, which he knew assured Cass's victory in South Carolina, Simms again spoke before the Taylor organization on September 14. He cautioned the state against joining another national party, and he urged his fellow campaigners to think first of a united South, and only secondarily of particular candidates. Taking stock of local politics, Simms told the Taylor supporters to advocate the popular elections of Presidential electors. Since the people of the state were true to the South and above the petty politics of the Rhetts and Elmores, Simms was certain that they would elect Taylor.[32]

Simms was confident that the Taylor forces would at least carry Charleston and the Neck, and in late September he departed for New York, to fulfill some editorial commitments and to work on a collection of poems, *Charleston and Her Satirists*. Supposedly written in response to a Northern attack on the cultural life of Charleston, Simms' poems were actually part of the Taylor campaign. Unfortunately, said Simms, the person who had written *Charleston: A Poem* had made some perceptive comments on the faults of his native city. He agreed that Charleston had many faults; it was vulnerable to criticism, especially in its political life.[33] In his poems Simms wanted to expose the Cass Democrats. He was convinced that they bore no real love for Calhoun, whom they used to wipe out opposition to themselves. By destroying their opponents, the Carolina "Hunkers" stifled the emergence of gifted and talented young leaders in South Carolina. Simms hoped that the youth of the state would rebel against the hypocritical Cass forces and destroy the Bank of the State. In clumsy poetical but shrewd political fashion, Simms showed the power that money could have in the state. To save South Carolina economically, to keep it from losing its potential leadership to the West, Simms called for renewed efforts for Taylor and for destruction of the entrenched powers.[34]

Through his verse Simms showed that he agreed with much of the Northern attack on his state. A young politician who refused to obey the entrenched powers became "a stranger in the land," forced to migrate westward to exercise his freedoms. Simms said that because they lacked the incentive to experiment, the young neglected their fields and followed the reactionary agricultural dictates of the state. Many were in debt to the Bank, and they allowed their slaves to wander off the plantation, while they themselves sought richer lands. To protect the South he urged Southerners to regain their pride by agricultural experimentation and economic diversification. Simms believed that the economic revitalization of the South would not only put an end to "Hunker" control, but would eliminate the need for young men of talent to emigrate westward or to neglect the arts.[35]

Although Simms found fault with his native South, *Charleston and Her Satirists* reflected his conservatism in a time of progressive democratic thought and his growing animosity toward the North. He saw the North as "dark and dank," a place filled with weird revolutionary ideas. He condemned the movement for women's rights, belittled weak Northern poets, and denounced the lunatic ideas of Fourierism and Frances Wright. He called the North a place of divorce, murder, and adultery. He accused Northerners of being too materialistic and Southerners of not being sufficiently competitive or practical. Simms did not want the planter to become crass and materialistic, but he admonished the Southern planter to compete favorably with the Northern merchant, lest he lose his way of life. He again thanked the Northern satirist for opening the South's eyes.[36]

Simms returned to Charleston in mid-October and made one last speech in favor of Taylor's candidacy. At a public meeting of Democrats for Taylor, he called for the formation of a Southern State Rights Republican party. At last Simms, Henry DeSaussure, James Simons, and other allies had abandoned any pretense of hoping for reform within the local Democratic party. Simms personally wrote two of the resolutions at the meeting, and he helped to write a pamphlet which circulated throughout the state. The resolutions called for an independent Southern party with South Carolina as the organizer but not the sole participant. Simms' idea was to unite with other like-minded Southerners in a show of strength to air the South's grievances. Simms was convinced that regardless of the national results, the state would benefit from the exposé of Elmore and the Bank, the destruction of the "Hunkers," the election of a Taylorite, Isaac E. Holmes, to Congress, and the movement for a new party. He confidently awaited the election returns, knowing that the South would be safer with Taylor as President, and that he might be rewarded for his political activities. It seemed that Taylor's election was unimportant compared to this beginning of Southern unity.[37]

After the election results were in, Simms temporarily moderated his Southern Rights Party views and asked Calhoun to suggest qualified counselors for Taylor. Simms felt certain that the new President would look to the South for his close advisers and administrators, and he expected an ambassadorial appointment for himself. He asked Robert Toombs and Hammond to promote his appointment, because he needed the mission. The diplomatic post would save him financially as well as give him a change of perspective and perhaps even some new literary material. Turning down an offer to become lieutenant governor of South Carolina, an honorary office without power, Simms was confident that he would receive a foreign mission. Hammond cautioned the writer to avoid optimism, and he wondered whether Simms' recent appointment as editor of the *Southern Quarterly Review* had not entangled him too much in local affairs for him to take a foreign office. His advice proved to be correct; Taylor named another candidate to the diplomatic post which Simms wanted.[38]

Losing the foreign mission did not disturb Simms, since he was too busy campaigning for the United States Congress. A caucus of Taylor Democrats in Charleston had nominated him to succeed Holmes in the House, and he happily consented to make the race. He explained that he would accept a local Democratic nomination, but that he no longer felt any loyalty to the national party. Having the advantage over most politicians, Simms used his facility for political fiction to promote his candidacy. To that end he published in the *Mercury* "The Home Tourist," a series of dialogues between a Father Abbott and his acolytes about the economic and political future of Charleston.[39]

In an effort to reconcile the city's warring parties, Father Abbott hoped that political differences could be settled in order to begin the restoration of Charleston's economic dominance of the Eastern seaboard. The Charleston beaches were deserted, for there was no longer even a bridge across the Ashley River to connect Charleston with the rich low country to the south. Once a commercial port rivaling even Liverpool, Charleston had sunk into economic apathy. There were fish in abundance for the sportsman, but no one was energetic enough to advertise the fact. Charleston's revival necessitated a truce between the "Hunkers" and the young talent in the city.[40] Father Abbott urged his young colleagues to experiment, and he told them that if the city had a bridge and more hotels, it could become a popular resort area. He said that railroads could open the "measureless" interior of the state to development, and the creation of a line of commercial intercourse could restore the city's economic ties with Europe. Father Abbott hoped to see many cotton factories rise near Charleston. With zeal, earnestness, imagination, hard work, and the combination of a great commercial and agricultural center connecting Charleston to the interior, the good father claimed that the South would cease to be a victim of Northern exploitation.[41]

After he retired, Father Abbott chose to settle amid the natural beauty of the Southwest, away from the activity of the urban environment in which he had spent his life. He predicted that the key to the future of the South lay in finding the kind of leader who loved the beauty of nature and yet thrived in the utilitarian atmosphere of mercantile Charleston. Although Father Abbott was most attached to the South as a place where stationary people were content merely to cultivate the gifts of nature, he knew that his section could protect its agricultural ideal only by actively competing with the commercial North. But he had no fear that the type of statesman who could combine such virtues would succumb to materialistic ambition. He also knew that the slave system was the South's stabilizing factor, because the planter learned the importance of making decisions for his fellow man. Thus the hero, the man who would create a Southern nation, had to run for political office, in order to promote the idyllic nineteenth-century agrarian dream through the use of practical, utilitarian demands for economic diversification.[42]

Splendid piece of campaign propaganda that it was, *Father Abbott* did not succeed in electing Simms to Congress. Simms shifted his concern to national affairs in order to survey the activities of the new President, for whom he had devoted so much political energy. He could not understand why Taylor, a slaveholder, was noncommittal on the vital slavery extension question in his inaugural address, and he was appalled at Taylor's choice of the abolitionist and New York Whig William Henry Seward, as a close political adviser. Simms' final disillusionment came with Taylor's first annual message to Congress, when the President insisted that California become a free state. The fact that such an action would completely disrupt the North-South sectional balance in no way upset Taylor. Simms bitterly speculated that New Mexico and Utah would follow California as free states and that the South would forever remain a numerical minority in Congress. The man who was to have been the South's savior became anathema to all Southern expansionists.[43]

The disillusionment over Taylor was soon apparent in Simms' own activities. He realized that the South had no constitutional guarantees in the Union, and he reiterated his call for a Southern union by supporting Calhoun's proposal for a convention of the Southern states.[44] South Carolina prepared for convention, and the state legislature moved to elect delegates. Simms told Hammond that he would like to be a delegate. He had used the Taylor campaign to call for Southern unity in 1848. Since Taylor, a Southern slaveholder and the supposed heir to Jackson's mantle, had betrayed the South, there was no need for Simms to mitigate his Southern-rights views. If anything, Simms' disappointment in Taylor made him a more rabid sectionalist and left him bordering on radical, immediate secession.[45] But as a practical man, he saw the need for caution in achieving political unity.

Simms' belief in the importance of Southern sectional unity had emerged in his writing and politics over the last decade. Motivated by a deep loyalty to his native state because of a myriad of social, economic, political, and even emotional attachments, he had given up hope for the South's survival in the Union. As a legislator he had encouraged the radical Bluffton movement and had introduced resolutions for a Southern convention to ponder the value of the Union. With victory over Mexico and hopes of further Southern expansion, his radicalism temporarily abated. Still, he agitated for the election of a Southern President in order to ensure the South's safety and power within the Union. Simms finally realized that the South could not maintain its equal position in the Union when his Southern hero, Zachary Taylor, betrayed the South on expansion and territorial integrity. In his political activity and writings during the following decade, he displayed a vigorous Southern nationalism. Counseling against South Carolina's openly leading a secessionist movement, he became a political theorist in the 1850s, assisting in the development of a political formula for Southern cooperation. Unwilling to wait too long for a united South to realize that it could become a separate nation he spent the years before the Civil War actively proselytizing for a Southern nation which would pursue common goals outside the Union.[46]

NOTES

1. Simms used the term "Hunker" to refer to the Bank-controlled Southern Democratic party of Calhoun, Elmore, and, at times, Rhett. His reason for regarding Calhoun as too conservative was Calhoun's late recognition of the need for Southern cooperation.

2. William Gilmore Simms, *Self-Development* (Milledgeville, Ga., 1847), pp. 40-44.

3. Ibid., pp. 6, 9, 11, 13, 16, 20, 23, 25, 29, 30, 32, 34-35, 39, 40; Hammond to Simms, Nov. 17, 1847, Hammond Papers, Library of Congress; *Mercury*, Feb. 9, 1848.

4. Bohner, *John Pendleton Kennedy*, p. 177; Canby, *Walt Whitman*, pp. 45, 53, 69, 76, 78; Miller, *Raven and the Whale*, pp. 170, 214, 228, 230, 237, 264; John Bigelow, *William Cullen Bryant* (Boston, 1890), p. 104; F. O. Mathiessen, *American Renaissance* (New York, 1941).

5. *Mercury*, July 16, 1846, Apr. 9, 13, 1847; Brainerd Dyer, *Zachary Taylor* (Baton Rouge, 1946), pp. 266-267.

6. Again Simms' fear of westward settlement was tempered by political necessity. See *Simms Letters*, 2: 267, 287-289, 296, 297, 331-332, 333, 353, 372; *Self-Development*, p. 22; Smith, *Forces*, p. 129; Dyer, *Zachary Taylor*, pp. 272, 289, 291-292.

7. William Gilmore Simms, *Lays of the Palmetto* (Charleston, 1848), advertisement, pp. 8, 11, 18; *Mercury*, Feb. 1, 1848.

8. Dyer, *Zachary Taylor*, pp. 278-280, 294; also see pp. 272-273, 277.

9. *Simms Letters*, 2: 290-291, 311, 367; Hammond to Simms, July 23, 1847, Hammond Papers, Library of Congress. (See the author's forthcoming article on the Taylor Democrats of Charleston.)

10. *Simms Letters*, 2: 206, 244-245, 255, 278-279, 309, 311, 317, 344, 354, 373, 377, 379, 384; Hammond to Simms, Jan. 11, Oct. 31, 1847, Simms to Hammond, Jan. 2, 7, Nov. 7, 1847, Hammond Papers, Library of Congress; Hammond Diary, Jan. 1847, p. 34, Hammond Papers, University of South Carolina.

11. *Simms Letters*, 2: 311, 319, 332.

12. Simms always took an ambivalent attitude toward Calhoun's presidential ambitions. He knew that it was political suicide to oppose Calhoun openly in South Carolina. *Simms Letters*, 2: 240-241, 245-246, 294-295, 297, 310; Hammond to Simms, Apr. 4, 1847, Hammond Papers, Library of Congress; Duff Green to Calhoun, March 6, 1847, Calhoun Papers, University of South Carolina. The most careful study of Calhoun's presidential politics is Joseph G. Raybeck, "The Presidential Aspirations of John C. Calhoun, 1844-1848," *JSH* 14 (1948): 331-356; also see Capers, *Calhoun*, pp. 233, 234.

13. Boucher and Brooks, eds., "Correspondence to Calhoun," pp. 293, 326, 338-339; Meigs, *Life of John C. Calhoun* II, 286.

14. Calhoun to Hammond, Jan. 23, 1846, Hammond Papers, Library of Congress; Jameson, ed., "Calhoun Correspondence," pp. 708, 712; White, p. 86.

15. *Simms Letters*, 2: 267; *Lays of the Palmetto*, pp. 8, 11; Hammond to Simms, Feb. 23, 1847, Hammond Papers, Library of Congress; Capers, *Calhoun*, pp. 233-234; Current, *John C. Calhoun*, pp. 28-29; Daniel Wallace, *The Political Life and Services of the Honorable Robert Barnwell Rhett* (Cahaba, Ala., 1859), p. 22.

16. Beverly Tucker to Hammond, March 13, 1847, Hammond Papers, Library of Congress; Hammond Diary, March 1, 1847, Hammond Papers, University of South Carolina; Milo Milton Quaife, ed., *The Diary of James Knox Polk, during His Presidency, 1845 to 1849* 4 vols. (Chicago, 1910), 2: 378; Charles Henry Ambler, *Thomas Ritchie; a Study in Virginia Politics* (Richmond, 1913), p. 269.

17. *Congressional Globe*, 29th Cong., 2 sess., p. 455; George Parks to E. M. Snow, Nov. 13, 1847, MSS, George Parks Papers, South Caroliniana Library, University of South Carolina; Simms to Hammond, March 2, 29, 1847, Hammond Papers, Library of Congress; Thomas Hart Benton, *Thirty Years' View* 2 vols. (New York, 1856), 2: 699, 713.

18. Richard K. Crallé, ed., *The Works of John C. Calhoun* 6 vols. (New York, 1851-1870), 4: 383-384, 386-387, 388, 390-391, 394; *SQR* 12 (July 1847): 91-134; Simms to Hammond, March 29, 1847, Apr. 2, 1847, Hammond to Simms, Apr. 1, 1847, Hammond Papers, Library of Congress. Simms was furious over Calhoun's late acceptance of cooperation. The entire secessionist-cooperation movement needs careful revision. For the prevailing views see Herman V. Ames, "John C. Calhoun and the Secession Movement of 1850," *American Antiquarian Society* (Apr. 1918), p. 24; Howard C. Perkins, "A Neglected Phase of the Movement for Southern Unity, 1847-1852," *JSH* 12 (May 1946): 156; Chauncey S. Boucher, *The Secession and Co-operation Movements in South Carolina, 1848 to 1852* ("Washington University Studies," Vol. V, No. 2; St. Louis, 1918), pp. 69-74.

19. Circular sent to Hammond by I. W. Hayne, Aug. 2, 1847, Hammond to Simms, Nov. 1, 1847, Simms to Hammond, Oct. 20, 1847, Hammond Papers, Library of Congress; *Mercury* Sept. 5, 1848; Jameson, ed., "Calhoun Correspondence," pp. 1114-1116, 1117, 718-720, 1184; Boucher and Brooks, eds., "Correspondence to Calhoun," pp. 375-376, 453-454, 468-469; Wiltse, *John C. Calhoun* III, 372.

20. My major source for Simms' role in the Charleston campaign for Taylor is the *Palo Alto*. With the assistance of Mr. Les Inabinett of the South Caroliniana Library, I discovered this newspaper. (It is obvious that Simms felt that he had more of a part in the campaign than he had in fact.)

21. *Courier*, Feb. 3, June 20, 1848; *Simms Letters*, 2: 319, 333-334, 411-412; *Mercury*, Aug. 21, 1848; Simms to Hammond, May 1, 1847, Hammond to Simms, May 15, 1847, Hammond Papers, Library of Congress; Carson, pp. 265, 275-

276; Mrs. Perry to Perry, late in 1848, MSS, Benjamin F. Perry Papers, South Caroliniana Library, University of South Carolina; Lillian Adele Kibler, *Benjamin F. Perry, South Carolina Unionist* (Durham, N. C., 1946), pp. 222-225; see also Holman Hamilton, *Zachary Taylor* 2 vols. (Indianapolis, 1941-1951), 2: 45-46.

22. Washington Allston to Calhoun, Apr. 18, 1848, Calhoun Papers, University of South Carolina; Wiltse, *John C. Calhoun* III, 361.

23. *Mercury*, July 15, Aug. 7, 21, 1848; A. G. Summer to F. H. Elmore, June 23, 1848, Calhoun Papers, University of South Carolina; Raybeck, p. 350.

24. *Courier*, July 20, 1848; *Simms Letters*, 2: 415.

25. *Palo Alto*, 1: 1, Aug. 5, 1848; *Courier*, July 21, 1848; *Mercury*, July 21, 1848; *Simms Letters*, 2: 426, 430; James M. Walker to Hammond, July 21, 1848; Simms to Hammond, Aug. 10, 1848, Hammond Papers, Library of Congress.

26. Rhett and Elmore again worked together in behalf of Cass. See *Simms Letters*, 2: 418-421.

27. *Simms Letters*, 2: 421, 433, 424, 428, 433-434, 439; Columbia *South Carolinian*, July 28, 1848; Hammond to Simms, July 26, 1848, Hammond Papers, Library of Congress; for a study of Hammond's vacillation see Merritt, *James Henry Hammond*, pp. 82-85, 87.

28. *Simms Letters*, 2: 423, 428, 436, 440; Hammond to Simms, May 29, June 20, 1848, Simms to Hammond, June 15, 1848, Hammond Papers, Library of Congress.

29. *Courier*, Aug. 26, 1848; *Mercury*, Aug. 31, 1848; Hammond to Simms, Aug. 13, Sept. 7, 1848, Simms to Hammond, Aug. 29, Sept. 14, Dec. 11, 1848; Hammond Diary, Sept. 22, 1848, note on "General Taylor and His Administration," Hammond Papers, University of South Carolina.

30. See *Mercury*, Aug. 30, 1848 for attack on *Palo Alto*; *Palo Alto*, Aug. 5, 12, 16, 26, Sept. 2, Oct. 7, 1848; *Simms Letters*, 2: 441. Simms told Hammond that he merely edited and added a few points to the young editors' arguments. It is incalculable just how much lasting political influence Simms had on the many anonymous editors of the *Palo Alto*.

31. *Simms Letters*, 2: 431, 440; *Palo Alto*, Aug. 5, 9, 12, 30, Sept. 6, 9, 1848. The paper seemed to print every speech Simms gave in the month of August.

32. *Simms Letters*, 2: 441, 445-446; *Palo Alto*, Sept. 13, 16, 1848; *Courier*, Sept. 16, 1848; *Mercury*, Sept. 16, 1848; for the Calhoun forces' reaction to the *Palo Alto* and Simms see Whitemarsh Seabrook to Calhoun, Oct. 22, 1848, Lawrence M. Keitt to Calhoun, Oct. 25, 1848, Calhoun Papers, University of South Carolina.

33. William Gilmore Simms, *Charleston, and Her Satirists* (Charleston, 1848), p. 3; *Simms Letters*, 2: 447, 451.

34. *Charleston, and Her Satirists*, pp. 11, 48-52.

35. Ibid., pp. 52-55, 41-42, 43-44, 11.

36. *Simms Letters*, 2: 555; *Charleston, and Her Satirists*, pp. 6, 12, 15, 20, 24, 26, 28, 32, 33, 38, 40, 41, 43, 46, 48.

37. *Courier*, Nov. 2, 1848; *Simms Letters*, 2: 448, 449, 451, 455, 457, 458-459, 465; James M. Walker to Hammond, Aug. 22, 1848, Simms to Hammond, Nov. 11, 1848, Hammond to Simms, Jan. 7, 1849, Hammond Papers, Library of Congress. Years later in an article entitled "The State of Parties in the Country," *SQR* 8 n. s. (July 1853): 16, 20, 21, 28, 29, Simms reiterated that he had not supported Taylor for personal political gain.

38. *Simms Letters*, 2: 469, 475, 482-483, 532; Crallé, *Works of Calhoun* 6: 290-313; Hammond to Simms, Nov. 17, Dec. 1, 1848, Feb. 10, March 9, June 15, July 9, 1849, Simms to Hammond, Nov. 24, Dec. 3, Dec. 15, 1848, Hammond Papers, Library of Congress; for a comparison see Bancroft's

behavior at not receiving an appointment to the London consulate, Nye, *George Bancroft*, pp. 177, 179-180.

39. *Simms Letters*, 2: 554, 563, 565, 570; William Gilmore Simms, *Father Abbott* (Charleston, 1849), pp. 3-4; *Father Abbott* was first published in the *Mercury* during September, October, and November of 1848.

40. *Father Abbott*, pp. 9, 20, 25, 26-27, 31, 32, 33, 57, 106, 111, 120, 149, 150.

41. Ibid., pp. 145, 146, 148, 168, 182, 185, 192, 202, 203-204, 205, 206, 211, 220. In November 1849, Simms had the opportunity to test his theories. He was appointed to the board of the Industrial Institute Fair in Charleston; see *Simms Letters*, 2: 569.

42. *Father Abbott*, pp. 208, 232, 234, 235, 17, 178, 224, 226, 220.

43. *Father Abbot*, p. 221; *Mercury*, Jan 22, Feb. 7, Dec. 27, 28, 1849; *Courier*, June 22, 26, 1849; *Simms Letters* 2: 483; James D. Richardson, ed., *A Compilation of the Messages and Papers of the Presidents, 1789-1902* 20 vols. (Washington, 1903), 5: 4-7, 9-29; Benton, *Thirty Years View* II, 741; Wiltse, *John C. Calhoun* III, 405.

44. *Simms Letters*, 2: 482, 537; Hammond to Calhoun, Feb. 19, 1849, Hammond Papers, Library of Congress.

45. *Simms Letters*, 2: 574-575, 577; Calhoun to Hammond, Dec. 7, 1849, Hammond Papers, Library of Congress; *SQR* 8 n. s. (July 1853): 28; see also Higham, "Changing Loyalties of William Gilmore Simms," p. 220; Norvel Neil Luxon, *Niles' Weekly Register, News Magazine of the Nineteenth Century* (Baton Rouge, 1947), pp. 286-287; Jesse Macy, *Political Parties in the United States, 1846-1861* (New York, 1917), pp. 127, 186.

46. If there was any shift in Simms' career it was only a matter of more sober political analysis. His radical secession sentiment became more practical as the South moved toward separation.

6 A Political Theorist of Southern Nationalism

WHEN PRESIDENT TAYLOR failed to demonstrate his good will toward the South, Simms began to reexamine his own thoughts on Southern unity. When South Carolina and the rest of the South failed to resolve the secessionist-cooperationist controversy of 1850-1852, Simms' need to clarify his political philosophy seemed to take on added urgency. In his later Revolutionary romances, *The Golden Christmas* and *Southward Ho!*, his revised version of "Miss Martineau on Slavery," and many lectures, Simms quantified his theories of political behavior. His topics included the value of political parties, the South's continued need for a leader, the relationship of Southern economy to society, and the value of slavery. His efforts exhibited an unsystematic combination of practical and romantic political theory. Simms' one serious attempt to clarify his political philosophy was *Egeria*, a collection of aphorisms concerning the nature of man's obligation to society. Nevertheless, Simms was a perceptive political theorist in an age when only a few novelists cared about either man's place or significance in the social and political system.[1]

Although he no longer held office or managed political campaigns, Simms was by no means removed from active political life. A Charleston newspaper again nominated him to represent the city in Congress, but his radicalism and political independence, combined with his antagonism toward the Bank

faction, made him an unacceptable candidate. He also continued to serve as an adviser for delegates to various political
and commercial conventions, and he became especially close to
the Virginian, Beverly Tucker. Through both Tucker and Hammond, Simms kept a close watch on the political antics of the
Southern convention movement in 1850. He politicked for the
presidency of the South Carolina College in Columbia and was
pleased when the Charleston *Courier* seconded his nomination.
Many of his friends encouraged the trustees to turn the College
into an agent for Southern unity and to name the South's most
talented man of letters to its highest post. Simms actively
sought a nomination to the first Nashville Convention, but
when his candidacy was rejected, he urged friends to serve as
delegates.[2]

Since Simms was unable to participate in the Nashville
Convention, he vicariously celebrated the hopes of Southern
unity by corresponding with Hammond and Tucker. His loss of
faith in President Taylor and his anxiety over the admission of
California as a free state led him to condemn any compromise
with the national government. Although chagrined at the
lateness of Calhoun's actions, Simms supported the statesman's
call for a Southern convention to found a united party which
would hopefully combat Northern power and secure the future
of the South. Simms was convinced that separation was
inevitable and that it was the South's only means of maintaining its independence. He was delighted that other Southern
states were also disgusted with the politics of compromise and
that they seemed more than willing to support the convention.
For once, South Carolina would not have to appear radical and
too far ahead of the rest of the South.[3]

Active in pre-convention meetings, Simms spoke and
wrote for a Southern confederacy. But Simms was a wise politician who feared the power of persuasion of national parties
bent on compromise. He was not convinced that Virginia, Kentucky, and Tennessee would support a secession movement, yet
he hoped that a prevailing spirit of sectional interest would
emerge, and he was pleased that Southern states were meeting.
Simms correctly predicted the defections, since with Taylor's
death and the compromise work of Clay and Douglas, the national parties began to erode the convention's unity. Only nine
Southern states participated in the convention, and the South

Carolina and Mississippi delegations found moderation to be
the trend at Nashville. Simms was disappointed, but a second
Nashville Convention was planned. He was consoled that
Southern states had met together in convention and that many
Southerners, although opposed to secession, began to see the
need for Southern unity. But he advised Hammond not to attend the second Nashville Convention, because he believed that
nothing would be accomplished there.[4]

His prediction proved to be correct. The failure of the second Nashville Convention produced a hotly debated contest in
the South Carolina legislature. On the one side were those who
wanted immediate single-state secession, while the other, more
practical faction advocated South Carolina's continuing to
work with other Southern states. Without thought of Southern
unity, Rhett, Governor John H. Means, and other fire-eaters
determined to force a bill for a state secession convention. At
the same time, Benjamin F. Perry and Waddy Thompson of
Greenville began a cooperationist newspaper, the *Southern
Patriot*, and supported a call for a united Southern convention.
The issue in the radical-dominated legislature was never union
or disunion, but single-state or united Southern secession. Because of the two-thirds rule, the cooperationists were able to
stall the legislative radicals in their call for a state convention.
A compromise measure was passed which called for a Southern
convention to meet in Montgomery, Alabama, in January
1852, the delegates to be elected in October 1851. A second
part of the compromise bill provided for a state convention to
meet in order to pass on the actions of the Southern convention. Delegates to the state convention were to be elected in
February 1851. The immediate secessionists were in the majority, but their power had been temporarily stalled through the
action of the legislature.[5]

The Charleston *Mercury* nominated Simms along with Alfred P. Aldrich, Hammond, and Samuel W. Trotti as delegates
from Barnwell to the state convention, but the writer declined.
As a delegate to a Southern Rights Association meeting in October 1850, Simms had advocated the construction of a
Southern confederacy, and barring that, immediate "measures
to meet the existing crisis." But when he saw that the Georgia
legislature had refused to support a convention, he was con-

vinced that South Carolina should avoid any precipitate action until the rest of the South could be persuaded that unity was necessary. While he praised Rhett, he was certain that the state convention would move too quickly for the rest of the South. Simms advised Beverly Tucker to avoid extremism in Virginia until after the next national election. Convinced that time was on the side of secession, he believed that the national Democratic party would turn against the South and that the abolitionists would continue to grow in strength, thus creating a militant and united South. Predicting secession in five years, he advised his native state against pushing the South too soon. His personal sentiments were for immediate secession, even alone if necessary, but the practical side of his politics prevailed. Like many other politicians, he remembered South Carolina's embarrassment in 1833, and he felt that any immediate action would only create a wider breach in the relations of the Southern states. The rest of the South was jealous of South Carolina's continued leadership, so Simms declined nomination to a convention that would only antagonize most of the South. His plan was to push for unity by constantly reiterating the South's common heritage and its common need to protect slavery.[6]

Although the state was no longer split over the ultimate objective, there was disagreement over the means of achieving secession. The February election for delegates to the future state convention produced 127 single-state secessionists out of the 169 delegates elected. But it was a deceptive vote, because many of the so-called single-state secessionists believed that Georgia and Mississippi were prepared to follow South Carolina. There ensued throughout the state a series of special meetings, mainly to keep emotions running high in preparation for the October election of delegates to the proposed convention in Montgomery. The Charleston *Mercury* and other secessionist papers continued to agitate for secession. In May, Rhett called a Southern Rights Association meeting to argue the case for single-state secession. On the surface the meeting was a success, because it produced an overwhelming vote to disregard the action of other Southern states and secede alone if necessary.[7]

But at that Charleston meeting the Rhett forces had

reached their peak. James L. Orr, who had become a National Democrat, made a divisive speech at the association meeting. He was aware that there was little chance to achieve a redress of grievances in Congress, and he wanted to create a Southern union. But Orr knew that South Carolina could not secede alone, and that for the time being, no other Southern state would follow.[8] Rhett was furious. But it was Alfred P. Aldrich, under the careful tutelage of Hammond and Simms, who really put doubt in the immediate secessionist camp. He presented Hammond's "plan of state action," which advocated a boycott and separation of business interests from the North, but cautioned against the foolhardiness of separate action. Pleased with the results of the meeting, Simms knew that South Carolina's future action was no longer in the hands of Rhett and that cooperation would prevail.[9]

A strong opposition party was formed with its nucleus in Charleston. Robert W. Barnwell, a converted single-state secessionist, spoke of his loyalty to South Carolina. He vowed to follow the state in any action, but he requested time to convince the South to join in united action.[10] The cooperationists continued to gain strength as Simms began to write political commentary for the Charleston *Evening News*. He urged North Carolinians to unite with South Carolina in their common cause, but he dismissed Virginia as a tool of political parties, corrupted by its proximity to Washington. Simms cautioned his own state to become diplomatic in its political actions. The articles covered his travels throughout the Southeast, and they enlightened South Carolina as to the behavior of other Southern states. Simms also realized that the only way the South could secede was for South Carolina to follow, not lead, the rest of the South. Expediency was the cooperationists' main issue, and even the Charleston *Mercury* finally realized the necessity of Southern unity. The *Mercury* affirmed that the cooperationists were true secessionists, and that single-state secession was unattainable. When the October election was held, the immediate secessionists were soundly defeated, since the state rejected the idea of a Montgomery convention altogether.[11] The crisis was over. Secession was averted, and Simms' hope for a conciliatory attitude toward the rest of the South was finally realized.

When the state legislature met in December 1851, it had to schedule the state convention, which was no longer necessary, since the Southern convention would not be called. The only remaining reason for holding a state convention was to unify South Carolina by soothing the various dissident elements in the state. When the state convention convened in April 1852, few important political figures bothered to attend. Maxcy Gregg struck the tone of the convention when he cautioned the state to bide its time and to await an opportunity to strike at the North with a united South. Governor John H. Means was certain that all South Carolina was united on the state's right to secede.[12] Benjamin F. Perry agreed with the convention resolutions on the right of secession based on "the sufficiency of the causes." He sounded the unifying factor for the entire South when he called slavery "moral and correct" and stated that it "will be maintained by South Carolina at all hazard."[13] Since the radical Rhett faction was forced from leadership in the state, the convention was considered a success. In his inaugural address as governor, John L. Manning advocated an end to all factious agitation in South Carolina.[14]

If Simms was pleased with the recent events in the state, he was disappointed at the quality of leadership which seemed to be emerging in South Carolina. He felt that a new breed of mediocrity was replacing intelligent politicians and statesmen in a period of extreme crisis. Instead of leaders, men who played up to mass sentiment were everywhere in evidence. Simms continued with renewed impatience his search for a young Hickory, a prophet to carry the South out of the wilderness. In a time when Washingtons, Pinckneys, and McDuffies were needed, Simms was disturbed that as far as he was concerned, South Carolina was governed by radical Rhetts, compromising Elmores, and party hacks such as Orr. What had happened to the proud combination of brilliance and leadership in a state which had once overflowed with heroes? As Simms said, "souls for trying times" were sorely needed.[15]

The death of Calhoun was partly responsible for the failure of leadership in South Carolina, for it had deprived the state of its most brilliant defender in the Union. Simms, like many other former opponents of the living Calhoun, envisioned

the dead statesman as the symbol of Southern integrity and nationalism. Calhoun's final speech on the fourth of March,
1850, had sounded the necessity for Southern unity. Simms
used that speech to stress the importance of Calhoun to the
South, and he wrote that Calhoun was a man who had
sacrificed his own ambition and had driven himself to death in
pursuing the best interests of the South.[16] Writing as "Lorris" in the *Mercury*, Simms castigated Thomas Hart Benton
and other politicians for their unfair view of Calhoun's career.
Simms called for the publication of Calhoun's works and the
writing of his biography in order to give the South a guide for
united effort. "Lorris" also reviewed Richard K. Crallé's edition of Calhoun's works and praised them for their careful attention to the relations of the states to the federal government.
He maintained that Calhoun's ideas, especially the concept of
how to protect minority rights within or without the Union,
were mandatory reading for all Southern politicians. Simms
considered Calhoun a profound political theorist who left writings which were of utmost importance in the movement for
Southern nationalism.[17]

When the city council of Charleston selected Hammond to
give the funeral eulogy for Calhoun, Simms volunteered to sup-
ply much of the biographical material and edit the speech. Although Hammond had no true feeling for Calhoun, Simms considered the opportunity to advance Hammond's own career too
important to refuse. He advised Hammond to review Calhoun's
family life and education, then to develop his years of public
service and dedication to the South's defense. He wanted Hammond to stress that since Calhoun had died in office, he was
even more of a martyr to the cause than if he had shunned
public responsibility. Cautioning against the pathetic or con-
ventionally flowery but false sentimentality of most orations,
Simms suggested that Hammond emphasize Calhoun's heroic
qualities. He also advised Hammond to conclude with a comment on Calhoun's "singleness in his devotion to the
South."[18]

More useful to the South in death than he had been in life,
Calhoun was nevertheless partly responsible for the leadership
vacuum created in South Carolina by his death. A mad scramble ensued for his Senate seat and the choice of his successor as

the state's political leader. Simms was not pleased by the prospect of a transition period in which mediocre men would battle for state leadership. He wanted Hammond, whom he regarded as the most intelligent and talented politician in the state, to take Calhoun's place in the Senate. But through political chicanery Governor Whitemarsh Seabrook chose Simms' longtime rival, Franklin Harper Elmore, as Senator. Ill and unwilling to relinquish his powerful Bank presidency, Elmore was forced to accept, only to die in Washington a few months later.[19] In the fall, a radical state legislature named Rhett to the Senate. Simms believed that a truly strong leader such as Hammond had no chance to win office. The weak always resented a Hammond, and Calhoun had so dominated the state's politics that few men of intelligence were in a position to elect a capable man to office. Hammond was not elected in this important period, when a figure was needed who could unite the South and "bring on the catastrophe."[20] Simms persistently campaigned to place men of ability in the state's hierarchy. While he cursed Calhoun, he planned long letters to instruct men such as James Chesnut, Perry, Orr, William Porcher Miles, and Hammond on their role in the defense of the South.

Simms gradually developed a concept of leadership which was more sophisticated than his previous romantic attraction to military heroes. He advised Henry S. Randall, the biographer of Thomas Jefferson, to stress Jefferson's Southernness and to emphasize the relevance of the Declaration of Independence to the South in the 1850s. Simms insisted that Southerners have models for their political behavior, and he encouraged Beverly Tucker to write a life of John Randolph of Roanoke, Hammond to study the career of George McDuffie, and John Pendleton Kennedy to write on his kinsman William Wirt.[21] In one of his poems, Simms stressed Jackson's Southernness and his defense of the Southern city of New Orleans. His Jackson was a native Carolinian whose greatest strength was in guarding his homeland. Simms praised the fanatic who could inspire men to action through his powers of concentration. For Simms himself, the object of concentration was the defense of the South.[22]

The primary qualities of true greatness, according to

Simms, were constantly to strive for truth and "consumation" of the final object and to refuse to succumb to stupidity or errors of judgment. He said that a good leader should be willing to accept censure and to have his motives misunderstood by his own generation. He believed that the shrewdest politician should never assert his popularity, but he should use it to its fullest extent. Simms knew that mediocre men delighted in destroying their moral and intellectual superiors. His true leader was one who watched his followers and promoted his own views. Simms thought that a practical sense of justice and a need to follow the leader who could ensure its preservation were inherent in the nature of man. In his opinion, working on behalf of the rare, selfless dedication to unity of interest without slipping in one's own beliefs constituted "the only sure claim upon which we may reasonably expect the gratitude either of our fellows or of the future."[23]

Simms had devised a philosophy of leadership which was practical, dedicated, and fanatical, and he was willing to devote his life not only to finding but to educating these leaders. He also realized that to create men of vision and to further the cause of Southern nationalism, the national party system which he had rejected in 1848 should continually be exposed as inimical to Southern interests. Besides perceiving the foolhardy existence of a viable party structure in a growing and expanding country, Simms knew that the growth of bureaucracy made Washington a haven for devious politicians who never allowed political principles to interfere with the gratuities of party loyalty. Because of the party system, Congress not only bred poor political leaders but served as a debating society for party intrigue. Above all, Simms was alarmed that the national government behaved as a tool of the national party system, thus working against his personal wish for a sectional party to unite the South. His opposition to political parties was based on the South's inability to control one of the existing parties, not a romantic antipathy to the deviousness of the party system.[24]

Dislike of national parties carried over to Simms' view of the 1852 Presidential election and the electoral process. While other literary men became enthusiastic over the virtues of Franklin Pierce, and many Southerners were pleased at his pro-Southern attitudes, Simms was unable to find any reason to support openly the New Englander's candidacy. Suspicious of Pierce's home state of New Hampshire, an abolitionist stronghold, Simms feared that Pierce would become another Zachary Taylor. Although he still advocated popular elections, he began to temper his practical political views of democracy. Simms sought a new form of conservatism which would be dedicated to unity of the South and antagonistic to national politicians and parties. Once he would have ardently supported Pierce, but he had grown suspicious of the "virtue of numbers." Since he equated the Democratic party with a strong support of majority rule, he cut loose from that party and questioned the democratic spirit. Although he continued to favor Pierce over his Whig opponent, he no longer held any faith in the Democratic party, and Pierce's pro-slavery statements in defense of fugitive slave laws were not enough to move Simms to political activity.[25]

In part Simms' renewed interest in the pro-slavery controversy was also designed to exploit the slave states' fear of the abolitionist movement. Cautioning his friend John P. Kennedy to forget abstract theories of freedom and to defend the slave question, Simms continued to stress slavery as a positive good. He revised the pro-slavery essay on Miss Martineau, wrote lengthy book reviews of works favorable to slavery, and forcefully attacked abolitionism.[26] Simms' view of slavery was hardly original, since most of his work merely reflected the prevailing views of his period. But his bold political approach to slavery was unique. Few Southerners at that time recognized the usefulness of slavery in bringing on the long-awaited Southern unity movement. And Simms was unusual in that he was able to use both fiction and the essay to create a theory of Southern society with slavery as its cornerstone.

Included with a group of eminent Southerners' articles in *The Pro-Slavery Argument*, Simms' revision of his essay on Miss Martineau was entitled "The Morals of Slavery." In the introduction he stated that in 1837 the issue of slavery "had not so greatly engaged the attention of the Southern people," because the abolitionists had been relatively ineffectual. But by the 1850s they were in a position to form their own party and to endanger Southern society. Simms thanked the abolitionists for making the South more aware of its social obligation to retain slavery. Using Harriet Beecher Stowe as a new foil, Simms defended the benevolence of the system. Far from being cruel, slaveowners were kind masters, he said. He invited the skeptical Martineaus and Stowes to observe the system in operation, to judge slavery for themselves, and to understand the moral uplift which the system gave to the slaveholder himself.[27]

If domestic slavery was uplifting, Simms also believed that it was legally justified through the democratic belief in private property as found in the Declaration of Independence. Simms, a firm believer in property rights based on laissez-faire economics and natural law, was convinced that society thrived on the guaranteed results of hard labor. The result of labor was property. Natural law guaranteed the protection of property, and property for the Southern planter consisted of his land and his slaves. Simms also claimed that the concept of equality in the Declaration of Independence did not apply to slaves. He said that the founding fathers were democratic, but that their notion of democracy "was not levelling in its character." Whites were guaranteed equal opportunity to compete with one another, but the slave as property was bound to a collective society based on paternalism.[28]

Simms also used the essay and fiction to attack the abolitionists. Even Mrs. Stowe, he cautioned Miss Martineau, could not praise the abolitionists. She had made the villain of *Uncle Tom's Cabin* a Yankee, and she found abolitionists a disruptive and evil force in society.[29] Writing as "Lorris," Simms accused William Henry Seward of fomenting unrest, but he realized that Seward's agitation for a new party would result in united Southern secession. Simms, who was antipathetic to hypocritical Northern morality, repeatedly berated the New England abolitionists. Historically, he insisted, that section had profited from the slave trade, but the grandsons of slave traders virtuously advocated abolition in Congress. In *Michael Bonham*, Simms' verse play about the Mexican War, the legendary Davy Crockett reminisced of his days in Congress and singled out John Quincy Adams as an arch-villain. Since the center of abolitionism was New England, Simms wondered why that section did not concentrate on educating its own, rather than sending school teachers to lecture the South on morality.[30]

Using a conventional story line of passengers aboard a ship heading south, amusing themselves with tales of adventure, in *Southward Ho!* Simms allowed people from all parts of the South to speak out against the entire North. Maintaining that Unionist sentiment in the South no longer existed, Simms sought to widen the breach by reciting the evils of the abolition "mania." He called for Southerners to stay at home and asked, "Why spend time and money on people who defame our character and destroy our institutions?" He admitted that abolitionists were still a minority, yet he insisted that they were increasingly shaping law and dictating Northern policy, especially in their encouragement of runaway slaves. He summoned Southerners to unite against fanaticism and radicalism and to refuse to submit to Northern standards. A separate South, free of outside oppression, could develop its slave civilization and become one of the world's most affluent and cultured societies, he claimed.[31]

The result of this aggressive defense was a positive view of slavery as a necessary part of a conservative society. Much has been written about the relationship between the famous Lieutenant Porgy and his slave Tom, especially about Tom's loyalty to Porgy in refusing to accept liberty.[32] But Simms' other plantation stories more realistically captured his view of the role of slavery in Southern society. Simms fully realized that slavery was a burden to the planter. Many of his friends kept more slaves than they needed, because they did not want to break up families. He also knew that many slaves did not work to capacity, but a staple crop economy needed gang labor. Simms captured the effect of slavery on the slaveholder in his characterization of Major Bulmer, the fierce secessionist in *The Golden Christmas*, who wanted to protect the old plantation system from outside forces which sought to change it. There were social virtues to be gained from the obligation of ruling other men, and this concept of noblesse oblige was not to be surrendered without a struggle. The Major was a wise politician and romantic hero, fond of his Anglo-Saxon blood and attached to the medieval concept of honor; he cared for his slaves. Protected against cold and hunger, his workload adapted to his capacities, the slave was happy and secure at "Bulmer Barony." Simms was not romanticizing the slave system, for he had pointed out the pitfalls as well as the advantages of slavery. No longer willing to countenance "Mr. Jefferson's Gallic vagaries, that it [slavery] was immoral, evil, and without proper sanction," Simms regarded slavery as the finest of economic systems for a race destined to accomplish much in the history of civilization.[33]

From his combined realistic and romantic view of slavery and his desire to create the bonds for a Southern union, Simms developed his theory of the function of a society and man's place in that society. Always considering himself a conservative, Simms explained that conservatives believed in the progress of mankind and did not want to keep things as they were. The true conservative controlled progress in order to use the future for his own interests. But Simms defined conservatism as meaning respect for an ordered society, and he became increasingly conscious of one's "place" in society. He even claimed that the primary responsibility of an intellectual was to instruct his fellow man on the proper respect for authority. He opposed almost all revolution, condemning revolutionaries as fools "who seek by madness to recover what they have lost by blindness." Simms had not completely repudiated his Jacksonian view of a man of humble background rising to a position of leadership, but he had tempered the idea of a natural aristocracy with a belief in a more stratified, controlled, hierarchical society.[34] There was obviously some conflict between the actual and the ideal in Simms' social philosophy.

In his later Revolutionary romances Simms was conscious of the concept of status, particularly as it affected the need for qualified leaders in times of crisis. He used the Revolutionary setting to delineate the social world of South Carolina in hopes of constructing a set of values under which leaders could govern their society. He even subordinated historical narrative "to illustrate the social conditions of the country, under the influence of those strifes and trials" which gave meaning to the most ordinary events. Simms' themes were shaped less by class conflict or by his view of his own status in South Carolina society than by his interpretation of the need for unity in the state after the Revolutionary War. To build its power inside or outside the Union, South Carolina had to demonstrate that the

Revolution had unified the state. Simms felt that it was particularly important for the average citizen to accept the leadership of the conservative and privileged elite in tumultuous times.[35]

If the Revolution created leaders, it also gave some lower-class Carolinians an opportunity to raise their status. This attempt to shift status gave Simms an opportunity to present his conservative view of the South's lower classes. In *The Forayers*, Richard Inglehart, a poor boy seeking power and position, had joined the Loyalists in a time "destructive of most conventionalities," only to lose his life because of ambition. By the 1850s Simms seemed to be warning that the failure to observe class distinctions would bring sorrow and mortification to those who sought to raise their station in life. In a similar instance, the aristocratic Major Sinclair lowered his class standing by marrying a common overseer's daughter. Although his father was furious, the heroic deeds of young Bertha Travis enabled Sinclair to marry her. To make the Travis family fully acceptable, Simms had to create in *Eutaw* a role for Bertha's brother, the famous Colonel Henry Travis of the War of 1812. The lower classes conspicuously, in an effort to raise their status, flirted with and often joined the English forces, hoping that they would conquer the United States and place the poor in power. Simms damned them and all who would try to disrupt the natural hierarchy of South Carolina.[36]

Quite the opposite position emerged when Simms studied the old landholding patriarchs of Revolutionary South Carolina. Most of them, like Colonel Walton, father of the heroine of *Katherine Walton*, felt more loyalty to conservative England and distrusted the Revolutionary change. Set near Charleston, the novel portrayed the split and final reconciliation between generations. Katherine, every bit a colonial aristocrat, took pride in her ancestors but supported the Whigs in the Revolution. Her father, at first loyal to England, gradually shifted to the American side. He was captured, imprisoned in Charleston, and finally hanged as a traitor to England. With the aid of a fictional David Ramsay, the Revolutionary historian, Simms praised the truly magnificent patriotism of most of Charleston's aristocracy, the great majority of whom had spent some time in the city's prisons. In addition, Simms ceased being

the pure American Whig. He saw much advantage in the conservative tradition of England's church, form of government,
and legal system. He became more objective toward the British,
and symbolically depicted soldiers from both sides being buried
in a common grave.[37]

The key character for understanding Simms' attitudes on
South Carolina society was Major Sinclair's father, a virtual
feudal baron of the low country. The patriarch, ideal-
istically loyal to England, was set in his ways, and perfectly
happy as one of the colonies' largest and most respected land-
holders. An English squire, gout-ridden and stubborn, the
elder Sinclair had furious debates with his son over the nature
of loyalty and liberty. In one of their many arguments about
class, he told young William, "Once break down the barrier of
rightful authority, and there is an end to all security—all
right—all liberty!" But blood was thicker than water, and the
elder Sinclair, fearful of his son's safety, refused to give aid and
information to British troops. Unable to war against his
English heritage, he vowed to remain a neutral and, toward the
end of the war, saw some merit in the Revolutionary cause.
What he really saw was the retention of aristocratic control
among the colonists, and he finally submitted to the new
generation, realizing that his way of life would be preserved.
Simms ended most of the later Revolutionary romances not
only with a reconciliation of the generations, but also with a
unified South Carolina. Former Loyalists, with less of an
ideological belief than old Sinclair, joined ranks with the Whigs
when American victory was assured. A show of loyalty to one's
homeland was of utmost importance; even the elder Sinclair
never believed himself disloyal to South Carolina.[38]

In his border tales set in the post-Revolutionary South,
Simms discussed the plantation as a viable social system. He
sought to create an impression of Southern unity based on the
common defense of an agricultural society. Although he was
still infatuated with young men of noble stature who had
emigrated to the frontier to make a new place in society, Simms
returned to his earlier doubts that the frontier was a suitable
place for civilized Southerners. Lacking proper education or
communication, frontier planters lived too far apart to achieve
a unity of interest. The uncivilized frontier was the scene for so-

cial disruption and violence. A sedentary population with an opportunity to grow in numbers and wealth again replaced Simms' earlier rromntic attachment to the wilderness. An agricultural population, living on large plantations near cities, was his ideal society. For Simms, the plantation system embodied opportunity to think, to learn, to build a new society based on conservative principles; it alone could preserve the Southern way of life.[39]

Not only was the plantation system the finest and highest form of civilization known to man, but Simms found it useful to oppose Northern aggression. "Lorris" wrote of moral and political decay in Europe and predicted the same for Northern cities. But agricultural interests allowed the South to escape the calamity, maintaining its institutions. Cities bred corruption, while the plantation promoted a superior behavior. Realizing that a vigorous defense of the plantation aided the drive for unity, Simms often attacked the Northern enemies who sought to change the South. Major Bulmer wanted to maintain "those social virtues which constituted the rare excellence of our old plantation life in the South." When Northerners claimed that the South was an agricultural desert, Simms jumped to its defense. Northerners judged only externals and knew nothing but city life, he claimed. Since every plantation was a self-sustaining village, the South needed no large cities. When the prosperity of staple crop cultivation was attacked, he quickly jumped to the defense of Southern agriculture. Taking the offense, he pointed out that in contrast to the North, poverty was nonexistent in the South.[40] Simms was more than willing to unite the South by exposing Northern attacks upon its institutions.

But the romantic and propagandistic side of Southern agricultural civilization never overshadowed Simms' practical view of the plantation. He knew that if the plantation system were to survive it had to concentrate upon diversification and improvements. Citing his own failure to market a successful cotton crop, he urged Southerners to plant scientifically. Economy was not a virtue of the Southern planter, and he rarely planned for lean years, being either too lackadaisical or too philosophical about the whims of nature. Colonel Openheart from *Maize in Milk* was constantly in debt, rarely able to go two years without crop failure, and unwilling to attempt the cultivation of his swamps. Always confident about next season, he depended on foreign markets for his prices. His estate was saved in the romantic tradition of marrying an offspring into a wealthy family. Hardly the epitome of the successful planter was the much-loved but frankly incompetent Porgy. No businessman and always in debt, Porgy was a foolish farmer. He would have gladly died for Glen-Eberly, his plantation, but sentiment could not remedy the ills of an excessively large slave population or compensate for his inability to make the best use of his land.[41]

Recognizing the romantic, impractical side of the South as anything but a virtue, Simms often stressed the need for a more utilitarian philosophy among the planters. Millhouse warned Porgy to make himself useful, to study crop raising and rotation, to market his own product, and to learn something of the business of running his plantation. Simms did not want the planter to emulate the Northern businessman, but sound economic practices often required some compromise of romantic principles. In a lengthy study of scientific planting "for those who would elevate the dignity, and increase the results, of our agricultural enterprise," he called for experimental nurseries and special schools to train young farmers. He never failed to praise industrious and hard-working planters, and he rejected any dependence upon foreign labor. He urged planters to anticipate cycles of drought and low prices and to prepare for lean seasons through the development of storehouses. He even encouraged local manufacturing to fill the South's own needs, "that we may be perfectly independent of our Northern brethren."[42] Simms' fictional characterizations, which he used as lessons for the South, showed that he was well aware of what the South had to do economically in order to preserve its way of life.

To strengthen the slave society Simms turned from agriculture to state political power in order to clarify South Carolina's position in the coming sectional crisis, to construct a more cogent argument for cooperation among Southern states, and to formulate a position on the Presidential election of 1856. Perhaps more than any other South Carolinian, Simms knew "the faults and foibles" of his own state. But he was unwilling to disparage the state, because he realized that only South Carolina could lead the South into a confederacy. In Simms' view, history proved that South Carolina, the proud preserver of the past, had moved too fast for the rest of the South. While Simms was at times almost metaphysical in glorifying the state, a hard core of practicality dictated his views. The duties of the state were to guard its sovereignty, to realize its heritage, and to protect its people. Aware that South Carolina was unable to accomplish these objectives in the Union and since it was unable to force its own views upon another state, he called for the adoption of a plan to urge the need for unity throughout the South.[43]

Simms' own cautious formula for cooperation and eventual secession slowly took shape. South Carolina should advocate secession but hesitate to force or to appear to lead other Southern states; "it is essential to the common cause that we should be civil to each other." If the South could not yet see its future together, it was necessary to point out that it would soon *"pull* together." For this reason Simms' mythical traveler in *Southward Ho!* assured the North Carolina farmer that the secession movement was genuine. Warning him that there was a near-majority in South Carolina for separate state secession, he urged the farmer to work for cooperation in North Carolina. He wanted secessionists to avoid jealousy, to work together, and to organize committees to influence the rest of the South. In that work Simms reiterated that there was no chance for the South, "unless we cut loose from the whole Yankee consarn."[44]

Applying his views of secession and Southern society to the Presidential election of 1856, Simms wrote articles and letters and lectured on the merits of supporting no national candidate for office. "Lorris" was convinced that Seward would be the abolitionist candidate and that Sam Houston would campaign on the newly organized Know-Nothing ticket. Unabashedly favoring Seward's election, Simms knew that Seward would force the slavery issue and thus hasten secession. He felt that neither the Whigs nor the Democrats could offer candidates acceptable to the South, and he blamed the Democrats for bringing this failure upon themselves. He deplored the rise of the Know-Nothings as a divisive factor in the Southern

Rights movement. An open opponent of a state Democratic convention, Simms wanted South Carolina to abstain from all national elections. Simms' aim was to reduce Presidential power to that of a state governor, thus making the office impotent, and ending the mad scramble every four years for the Presidency. He cautioned his friend James L. Orr to "calculate the value, at once to yourself and the South, of the Democratic Party." He was certain that James Buchanan would win and carry a substantial portion of the South, but the election of another Southern sympathizer was no longer an issue. He urged Orr to join the sectional party system and to help unite the South. He predicted that the existing party system would fall apart under the strife of sectional battles. Simms opted for the extreme Southern wing of Congress to exert itself, and he felt no joy when Buchanan was finally elected.[45]

Simms' years of effort in eulogizing South Carolina's past, in constructing a theory of Southern society, and in lecturing on the necessity of unity, were appreciated in his home state.[46] His popularity was manifested in the invitations he received to speak before various political, social, and learned organizations throughout the South. In February 1854, he was a guest speaker at the Smithsonian Institute in Washington and lectured on his usual interests—poetry, the theater, and the practical use of languages. As often happened, he scheduled speaking performances in various Southern towns on his way home in order to pick up extra money. Repeating his Smithsonian lectures in Richmond and later in Savannah, he also spoke on the copyright issue which was before Congress.[47] Not to be outdone, a group of Charleston's intellectual leaders asked Simms to deliver lectures in that city during the late spring of 1854. Hoping for a large audience to hear its distinguished citizen, both papers praised his speaking abilities. Again addressing his remarks to the practical uses of poetry and other topics, Simms delivered three lectures in Charleston. When he discussed the American Revolution, he re-emphasized the state's glorious role in what for South Carolina had been a civil war. He cautioned the South against becoming too materialistic and thus forsaking imagination and creativity in the pursuit of wealth. Lecturing on his familiar view of Southern society, Simms praised the people for their love of nature and closeness to the soil. Always the teacher, he made certain to point out the poetical qualities of Calhoun, qualities which many politicians considered methodical and argumentative. Calhoun, a master of intuitive analysis, had found that people could only understand dull discourse.[48] In that manner Simms sought to create a unity of cultural feeling among his fellow Southerners and re-create the importance of the South's heritage for practical political purposes.

Simms readily accepted requests to speak before college students. The Chrestomathic Society of the College of Charleston asked him to speak in February of 1855. Choosing "The Choice of a Profession" as his topic, he spoke on the aims and expectations of young men entering public life. He urged the students to strike a balance between too much and too little competitive spirit. Stressing the importance of industrial enterprise, he regarded the youth of South Carolina as the hope for its future.[49] In the same vein, he delivered an inaugural address on the purpose of education before the students of the Spartanburg Female College on August 22, 1855. He emphasized that proper education served the growth and strength of the state, and he called for the education of Southern children to protect them from outside interference. Since many of the young women in the audience were future teachers, Simms wanted them to know and understand their state's history. Predicting the ultimate secession of the South, he concluded by emphasizing the importance of Southerners' practicing their section's traditions.[50]

Best of all, Simms enjoyed lecturing before political audiences, where he could sway the views of the state's leading politicians. During the summer of 1855 he lectured in the many small up-country towns between Greenville and Spartanburg, where he had the opportunity to travel and chat with James Orr and Preston Brooks. At a special testimonial dinner for Orr in Anderson he praised Orr's leadership of the Southern forces in Congress and probably cautioned him against remaining loyal to the Democratic party. Simms also managed to have long chats with the able politician Lawrence M. Keitt. In Pendleton he spoke on colonial history and surely influenced the historical views of Preston Brooks, who was particularly fascinated by his description of the Revolutionary battle at King's Mountain.

Simms' idea of history undoubtedly inspired Keitt to defend
South Carolina's past role in the United States Congress. And
Simms' presence in the up country certainly must have made
Brooks a more tenacious advocate of the state's heroic role in
the Revolution, perhaps even provoking his outburst against
Charles Sumner the following year.[51]

Although he was tired from many lecture tours, editorial
obligations, and political meetings, Simms agreed to a speaking
tour in the North in the fall of 1856. He planned in his lectures
to stress the habits and manners of Southern society. He was
certain that when the North knew more about the South, it
would understand the necessity of not disturbing Southern
institutions. He also chose to speak on the South's role in the
American Revolution, particularly to vindicate the honor of
South Carolina, and to expose the Northern refusal to aid the
South during the Revolution.[52] Simms was confident of success, and he was overjoyed at the opportunity to speak before
learned audiences and to see his old friends George Bancroft
and William Cullen Bryant. He meant to tell Northerners the
truth about the South.[53]

Speaking with fervor, often departing from his prepared
text, Simms prefaced his lectures on the Revolution with harsh
comments about Charles Sumner. He accused contemporary
Northern politicians of slandering South Carolina's role in the
Revolution. Demanding justice for the South, which had been
faithful to the Union, he said that if the South were to perish, it
would not fall easily. He accused the North of fomenting
discontent, and he maintained that "only a fratricidal hand
would destroy this Family." He claimed a Southern national
feeling that was growing stronger than the Union itself. Then,
realizing that he had gone too far, Simms quickly apologized,
saying that he had spoken heatedly only because he loved the
South.[54]

Simms had made a fatal mistake. He had actually preached
Southern nationalism to a Northern audience. The second
lecture was poorly attended and, to save face and money, he
was forced to cancel the series. Northern newspapers attacked
him viciously as no more than a special pleader for the South.
Although bewildered and partly ashamed of his behavior,
Simms discovered that his pride as a Southerner overrode his

personal feelings. The Northern response was not only a personal insult but an insult to South Carolina. He accused the North of using any pretext for an assault "upon my State and people." As a matter of pride, he refused further to "obtrude myself upon any community" that misrepresented his own views and insulted his beloved South.[55]

Although Simms agreed with James Henry Hammond that the South would in no way reward his services, he could not escape his duty. For too long he had been accustomed to toil and sacrifice for the South. But the South reacted favorably to the man who insisted upon telling the truth about Southern society. Congratulations came from as far away as Missouri. A minor hero in Southern eyes, he received more invitations to lecture in the South than he could possibly accommodate. The writer who had developed theories of society and political action had also contributed to the cause of Southern nationalism.[56] But the theoretical politician also served his section as an active propagandist. For while he was developing a political theory of Southern society, he assumed the editorship of the *Southern Quarterly Review*. As editor he applied his years of theorizing to turn the *Southern Quarterly* into the South's leading political journal and exponent of Southern unity.

NOTES

1. William Gilmore Simms, *Egeria*, pp. xi, xii, 13. For views of Simms' fellow authors who were also concerned with political and social questions see Yehoshua Arieli, *Individualism and Nationalism in American Ideology* (Cambridge, Mass., 1964) and A. N. Kaul, *The American Vision* (New Haven, 1963).

2. *Courier*, Jan. 2, Oct. 2, 1851; *Egeria*, p. 294; Charleston *Sun*, Oct. 5, 1850; *Simms Letters*, 3: 9, 14, 19, 40-41, 69, 85, 88, 150. (Simms finally turned down the offer of the presidency of South Carolina College, claiming he could not afford it financially.) See also Hammond to James L. Orr, June 19, 1854, MSS, Orr-Patterson Papers, Southern Historical Collection, University of North Carolina; Hammond to Simms, Feb. 13, July 9, Dec. 10, 1850, James M. Walker to Hammond, June 21, 1850, Hammond Papers, Library of Congress; William Gilmore Simms, *Flirtation at the Moultrie House* (Charleston, 1850), p. 9. (Professor Guilds tells me that Simms may not have been the author of this book.)

3. *Courier*, Feb. 27, 1850; Crallé, *Works of Calhoun* IV, 573 (also see 542-572); Jameson, ed., "Calhoun Correspondence," pp. 765, 766, 773, 775-776, 787, 1209-1210; Ames, "Calhoun and Secessionist Movement of 1850," pp. 23, 32-33; Capers, *Calhoun*, pp. 240, 244, 252-253; Jesse T. Carpenter, *The South as a Conscious Minority, 1789-1861* (New York, 1930), p. 185.

4. *Simms Letters*, 3: 8, 9, 13-14, 43, 64-65; Hammond Diary, March 17, Aug. 10, Nov. 30, 1850, Jan. 25, 1851, Hammond Papers, University of South Carolina; *Courier*, Oct. 4, 1850, Jan. 21, 1851; Hammond to Simms, June 16, June 27, 1850, Hammond Papers, Library of Congress; *The Condensed Proceedings of the Southern Convention, held at Nashville, Tennessee, June, 1850* (Jackson, Miss., 1850), pp. 4-22; *The Resolutions and Address, Adopted by the Southern Convention Held at Nashville, Tennessee, June 3d to 12th Inclusive, in the Year 1850* (Nashville, 1850), pp. 5-26; Robert C. Tucker,

"James H. Hammond and the Southern Convention," *Proceedings of the South Carolina Historical Association, 1960*, pp. 9, 11-12; St. George L. Sioussat, "Tennessee, the Compromise of 1850, and the Nashville Convention," *MVHR* 2 (Dec. 1915): 330.

5. There is still much work needed on this phase of the cooperation movement in South Carolina. See Boucher, *Secession and Co-operation*, pp. 109-110, 111-114; White, *Robert Barnwell Rhett*, pp. 109, 113; Nathaniel W. Stephenson, "Southern Nationalism in South Carolina in 1851," *AHR* 36 (1931): 314-335; *Courier*, Nov. 30, Dec. 20, 21, 31, 1850; *Speech of the Hon. Benjamin F. Perry, of Greenville District, Delivered in the House of Representatives of South Carolina on the 11th December, 1850* (Charleston, 1851), pp. 5, 6, 28-29, 31, 34-36, 39.

6. *Simms Letters*, 3: 76-77, 85, 90-94, 99-100; 5: 412; *Courier*, Oct. 4, 1850, Jan. 21, 1851; Hammond Diary, Nov. 30, 1850, Jan. 2, 25, 1851, Hammond Papers, University of South Carolina.

7. *Mercury*, May 23, 1851; the fullest treatment of these events is in Harold S. Schultz, *Nationalism and Sectionalism in South Carolina, 1852-1860* (Durham, 1950).

8. Southern Rights Documents, *Speech of the Hon. James L. Orr, Before the Convention of Southern Rights Association, Held in Charleston, May 1851* (Charleston, 1851), pp. 1-16; Waddy Thompson to Orr, July 29, 1851, Robert Barnwell Rhett to Orr, Aug. 28, 1851, Orr-Patterson Papers.

9. Hammond Diary, May 25, 28, 1851, "Plan of Action," printed and privately circulated broadside, Hammond Papers, University of South Carolina. See also *Simms Letters*, 3: 121-123; *Mercury*, May 6, 7, 8, 1851.

10. *Proceedings of the Great Southern Co-operation and Anti-Secession Meeting Held in Charleston, September 23, 1851* (Charleston, 1851), p. 9; Hammond to Simms, July 1, 1851, Hammond Papers, Library of Congress; Schultz, *Nationalism and Sectionalism*, p. 31.

11. *Mercury*, June 11, Aug. 14, 15, 27, Sept. 27, Nov. 17, Dec. 6, 1851; *Courier*, June 10, 1851; Charleston *Evening News*, Aug. 13, 20, 21, 1851; *Simms Letters*, 3: 123, 133; Hammond Diary, Sept. 7, Nov. 30, Dec. 6, 1851, Hammond Papers, University of South Carolina; Simms to Hammond, June 9, 1851, Hammond to Simms, Oct. 11, 1851, Hammond Papers, Library of Congress; also see Boucher, *Secession and Co-operation*, p. 129.

12. *Journal of the State Convention of South Carolina; together with the Resolution and Ordinance* (Columbia, 1852), pp. 9-10; *Addenda to the Journal of the State Convention of South Carolina* (Columbia, 1852), p. 25; Hammond to Simms, Nov. 21, 1851, Hammond Papers, Library of Congress.

13. *Journal of the State Convention of South Carolina . . .*, pp. 18-19, 23, 24. Simms' fiction reflected his pleasure with the convention resolutions and the need for keeping secessionist sentiment alive; see William Gilmore Simms, *The Golden Christmas; a Chronicle of St. John's Berkeley* (Charleston, 1852), p. 139; William Gilmore Simms, *As Good as Comedy* (Philadelphia, 1852), pp. x, xiii; William Gilmore Simms, *Norman Maurice: or, The Man of the People* (Richmond, 1851); *Russell's Magazine* 2 (Dec. 1857): 178, 247, 251, 254.

14. Manning to Orr, Jan. 11, 1853, Orr-Patterson Papers; Wallace, *Political Life of Robert Barnwell Rhett*, p. 26; Boucher, *Secession and Co-operation*, p. 138; Schultz, *Nationalism and Sectionalism*, pp. 14, 41.

15. *Simms Letters*, 3: 77, 98, 128, 180; *Egeria*, pp. 111, 137-139, 140, 141, 225-226.

16. *Courier*, Apr. 1, 24, 1850; *United States Magazine and Democratic Review*, n. s. 26 (May 1850): 401, 402, 410, 414; James L. Orr to Robert Scoville, May 5, 1850, MSS, James Orr Papers, South Caroliniana Library, University of South Carolina; Wiltse, *John C. Calhoun* III, 460, 473-484. (See *Courier*, March 18, 1856 for what Calhoun came to mean for South Carolinians.)

17. Hammond Diary, Oct. 10, 1851, Hammond Papers, University of South Carolina; Benton, II, 787; *Mercury*, Dec. 23, 1854, Nov. 3, 1855; see also William Gilmore Simms, *History of South Carolina* (New York, 1860), pp. 430-431.

18. *Simms Letters*, 3: 23, 27, 29-30; Simms to Hammond, Apr. 13, 1850, Hammond to Simms, Apr. 26, 1850, Hammond Papers, Library of Congress; Hammond, *Letters and Speeches*, pp. 251-265. Following his own advice, Simms wrote a long poem in hopes of controlling and using the rapidly growing Calhoun legend in South Carolina; see *Simms Letters*, III, 73; William Gilmore Simms, *The City of the Silent: a Poem* (Charleston, 1850), pp. 24-25, 54; Rollin G. Osterweis, *Romanticism and Nationalism in the Old South* (New Haven, 1949), p. 144.

19. Simms to Hammond, Apr. 4, 1850, Hammond Papers, Library of Congress; Franklin H. Elmore to Whitemarsh B. Seabrook, Apr. 11, 1850, Elmore Papers, University of North Carolina; *Courier*, June 5, 1850.

20. Hammond Diary, Apr. 7, Dec. 14, 21, Jan. 2, 1851, Hammond Papers, University of South Carolina; *Simms Letters*, 3: 23, 24, 26, 41, 83, 88, 99, 106, 109, 124, 139, 158, 214, 222.

21. *Mercury*, May 4, 1855; *Simms Letters*, 3: 265, 77-78, 109.

22. *Egeria*, p. 25; *Courier*, July 29, 1854; *Lily and Totem*, p. 340; William Gilmore Simms, *Charlemont* (New York, 1856), p. 405.

23. *Egeria*, pp. 232, 230, 231, 177, 107, 25, 28, 35, 40-41, 47-48; *Charlemont*, p. 143. Also compare the 1842 and 1856 editions of *Beauchampe*.

24. *Michael Bonham*, pp. 6, 18; *Mercury*, Apr. 20, 1855; *Evening News*, Aug. 19, 1851; *Southward Ho!* (New York, 1854), pp. 106-108; *Egeria*, pp. 251-252.

25. *Egeria*, p. 57; *Courier*, July 5, 15, Aug. 13, May 17, Nov.

4, 6, 1852, March 9, 1853; *Simms Letters*, 3: 210-215, 293, 155, 160, 227; Simms to Hammond, May 10, 1852, Hammond to Simms, Dec. 15, 1852, Feb. 15, March 11, May 17, 1853, Hammond Papers, Library of Congress; Hammond to Orr, June 19, 1854, Orr-Patterson Papers.

26. *Simms Letters*, 3: 174, 256.

27. William Gilmore Simms, "The Morals of Salvery," in *The Pro-Slavery Argument* (Charleston, 1852), pp. 175, 177-178, 179; *The Golden Christmas*, pp. 152-153.

28. *Courier*, May 26, 1853; Simms, "Morals of Slavery," pp. 259, 260-262, 256, 250-251, 253-254, 257; Jenkins, *Pro-Slavery Thought in Old South*, p. 307; Arthur Young Lloyd, *The Slavery Controversy, 1831-1860* (Chapel Hill, 1939), pp. 156, 235.

29. "Morals of Slavery," pp. 198, 217, 219, 222.

30. *Mercury*, Dec. 25, 1854, May 2, 1855; *Michael Bonham*, p. 20; *The Sword and the Distaff* (New York, 1852), pp. 2-3, 519-520; *As Good as Comedy*, ix-xiii.

31. *Southward Ho!*, pp. 394-396, 388-389, 251-252, 398, 248-251; *Mercury*, Feb. 26, May 22, 1856; *As Good as Comedy*, p. 128; William Gilmore Simms, *The Forayers* (New York, 1855), p. 480.

32. *The Sword and the Distaff*, pp. 124, 149, 463, 580 (reissued as *Woodcraft* in 1854); *The Forayers*, p. 81.

33. *Mercury*, Jan. 25, 1855; *Evening News*, Sept. 20, 1851; *The Golden Christmas*, pp. 34, 115-116, 152-153; *Southward Ho!*, pp. 254-255; William Gilmore Simms, *Vasconselos, a Romance of the New World* (New York, 1853), p. 147; William Gilmore Simms, *Marie de Berniere* (Philadelphia, 1853), "Maize in Milk," pp. 336, 375, 401, 416, 418.

34. *The Sword and the Distaff*, p. 120; *Charlemont*, pp. 352-353; *Egeria*, pp. 51, 186-188, 237, 15-16. (It is doubtful that Simms reflected the view of most of the South's political writers in his conversation.)

35. Both the *Courier* and the *Mercury* understood the importance of Simms' later Revolutionary romances. See *Courier*, Sept. 11, 1851, Oct. 21, 1852; *Mercury*, Apr. 23, 1856; *The Forayers*, pp. 3-5; William Gilmore Simms, *Katherine Walton* (Philadelphia, 1851), pp. 3-4.

36. *The Forayers*, pp. 216-217, 293-295, 86, 89, 282, 291, 284-290, 303, 408; William Gilmore Simms, *Eutaw* (New York, 1856), pp. 201, 413, 581, 234-235, 70, 190, 218, 255-256.

37. *Katherine Walton*, pp. 43, 47, 55, 80, 79, 96, 129, 186. (In the second edition of 1854, Simms introduced the novel thus: "I Summon to my aid the muse of local History—the traditions of our home—the chronicles of our section—the deeds of our native heroes—the recollections of our noble ancestors.")

38. William Gilmore Simms, *The Scout, or The Black Riders of Congaree* (New York, 1854), p. 159. (*The Scout* was a reissue of the 1841 novel, *The Kinsmen;* see p. 173 to compare; Simms leaves out the importance of unity in the first version.) *The Forayers*, pp. 84, 110, 124, 147, 215, 218, 238, 414; *Eutaw*, pp. 415, 343, 321, 201.

39. *The Golden Christmas*, pp. 115-116; *Charlemont*, pp. 9-12, 8; *Richard Hurdis*, pp. 10-11 (in 1856 but not the 1838 edition); *Eutaw*, p. 172; *Egeria*, pp. 89-90, 234-235; *Mercury*, May 29, 1852.

40. *Mercury*, Jan. 29, Apr. 14, 1855; *The Golden Christmas*, p. 34; *Southward Ho!*, pp. 166-168, 170-172; *As Good as Comedy*, p. 65.

41. "Maize in Milk," pp. 321, 330, 351, 386-387, 390, 396, 399, 421-422; *The Sword and the Distaff*, pp. 111, 210, 343, 356, 388, 396, 489. For an interesting commentary on the Southern planter, see David Bertleson, *The Lazy South* (New York, 1967).

42. *Egeria*, pp. 150-155; *Mercury*, Jan. 29, 1856, Apr. 10, 12, 1855; *Southward Ho!*, p. 173; "Maize in Milk," p. 367; *The Sword and the Distaff*, pp. 327-328.

43. *Southward Ho!*, pp. 254, 441-445, 439, 440; *Courier*, Nov. 28, 1854.

44. *Simms Letters*, 3: 340, 341, 385, 417, 471; Hammond to Simms, Aug. 31, 1854, Hammond Papers, Library of Congress; *Egeria*, p. 270; *Southward Ho!*, pp. 176, 175, 322-323.

45. *Mercury*, March 14, May 2, 7, July 9, Sept. 21, 1855; *Courier*, May 9, 1856; *Simms Letters*, 3: 440-442; Preston Brooks to James L. Orr, Nov. 10, 1855, Brooks to O. R. Broyles, July 22, 1855, Orr-Patterson Papers. Also see *Proceedings of the Democratic State Convention of South Carolina . . . 5th and 6th of May 1856 . . .* (Columbia, 1856), pp. 18, 21, 22-23, 25, 28; *SLM* 22 (June 1856): 422-425; William Darrell Overdyke, *The Know-Nothing Party in the South* (Baton Rouge, 1950), pp. 70, 95-96; William A. Foran, "Southern Legend: Climate or Climate of Opinion," *Proceedings of the South Carolina Historical Association, 1956*, p. 18.

46. *Southward Ho!*, pp. 130, 381-382; *Vasconselos*, pp. 1-2, 180-181; *Katherine Walton*, pp. 102, 186; *Egeria*, pp. 61-66, 67-69; *Evening News*, Aug. 7, 21, 1851; *Mercury*, Feb. 20, 1856, Apr. 6, 1855, Dec. 13, 1854, Feb. 6, 1855, June 4, 1855, Sept. 14, 1853, July 30, Aug. 27, 1856, March 26, 29, 1855; *Courier*, July 31, 1855, July 7, March 26, 19, Feb. 20, Nov. 6, 1856, Jan. 6, 9, Feb. 12, 1854.

47. *Simms Letters*, 3: 292; *Courier*, Feb. 2, 20, 1854.

48. For a complete list of the Charleston sponsors, see *Courier*, May 30, 1854; also see *Courier*, May. 27, 29, June 1, 6, 9, 1854; *Mercury*, May 26, 27, 30, 31, June 1, 9, 1854; *Simms Letters*, 3: 300-301.

49. *Mercury*, Feb. 23, 1855; *Courier*, Feb. 23, 24, 1855; *Simms Letters*, 3: 302, 342, 365.

50. William Gilmore Simms, *Inauguration of the Spartanburg Female College, on the 22nd August, 1855 . . .* (Spartanburg, S.C., 1855), pp. 13-15, 28, 60; *Mercury*, Jan. 10, 1856.

51. *Simms Letters*, 3: 392, 393-394, 399, 402, 417 (also p. 390, quoting from the Anderson *Gazette and Advocate*, July 25, 1855); *Mercury*, Apr. 7, Aug. 1, 1856. Also see Van Tassell, *Reading America's Past*, pp. 136-137, and *supra*, chap. 4, p. 146.

52. *Simms Letters*, 3: 422-423, 426; Simms to Hammond, Sept. 7, 1856, Hammond Papers, Library of Congress; *Mercury*, Apr. 23, 1856; *SLM* 22 (Oct. 1857): 307.

53. *Simms Letters*, 3: 454-455; *Mercury*, Aug. 27, 1856; *Courier*, Oct. 7, Nov. 3, 15, 1856 (in *Courier* of Nov. 3, 1856, Simms explained why he was going north—". . . to speak of my native region, in respect to which, I trust, I shall be able to disabuse the public of the North, of many mistaken impressions which do us wrong").

54. "Letters from Paul Hamilton Hayne to Horatio Woodman of Boston," *Proceedings of the Massachusetts Historical Society* (Oct. 1920-June 1921), pp. 180-181; *Courier*, May 30, June 7, 1856; *Simms Letters*, 3: 521, 523, 548-549.

55. *Mercury*, Nov. 28, Dec. 1, 2, 1856; *Courier*, Dec. 3, 1856; New York *Tribune*, Nov. 19, 1856; Simms to C. Belknap, Nov. 26, 1856, letter from Simms (addressee unknown), Nov. 21, 1856, Simms to Octavia Walton La Vert, Nov. 24, 1856, Charles Carroll Simms Papers.

56. Simms to Hammond, Dec. 8, 1856, Hammond Papers, Library of Congress; *Simms Letters*, 3: 474.

7 Use of Periodical Literature as Propaganda

AS EDITOR of the *Southern Quarterly Review* Simms continued to create his romantic view of Southern civilization, as well as his realistic appraisal of the South's relationship to the Union. In his historical and political essays, he sought to enlighten his fellow Carolinians and the entire South to the need for cooperation and eventual Southern unity. Simms' own peculiar idea of a Southern conservative tradition was reflected in articles which viciously attacked the trends toward modernism in government and individual rights, in the growing liberalism of the North, and especially in the chaos of European revolutions. His years of proselytizing produced articles from the South's most important political and intellectual leaders, as well as from a number of close personal friends, mainly low-country planters and professional people who comprised a select circle of Charleston's intellectual elite. Above all, Simms' ability to persuade powerful people to write for the *Southern Quarterly* gained the magazine a reputation as one of the most important periodicals of its generation.[1] Tragically, few of the authors found any basis for disagreement; rarely had so much intellectual talent contributed such uniformity of opinion. And rarely had a magazine so much influence in creating Southern unity.

No other man of letters was as prominent as Simms in using a periodical for almost purely political purposes. Such important literary personalities as Poe, Irving, Whittier, Lowell,

Emerson, and Paul Hamilton Hayne edited periodicals at some
time in their careers, but their interests were usually literary,
and they rarely concentrated on politics. Of the *Southern Quarterly Review*'s contemporaries, only the *North American Review*, Brownson's *Quarterly*, the *Democratic Review*, the
American Whig Review, and *DeBow's Review* even attempted
to match the *Southern Quarterly* in political interest and bias.
Even the famed *Southern Literary Messenger*, whose circulation far surpassed the *Southern Quarterly*'s, never devoted its
pages almost exclusively to politics. Always active on the
slavery question, the *Southern Literary Messenger* was reluc-
tant to become a political organ for Virginia secessionist sentiment until under the editorship of John R. Thompson it advocated secession at the close of 1860. Only the brilliant
Charlestonian, James Dunwoody Bronson DeBow, who wrote
no fiction and edited his *Review* in New Orleans, matched
Simms' interest in politics. "Almost a textbook on the Southern
view of the slavery question," *DeBow's Review* was an early
convert to secession but remained largely devoted to Southern
commercial unity. DeBow was more interested in statistics and
economic motivation than in propagandizing for secession. As
a man of letters, Simms ranked above DeBow and perhaps was
more instrumental in urging unity upon the South.[2]

Assuming the editorship of the *Southern Quarterly Review* in April 1849, Simms brought years of experience to the
magazine. Contributor to many journals both North and South,
he had also served as editor of the *Magnolia* and the *Southern
and Western Monthly Magazine and Review* during the early
1840s. The *Magnolia* had been moved from Savannah to
Charleston by the owner, Philip C. Pendleton, in hopes that
Simms' prestige and editorial ability could save his magazine.
Simms had accepted the editorship in hopes of promoting
Southern literature, and he had wanted the South's most important literary and social critics to write for the *Magnolia*. He had
realized that his duties as an editor were not limited to ac-
cepting or rejecting literary articles, and he had vowed to keep
up with political, historical, economic, and social change. He
had sought to improve Southern thought, maintaining that the
printed word could aid the South in its political and social
struggles. But although he had set an excellent standard for

literary and political reviewing and had learned much about editing and managing a periodical, Simms had been unable to raise enough subscriptions to continue the *Magnolia.* Southern printers were often underpaid, and the magazine had rarely appeared on time. Overburdened with the work of editing and rewriting articles, he had written the entire "Editor's Bureau" and most of the other articles. Unable to serve without pay, Simms had resigned as editor of the *Magnolia* in June 1843.[3]

Hoping to impart a more political complexion to Southern periodicals, Simms had started his own magazine, the *Southern and Western Monthly Magazine and Review,* commonly called *Simms's Magazine,* in January 1845. The *Southern and Western,* distinctly sectionalist in its outlook, had contained articles on agricultural improvement, Texas annexation, and debates on the major political issues of the day. Southern politicians had soon realized the political power of the *Southern and Western,* and Alfred P. Aldrich had even suggested that it serve as the propaganda organ for a Southern Anti-Abolitionist League in Congress. Although read in influential circles and praised for both its literary merits and political usefulness, the magazine was discontinued for financial reasons after one year. Simms' last editorial had called for faith in Southern genius and had cautioned against neglecting those who really cared for the South. Simms vowed never to edit another periodical.[4]

Because of loyalty to the Southern cause, Simms was unable to keep his vow. Barely four years later he became editor of the *Southern Quarterly Review,* and he transformed the periodical into one of the finest political quarterlies in the country. Begun in New Orleans in 1842 under Daniel K. Whitaker, the *Southern Quarterly Review* was soon moved to Charleston. Whitaker offered the editorship to Simms in 1843. He turned it down, but he promised to contribute at least one article to each issue, and he agreed to help establish a nationwide reputation for the periodical. The new associate editor, J. D. B. DeBow, turned the quarterly toward politics as he defended slavery and promoted railroad growth in the South. A staunch supporter of Texas annexation and war with Mexico, DeBow left the quarterly sometime in 1845, perhaps because of his radicalism.[5]

The *Southern Quarterly Review* soon achieved notoriety

in South Carolina. A famous article attacking Calhoun's support of internal improvements, said to be written by Francis W. Pickens, temporarily interrupted Pickens' career and possibly forced the Northerner Whitaker to sell out.[6] A Calhoun faction under J. Milton Clapp, associate editor of the Charleston *Mercury*, bought the magazine. When an article favoring a democratic election of Presidential electors infuriated Calhoun, even Clapp found it impossible to please the statesman. Clapp immediately promised Calhoun that a rejoinder stating the opposite case would soon appear in the magazine.[7]

Having written articles in the *Southern Quarterly Review* for years, Simms knew of its controversial politics and its importance to the South long before he finally accepted its editorship early in 1849. A joint company of Calhoun supporters, probably disgusted with Clapp's editorship, chose Simms as editor. Simms had, through previous editorial experience, learned the power such a magazine could have in influencing the Southern mind, both through the intellectual relationship between the editor and his contributors, and through the topical nature of the articles. From the beginning the tone and purpose of the *Review* were political, because Simms regarded the magazine as an important vehicle for political writing. He wanted Calhoun to find political writers, and he solicited lists of interested and independent subscribers in Washington and throughout the South who would take up the "cudgel" for the South through the medium of periodical literature. Resolved to instruct and enlighten Southerners as to their political obligations, he also listened to the advice of his close friend John P. Kennedy, who knew that the *Review* would become an influential Southern periodical. Kennedy suggested that Simms counsel moderation, because some of the South's zealous defenders were equally as dangerous to Southern unity and safety as were Northern abolitionists.[8] Unabashedly political with little literary analysis, under Simms the *Southern Quarterly Review* never swayed from its purpose.

Establishing the criteria under which the periodical would operate was one thing, but putting it on a paying basis and attracting brilliant and biased contributors was another. Listening to Hammond's advice to pay contributors and to check the printers' typographical errors, Simms resolved to pay himself for the articles he wrote.[9] Since first-rate contributors would also help to put the periodical on sound financial footing, Simms turned avidly to that task. He solicited Hammond's services as a contributor, knowing that Hammond could teach the South many political lessons. He wanted Marcellus Hammond to write articles on expansionist sentiment, Benjamin F. Perry to write on up-country agricultural opportunity, Beverly Tucker to explain his economic and political views, and William Elliott to defend slavery and to elucidate the South's character. Simms was busy throughout 1849, planning articles and asking various personalities to work for the *Review* and the South. Relentlessly he hounded his friends, knowing that their personal influence and keen minds would be sharpened by writing articles of sectional interest and that their contributions would help to unify the South.[10]

The Negro slave, his life on the plantation and his status in the South, was a central topic in the pages of the *Southern Quarterly Review*. Of the twenty-six issues Simms edited, fully fourteen had at least one article devoted to slavery. The low-country McCords were most active in writing about the importance of slavery to the plantation system and undoubtedly influenced their fellow planters. The shy Louisa McCord wrote essays which compared free labor to slave labor, a pseudo-scientific study of the "Diversity of Races," a stinging review of *Uncle Tom's Cabin*, and a lengthy, critical article on Henry C. Carey's *The Slave Trade, Domestic and Foreign*.[11] Besides the McCords, Simms had succeeded in bringing other Southerners into the argument over the positive merits of Negro slavery. From John A. Campbell, Alabama planter, scholar, and associate justice of the U.S. Supreme Court, he received "Rights of the Slave States," a manifesto which declared the necessity of non-interference in the territories, and "Slavery Throughout the World." John Tyler, Jr., a Virginia slaveholder and staunch Southern rights advocate, wrote on "Negro-Mania—Race." Ephraim M. Seabrook, a Charleston attorney and student of church history, attacked emancipation in the West Indies, while Simms' Barnwell neighbor, David F. Jamison, later president of the Secession Convention, compared British and American slavery.[12] A dialogue of well-known and influential Southerners, sometimes of high intellectual quality, but more often eclectic, pseudo-scientific, and mediocre, could not help but bring many Southerners to examine their own views on slavery and to question any reason for remaining in the Union, unless the preservation of the institution could be guaranteed.[13]

Not only did he stimulate other Southerners to clarify their views on the importance of slavery, but Simms himself wrote many pro-slavery articles which were designed to promote Southern unity. Never missing a chance to call attention to others who supported the system, he praised Thomas Carlyle's advocacy of a slave society. Enumerating the "intrinsic merits" of slavery, Simms cautioned the South to insist that the Negro received benevolent treatment on the plantation. More practically, he regarded Negro slavery as "the soul of cotton." He stated that a slave economy was the most thriving economic system a country could have, and he warned that the South could not economically survive its abolition. Succumbing to the pseudo-scientific view of race, Simms claimed that the South had moral title to the slave, based upon the Negro's inferior characteristics and savage nature. Created inferior, the "African race" had to serve the white man, or at least the entire white South, Simms claimed.[14]

Turning to the abolitionist attack on slavery, Simms contended that the South was accountable for its slave system only to God. He refused to submit the slavery question to the abolitionists' judgment. In an article entitled "Stearn's Notes on *Uncle Tom's Cabin*," he maintained that the South no longer found humor in abolitionism and the weak sentiments of Northern hypocrisy. He had argued in favor of slavery, both logically and morally, and he had tired of discussion. The South was well-armed with a potential fighting force, and the burgeoning Southern nation demanded respect for its institutions. Since Southern arguments were not accepted in the North, Simms believed that the final issue would be to make "a trial of strength between the people of the Southern states, and their philanthropic assailants." Meanwhile, Simms warned the people of the South to study their own writers, if they wanted to assert the benevolence of slavery and to protect their country from outside interference.[15]

The defense of slavery led Simms and other writers in the

Southern Quarterly Review to promote Southern economic growth. Many articles were written in favor of free trade, the necessity for Southern support of local manufacturing, Southern commercial conventions, and the financial prospects of the South.[16] Simms printed articles on soil care and devoted many pages to theories on improving the cotton crop and maximizing plantation profits. Love of the beauty of nature in the pastoral surroundings of a well-stocked plantation was also a common topic in the *Review*. Images of the cultured planter, living the life of the mind and enjoying the outdoor life of hunting and fishing, were often invoked. One such article, the "Prospect and Policy of the South," claimed that Southern progress depended upon protecting the planter's idyllic existence from the South's increasingly materialistic sentiment. The author, who supported Simms' most romantic anti-utilitarian views, opposed Southern commercial conventions, maintaining that they would subordinate and ultimately destroy the planter class.[17]

In a rare footnote to an article, Simms took exception to the author's conclusions. He wanted to preserve the plantation system, but he cautioned that most planters erroneously ascribed the South's intellectual greatness, political success, and economic strength exclusively to agriculture. This was nonsense, he declared. Simms said that the South's great patriots and statesmen were trained lawyers or merchants, as well as planters. Competition with their fellow men "sharpened and brightened" their minds and gave them the knowledge and courage to lead their fellow Southerners. Agriculture was their hobby, often their refuge from the toils of public life; the plantation became a place to develop their naturally conservative views. He cautioned that, far from aiding the South, the planter class, by refusing to adopt modern inventions and methods and to manufacture their own raw materials locally, inhibited economic growth.[18]

Always foremost in Simms' mind were the consideration of unity of Southern interests and final freedom from Northern oppression as he used the *Southern Quarterly Review* to support the South's emerging factory and manufacturing system. As a natural consequence of the South's exclusive occupation

with agriculture, Southerners had entrusted Northerners with
the fulfillment of all of their economic and social wants. Simms
believed that the South was the economic and social servant
of the North. If the South would mix agriculture with industry,
he believed that it could become both economically and socially
independent. He praised other Southern writers, especially
DeBow, who advocated economic independence. He felt that
DeBow helped to destroy the myth of the necessity for complete
Southern economic dependence on the North. Simms wanted to
protect the plantation system through Southern industry,
which someday would compete favorably with Northern manufacturing. Believing that the South would become a major
economic power in the world, he reiterated that unity of
economic interests was related to eventual secession.[19]

Simms' practicality as editor of the *Southern Quarterly
Review* also revealed itself in his interest in local social and cultural affairs. In a lengthy review, Congressman Andrew
Pickens Aldrich, long a member of Simms' political clique,
called for reform in the state's judiciary system. He found
judges overworked and trial procedures antiquated. David F.
Jamison, who spent much of his time in Charleston, argued for
penitentiary reform. In a period when few Northerners were
concerned with the penal system, Jamison stressed the need to
alleviate the overcrowded conditions of prisons, and he hoped
to accomplish something useful by preparing the prisoners to
rejoin society. Articles on the value of education emphasized
the need for more public schools in the state.[20] Some authors
concentrated on Charleston society and on the importance of
improving the status of letters in the city. In a stinging attack
on his native city, William Porcher Miles, professor of math-
ematics at Charleston College, who later served as both
mayor and Congressman, indicted Charleston society for
inhibiting Southern writers. As one of the city's leading
thinkers, he realized that Charleston's emphasis on propriety
stifled freedom of expression among local authors. Miles
warned that for the sake of Southern unity Charleston had to
adapt to the newer South. He wanted Charleston, an urban center important to the future of Southern business enterprise, to
reform its stodgy atmosphere and to contribute both monetarily

and intellectually to its own writers' literary endeavors.[21] Miles enunciated a theme which was consistent with Simms' efforts throughout his career as a public man of letters.

Although the *Southern Quarterly Review* published no fiction, Simms never hesitated to promote indigenous Southern writers, especially if their literature, essays, and speeches stressed the South's heritage and common features. Realizing that lectures were a form of political literature, Simms often reviewed orations delivered throughout South Carolina. He was aware of Southerners' love of the intricate logic and the legal terminology of the lecture, particularly as a means of arousing the South to a realization of its place in the Union. Simms believed that the lecturer could take an active part in current politics, and he exclaimed that the lecturer had to assume "the toils of the preacher," and his language had to become that "of the prophet." Even the sermon could serve as a form of literature and further the Southern cause. For Simms, sermons reflected "the common sentiment of the people of South Carolina." The enthusiasm and ability of a minister to unite a crowd behind the moral growth of sectionalism was a powerful weapon in the movement for independence, Simms claimed. As with fiction, essays, and lectures, Simms promised to aid religious leaders through reviewing and commenting on their sermons.[22]

Not only did Simms use Southern literature in its broadest scope to aid the cause, but he also singled out other periodicals for praise and condemnation according to their bias. Although he was at times displeased with the *Southern Literary Messenger*'s lack of political involvement, he always praised its interest in supporting the South. DeBow and the *Review* often received special praise for their firm loyalty to Southern unity. Simms also complimented Richard W. Habersham's Charleston periodical, *The Self-Instructor*, on its practical attempts to educate Southerners to their danger in the Union. But he felt that Northern periodicals could no longer be trusted to present the South in a truthful manner or to treat its position with justice. When *Harper's Monthly*, a magazine which prided itself on having no political interest, supported free-soil, Simms attacked *Harper's* as an abolitionist tract. Simms even questioned the loyalty of Southerners who continued to support

Northern periodicals which attempted to undermine Southern institutions. Assuring Southerners "freedom from insult and denunciation" in the pages of the *Southern Quarterly Review*, he maintained that his periodical would benefit the South much more than *Harper's* or *Putnam's*. The only Northern periodicals acceptable to him were those like Louis Godey's *Lady's Book*, which vehemently rejected abolition and praised Southern values.[23] Obviously Simms was trying to promote Southern talent and ideas. But in doing so, he gained a reputation as a fire-eating professional journalist, prejudiced and hypersensitive to any outside criticism.

In further pursuit of his own muse of history, Simms also made the *Southern Quarterly Review* into a magazine of historical criticism and scholarly research. He stressed reviews about the South's history, because writers in the South had seldom done justice to their own past and had left a vacuum in the education of Southern children, who were forced to learn history from Northern books. Simms had long before realized that Southern historians must take their past into their own hands. In the 1850s there was a sense of urgency in his appeal to Southern youth to develop their historical consciousness. He aimed to build a core of young patriots to promote the movement for Southern independence. The South's future was in the hands of the "unbought, unbiassed, the ardent and frank nature of the young." Simms said that with proper training, or proper propagandizing, "the loghouse shall yet rear its Patrick Henrys and the playground its Washingtons and Marions."[24]

In an effort to find common bonds between the Southern states, Simms reviewed the work of historians who chronicled their own states' past. He praised Charles Gayarré's history of colonial and Revolutionary Louisiana, but he reminded the author that the historian should not forget his mission to instruct rather than merely to describe. He criticized William J. Rivers, professor of Greek at the College of South Carolina, for writing on South Carolina's past without properly studying the historical documents. Simms felt that more than ever the state needed to understand its heritage and should not be misled by poor and inaccurate writing. Linking the Southwest to the Southeast's past, he praised J. G. M. Ramsay's *Annals of Tennessee* as a scholarly work which placed the South's western heritage in perspective. Clear, concise, and well-documented, Ramsay's work was a model for future historical study. His description of the South's progress into the West, which recreated the Southeastern migration to the frontier, depicted a united South, filled with people of a common origin and common views. Simms called for young scholars to emulate this work in which Southerners could claim a common heritage.[25]

As a close adviser to William Porcher Miles, Simms counseled him on sources to use for his Fourth of July oration in 1849. Miles planned to speak on South Carolina's role in the Revolution, and since E. L. Magoon had omitted John Rutledge from the list of orators in his book *Orators of the American Revolution*, Simms did not want him to use it as a source for his speech. Fiercely partisan in his oration, Miles drew parallels between Revolutionary action in South Carolina and the problems of the present. Reviewing the lecture, Simms elaborated on Miles' view and showed the similarities between the colonists' legal plight in 1776 and the lack of constitutional security for the South in the present Union. He pointed out that "there could be no better use made of the anniversary of American freedom, than habitually to compare its objects and its acquisitions with the degree of security [with] which we enjoy its supposed guarantees."[26] In this manner, continuous comparison of past freedom to present evils became an important theme in the *Southern Quarterly Review*.

Europe's past was also reviewed in the *Southern Quarterly Review*. Beverly Tucker wrote critically on Macaulay's history of England and followed with a stinging denunciation of European radicalism, which was denying its sound, conservative heritage. The *Review* included studies of both Napoleon's essays on the historical importance of Roman law and David F. Jamison's work on the French Girondists. Frederick A. Porcher, professor of history at the College of Charleston and a longtime friend and collaborator of Simms, contributed a philosophical essay on the "False Views of History" and wrote cogently on the history of Greek political institutions.[27] Simms himself reviewed Pierre Guizot's *Democracy in France*, which combined historical analysis with political philosophy. Guizot applauded the growth of strong central government in Europe and wanted the same to happen in the United States. According to

Simms, Guizot misunderstood American history. The country was originally divided into self-governing communities, and as states were formed, the people yielded no power to a federal government. Citing Guizot's views of democracy in order to express his own position, Simms was confident that America's principle of state's rights protected the people against centralism. The history of France demonstrated that excessive control of a country created domestic friction. Simms hoped that the South could profit from France's mistakes.[28]

Simms attempted to clarify what history should accomplish and how it should be written. He believed that the historian should not merely accumulate facts. "History implies art, system, arrangement, grouping," critical judgment, and the conclusions drawn from many conflicting accounts. Simms said that a historian should understand the character of his times, value the manners and habits of his people, and identify with the events which influenced their actions. Though hardly following his own example, Simms suggested that historians shift their interest from the single leader to the development of party power through popular support. The South's public leaders, usually from the upper classes, lived in Washington, and Simms claimed that the historian's duty was to teach them the importance of understanding past events to improve the defense of their section in the present. He was optimistic that if the Southern historian could follow those precepts, he would never have to worry about his people seeing history "through Northern eyes."[29]

But if the practical side of Simms viewed history in terms of mass movement and group leadership, the romantic side of him still yearned for the hero, the great man, to lead the South to secession. He reviewed many biographies in the *Southern Quarterly Review*. His intention was to analyze the thoughts and actions of public men, both to instruct contemporary leaders and to unify the South in its struggle for independence. Critical of the popular biographer who made fable out of the real drama of the past, he also questioned the writer who exalted an ordinary man. He preferred to find faults in the truly great, rather than to romanticize mediocrity. His criteria for biography centered around the usefulness of the historical figure as a symbol; the deeds and actions of his biographical

subjects had to be useful to a later generation. Simms' primary
example was Washington, who required no romantic biography
or falsification of the record; his life symbolized heroism in the
face of almost insurmountable odds. The life of Washington,
which illustrated Southern values, could instruct Southern
youth in their loyalty to the Southern cause.[30]

Each biography or biographical essay in the *Southern
Quarterly Review* had a special purpose for the South. For example, in an article on Hugh A. Garland's *Life of John Randolph of Roanoke*, Beverly Tucker found the author unable to
grasp Randolph's character. Both Tucker and Simms considered Randolph a great leader of the Southern cause and
feared that the South might never have another equally able
defender of its way of life. Simms spent years trying unsuccessfully to persuade John Pendleton Kennedy to write a
biography of Kennedy's relative, Philip Pendleton Cooke.
However, Simms did review Kennedy's *Life of William Wirt*,
and he cautioned Kennedy against excessive loyalty to the
Union, stating that a tyrannical government did not deserve
the support of its talented men. In his review of *The Life of the
Baron DeKalb*, Simms stated that the Revolutionary leader was
too ordinary a man to turn into a hero. He also was un-
charitable toward the Polish hero, Louis Kossuth, who had attempted to raise money for his nation's independence. Kossuth
had wanted the United States to interfere in another country's
internal relations, and Simms, living in a world where he constantly attacked the North for meddling in Southern affairs,
had little sympathy for Kossuth.[31] Obviously Simms' many
reviews of biographies were consistent with his own political
and social views.

Returning to an old theme, Simms accused South Carolinians of allowing their heroes to go unnoticed. He was convinced that only a Southerner could truly recapture the force-
fulness of the South's public men, and in the *Review* he urged
Southern writers to take up biography. He believed that the
South had been relegated to a subordinate position in the Union
partly because the actions of its leaders had often been interpreted by Northern writers. Especially at such a time when the
South's "individuality is threatened," the people deserved a

more reliable knowledge of their public leaders' duties and services.[32]

To that end Simms sought to spread Calhoun's fame throughout the South. The many funeral orations to Calhoun provided an excellent vehicle for biographical review in the *Southern Quarterly Review*. Simms called the Alabama politician George J. S. Walker's eulogy part of that "spontaneous outpouring of public feeling" over the entire South's loss. He praised Walker's perceptive understanding of Calhoun's great talent for "penetrating analysis, his perfect comprehension of the political system under which we live, . . . and the moral excellence of his life." Calhoun's career was the subject of specific essays in the *Review*, and some articles presented Calhoun's conservative views on government and society.[33] In his review of *Mardi*, Simms attacked Herman Melville for characterizing Calhoun as an evil slavedriver. He dismissed Melville as a biased political writer, undeserving of future comment.[34] Beverly Tucker's lengthy article on Robert Barnwell Rhett's and Hammond's eulogies to Calhoun, which Simms edited, indicated that South Carolina recognized its prophets, believed "in their inspiration," and planned to use them for the mission ahead.[35] Simms assisted the entire South in identifying Calhoun with the cause he so fervently espoused—the South's defense of its national interests.

Calhoun's example was enlisted and invoked in the search for new leaders. Simms wrote a lengthy review of Hammond's funeral oration on Calhoun, stating that only Hammond could accurately estimate Calhoun's genius or reveal what he meant to the South. He thought that Hammond's eulogy would survive as one of the state's most important historical documents, ranking with Calhoun's stand against the Force Bill and his Fourth of March speech. Simms was convinced that no better man than Hammond was available to replace Calhoun "as one of the very first statesmen of the confederacy—perhaps of the age." He asked Hammond to reenter public life and to assume the political leadership (which was rightfully his) in South Carolina and throughout the South.[36]

Under Simms the *Southern Quarterly Review* became the most partisan political periodical in the country. The political

articles which dominated each issue chronicled the evolution of
Simms' own political views on the important issues of the day.
He sought contributors whose sympathy and good faith in the
Southern cause equaled their active experience in public life.
Writers from all parts of the South created a dialogue in which
the South's future course was the dominant theme. Mostly in
moderate and persuasive logic, but sometimes in inflammatory,
radical tones, there emerged in the pages of the *Southern Quarterly Review* the concept of a cooperating South, searching for
common bonds of political relations and needs.[37] Simms
believed in sharpening political leaders' wits and defenses by
using journalism as political propaganda, and he alerted both
the politicians and the people of the South to their common
needs.

Although he was unable to attend the Nashville Convention because of editorial duties, Simms demonstrated the
political usefulness of the *Southern Quarterly Review* in his
study of that convention.[38] The article, entitled "The
Southern Convention," claimed that the convention met for the
dual purposes of citing Northern aggression and discovering
some way to defend the South. It was significant that many of
the Southern states had agreed to discuss their mutual
grievances as a united body, but the convention was bound to
the old two-party system, and the results of the sessions were
inconclusive. Simms fixed on the existing party system as the
major obstacle to a united South. Calling for a geographical
alignment of parties, he was sure that future events would
demonstrate the failure of the two-party system to cope with
the sectional crisis. As the *Review* became the leading propaganda organ for a one-party South, Simms continued to urge
the South to think only of the defense of "our very safety and
existence as a people."[39]

In many private discussions with Hammond, the two men
had previously reached an agreement on the future of North-
South relations. When they collaborated on Hammond's lecture
before the Two Societies of Charleston, an article on the future
relations between the North and South emerged. As students of
history, they both opposed immediate single-state disunion but
they emphasized that the South had nothing to fear from the
dissolution of the Union. Hammond's article compared the

relative strengths and weaknesses of the North and the South and each section's advantages within the Union. He claimed that the growing power of abolitionists in the North had made the South question the value of the Union. While Hammond counseled the South to strengthen its social and political system, he insisted that Southerners begin to prepare for the consequences of separation.[40] Hammond's article, the only piece he submitted to the *Review*, and Simms' essay on the "Southern Convention" set the tone and purpose of the magazine's active political role.

Articles which argued the relative merits of cooperation and immediate secession also appeared in the *Review*. Most of them dealt with what South Carolina could do to unite Southerners. Beverly Tucker, a radical secessionist, called for immediate action, yet he wanted the rest of the South to join South Carolina. Writing on "The Destinies of the South," James Chesnut, Jr. soon to enter the United States Senate questioned the desirability of trying to avert an eventual showdown between the North and South. Realizing that remote areas of the South had not yet felt Northern aggression, he hoped to enlighten the entire South to the advantage of eventual secession. Chesnut predicted that the antislavery movement would force the entire South to secede, and he was certain that the North would have to let the South depart in peace. Nevertheless, he called for a permanent military confederation for the "safety of the South." Louisa McCord cautioned that an act of separate secession would destroy any hope for a united South. Knowing that the South Carolina Convention of May 1851 was a failure, she suggested the calling of a state convention of moderates in order to gather a hard core of cooperationist leaders who would alert the South to its danger within the Union, yet counsel against South Carolina's seceding alone. As for preparing the entire South for secession, that was the duty of South Carolina's Congressmen. Mrs. McCord was convinced that disunion was the "only remedy to ills" and that the true leaders would work toward that end.[41] Those authors expressed Simms' own views and undoubtedly lent dignity to the entire cooperationist movement.

In his review of Francis W. Pickens' speech on secession, Simms complimented his more moderate contributors and

204 THE POLITICS OF A LITERARY MAN

disagreed with Pickens' theory of separate-state secession. He sought to conciliate the sensitive Pickens by praising his Southern patriotism. By no means, however, had Simms opposed secession; he believed with Pickens that the "experiment" of Union was almost over. Rather than allow South Carolina to initiate the action, he suggested that the abolitionists would force the struggle. He praised William Henry Trescot's timely article on *The Position and Course of the South*, because Trescot pointed out that most of the South was losing interest in the Union. Trescot wrote to agitate for the common interests of Southerners.[42] His reasoned article fulfilled one of the specific purposes of Simms in the *Review*: both men had studied the merits of Southern unity and had never hesitated to support cooperation throughout the South.

Because Simms recognized that the national party system divided Southern loyalties and impeded the movement for unity, he denounced political parties in the *Review*. James Chesnut fixed upon "the federal character and aims of our national parties and politicians, together with the distraction produced by Presidential elections," as the primary cause of the South's apathy in defense of its own interests. An anonymous author of the "State of Parties and the Country" held moderate views toward the national Democratic party and believed that the future of the South lay in that party's strength. But this author cautioned that the South would only support a Democratic party which was wholly Southern in its character.[43] In articles on a "History of the Polk Administration" and "The Whig-Abolitionist Attack," Simms supported Chesnut's repudiation of national parties and abandoned hope for any rapport with the Democrats. He was also furious with Southern Whigs, who only wanted office and had no loyalty for the South. When those Whigs accused Franklin Pierce of being an abolitionist, that only proved to Simms the deviousness of the national party system. Certain that Pierce, an honest politician, if such were possible, was probably loyal to the South, Simms still would not actively support any Northern candidate in 1852. Furious at the national parties' shameless grasping for power at the cost of ideas and accomplishment, Simms was convinced that the key to any political success was in achieving a balance of power. Since the South, being a minority section, could no longer hold the balance of power in national politics, the two major parties were useless to its interests. Therefore he decided that in future elections he would favor the most pro-Southern candidate, regardless of party affiliation.[44] In this way, he used the *Southern Quarterly Review* to agitate for a Southern party free of any national party affiliation.

When Virginia's Senator R. M. T. Hunter spoke out in Congress against Stephen A. Douglas' defense of the Kansas-Nebraska Bill, the *Southern Quarterly Review* printed his speech, and Simms wrote an essay on the Virginia politician. While he did not consider the bill of primary importance to the South, he believed that the territorial question would settle the South's problems as a minority section, because the issue of Western expansion, rising above the sophistry and conciliation of politicians, would destroy the Union. Fiery debates, such as those on the Kansas-Nebraska Bill, helped to weaken the Whig party by identifying it with abolitionism. Simms predicted that out of the ashes of the Whigs and Free-Soil Northern Democrats would grow a sectional abolitionist party to attack the South. Then the political struggle would cease to be one of national compromise over the territories and slavery, and the ensuing sectional battle would ensure united Southern secession.[45]

Although many Southern politicians regarded the *Southern Quarterly Review* as a useful propaganda organ, the magazine did not show a profit. Subscriptions at first grew, but Southerners were notorious for not paying their bills. The *Review* went further into debt, and Simms could no longer pay contributors. Forced to write many articles and all of the "Critical Notes," he even put some of his own funds into the *Review*. By October 1852, the magazine was in deep financial difficulty, and Simms solicited funds from many of his friends. With the aid of the Charleston newspapers, a committee of prominent political and intellectual figures from the city met to "devise and adopt measures for the increase of the circulation" of the *Review*. The prestige of Francis A. Porcher, Isaac W. Hayne, William J. Grayson, and William F. Colcock helped to give the magazine some degree of financial solvency. Knowing

that if he abandoned the magazine it would fail, Simms
resolved to keep the *Review* one more year, without salary,
receiving his pay from the magazine's profits.[46]

Temporarily the prospects of the periodical improved. But
late in 1853, a Northerner, Charles Mortimer, purchased the
magazine, and Simms rebelled at the new owner's attempts to
control its editorial policy. He resigned in late 1854, the October issue being the last number under his editorship. With the
opportunity to purchase part of the Charleston *Evening News*,
Simms thought his talents could be better used under his own
direction. He planned to make the *Evening News* a strong pro-
Southern political newspaper and to maintain many of the
features he had used in the *Review*. But the *Evening News* purchase fell through and Simms retired as editor, though not as a
writer, until 1857, when he became closely involved with the
publication of *Russell's Magazine*. Without Simms, the floundering *Southern Quarterly Review* deteriorated in quality, and
Mortimer soon began to print the magazine in Baltimore. The
Review, one of the antebellum South's most influential
periodicals, failed in 1857.[47]

Although the *Southern Quarterly Review* was a financial
failure, Simms was proud of his accomplishments. He had
aroused many dormant minds to question their values and their
views of the Union. Contributors to the magazine found themselves locked in debate and exchange of ideas, although the
debates were limited in their subject matter. The *Review* was a
forum for Southern nationalism; dialogue on the merits of unity
and moderation constantly appeared in its pages. As the
Courier put it, in the pages of the *Review* "our best writers are
stimulated to exertion in proportion to the influence and
authority wielded by the medium through which they communicate with the public." The *Review* was a tribute to Simms'
own "industry, zeal, and ability," as he constantly paraded the
South's leading political figures' ideas before the public. He had
presented the South with a model of "the vehicle through which
we must chiefly hope to combat hostile opinion." By defending
their institutions, Southerners developed and refined their arguments and came to understand the importance of their own section. The writers in the *Southern Quarterly Review* trained "the
home sentiment, enforce[d] the home opinion, unite[d] the

home population, [and] provide[d] them with the true argument for defence."[48] And if Simms had no other consolation, his use of the *Southern Quarterly Review* for political purposes influenced James Henry Hammond to come out of retirement and to re-enter politics. Hammond was named to the Senate in 1857. As his adviser and sometimes his alter-ego, Simms helped to achieve their long-sought dream of a Southern Confederacy.

NOTES

1. See Mott, *History of American Magazines* I, 727; the only attempt to study Simms as editor of the *SQR* is Frank W. Ryan, "The Opinions of Editor William Gilmore Simms of the *Southern Quarterly Review*, 1849-1854," *The Proceedings of the South Carolina Historical Association, 1959*, 25-35; Ryan, however, does not bother to analyze the political nature of Simms' editorship or the purposes for which Simms used the magazine. See also Taylor, *Cavalier and Yankee*, pp. 249, 258-259; for a view of who wrote for the magazine and why, see Louisa McCord to William P. Miles, May 2, June 12, 1848, Trescot to Miles, March 22, 1848, MSS, William Porcher Miles Papers, Southern Historical Collection, University of North Carolina. (Trent says Simms' best articles were on politics but fails to study them, *Simms*, pp. 74-76, 163, 166, 190.)

2. Simms wrote long review articles in his "Lorris" column on the value of *DeBow's* and the *SLM*; see *Mercury*, Jan. 2, July 11, 1856; Mott, *History of American Magazines* I, 750-752, 678-682, 685-688, 367-368, 344, 498, 382, 679, 455, 279-280, 171-172, 735, 457, 629-665, II, 136, 735, 488-492, 338-348. (I have used Mott's view of most of the Northern periodicals; what files I have read substantiate his findings.) Trent, *Simms*, p. 182; *Simms Letters*, III, 94. See also Arthur Schlesinger, Jr., *Orestes Brownson, a Pilgrim's Progress* (Boston, 1938); Otis C. Skipper, *DeBow, Magazinist of the Old South* (Athens, Ga., 1958); Benjamin Blake Minor, *The Southern Literary Messenger, 1834-1864* (New York, 1905).

3. *Simms Letters*, 1: 197-203, 318; 5: 366-367. *Magnolia* 4 (April 1842): 248-249; 4 (June 1842): 377-378; n. s. 2 (May 1843): 336; (June 1843): 400. A. B. Meek to Simms, July 1, 1843, Charles Carroll Simms Papers; Hammond to Simms, Nov. 12, 1842, Hammond Papers, Library of Congress; Hoole, "Simms's Career," pp. 47-54; Stoney, ed., "Memoirs of Porcher," *SCHM* 47 (1946): 95. See also *infra*, chap. 3.

4. *Simms Letters*, 1: 440, 442; 2: 110; *Southern and Western Monthly Magazine* 1 (Jan. 1845): 67 and advertisement; (June 1845): 363-364; 2 (July 1845): 58-60; 2 (July 1845): 71-72, 2 (Nov. 1845): 343-346; *SLM* 11 (Dec. 1845): 760-762; A. P. Aldrich to Hammond, July 1, 1845, Hammond Papers, Library of Congress; also see Clement Eaton, *The Freedom of Thought Struggle in the Old South* (New York, 1964), p. 62 and chap. 3.

5. *Mercury*, Feb. 4, 1846; Elmore to Calhoun, Feb. 5, 26, 1847, Calhoun Papers, University of South Carolina.

6. *Mercury*, Feb. 17, 1847; H. W. Conner to Pickens, Apr. 30, 1846, Francis W. Pickens Papers, Duke University.

7. Elmore to Calhoun, May 16, 20, 1847, H. W. Conner to Calhoun, May 14, 21, 1847, J. Milton Clapp to Calhoun, June 21, 1847, Calhoun Papers, University of South Carolina.

8. *Simms Letters*, 1: 369-370, 384-385; 2: 58, 482-483; *Courier*, June 26, 1849, May 23, 1850; Kennedy to Simms, Feb. 29, 1852, quoted in Bohner, *John Pendleton Kennedy*, pp. 226-227.

9. Hammond to Simms, Apr. 30, June 4, 1849, Simms to Hammond, Feb. 25, 1849, Hammond Papers, Library of Congress; *Simms Letters*, 3: 5, 21; *Courier*, Oct. 18, 1849.

10. *Simms Letters*, 2: 522, 81, 476-477, 479, 495-497; 3: 4; *Courier*, March 21, 1850; *Wheeler's Magazine*, n. s. 1 (July 1849): 1-6; *Prospectus of the Southern Quarterly Review*, Charles Carroll Simms Papers; Hammond Diary, March 11, 1849, pp. 53-54; Hammond to Marcellus Hammond, Hammond Papers, University of South Carolina; also see Osterweis, *Romanticism and Nationalism in the Old South*, p. 120.

11. See *SQR* (Oct. 1849), (Apr. 1851), (July 1851), (Jan. 1853), (Jan. 1854); *Simms Letters* 3: 267.

12. *SQR* (Jan 1851): pp. 101-148; (Apr. 1851): pp. 305-339;

(Jan. 1852): pp. 153-175; (Oct. 1853): pp. 369-411; (Apr. 1853): pp. 422-454.

13. *Courier*, May 18, 1853; *Mercury*, March 11, 1853; Jenkins, *Pro-Slavery Thought in the Old South*, p. 262; also see Frank Stanton, *The Leopard's Spots* (Chicago, 1960), *passim*; Frederickson, *The Black Image in the White Mind*, chap. 3.

14. *SQR* 1 n.s. (July 1850): 509; 5 n.s. (Jan. 1852): 209-212; (Jan. 1854): 185-205; *Simms Letters*, 3: 174-175; see also Alexander Cowie, *The Rise of the American Novel* (New York, 1948), p. 240; Trent, *Simms*, p. 173; Henry W. Simms, *Emotion at High Tide: Abolition as a Controversial Factor* (Richmond, 1960), p. 77; Jeannette Reed Tandy, "Pro-Slavery Propaganda in American Fiction of the Fifties," *South Atlantic Quarterly* 21 (1922): 170.

15. *SQR* 9 n.s. (Jan. 1854): 248-249 (see also 185-205).

16. Ibid., 10 n.s. (Oct. 1854), "Prospects and Policy of the South," (Oct. 1849), "Right to Labor," 1 n.s. (Apr. 1850): 251-252.

17. Ibid., 10 n.s. (Oct. 1854): 454 (see also 434-453).

18. Ibid., 10 n.s. (Oct. 1854): 454-457.

19. Ibid., 2, n.s. (Sept. 1850): 31; 9 n.s. (Apr. 1854): 530-531, 524-525; 3 n.s. (Apr. 1851): 537-538.

20. Ibid., 2 n.s. (Nov. 1850).

21. Ibid., 7 n.s. (Apr. 1853): 418-421.

22. *Courier*, May 18, 1853; *Mercury*, May 10, 1853; Hammond to Simms, March 26, 1851, Hammond Papers, Library of Congress; *SQR* 4 n.s. (Oct. 1851): 319, 322, 324; 1 n.s. (July 1850): 372; 3 n.s. (Apr. 1851): 555.

23. *Simms Letters*, 3: 16, 94, 200, 270; *Courier*, May 18,

1853; *SQR*, 20 n.s. (Nov. 1850): 544; 10 n.s. (Oct. 1854), 511, 505-510; 9 n.s. (Jan. 1854): 244. Simms reviewed the magazine *Self-Instructor* and gave its purpose: "The object of this periodical is mainly the proper education of the Southern people, and the diffusion among them, of a just knowledge of the resources and power of their section."

24. *Courier*, Jan. 9, 1854; *Simms Letters*, 5: 409; *SQR* 3 n.s. (Apr. 1851): 570-571; 5 n.s. (Jan. 1852): 119.

25. *Simms Letters*, 3: 34, 119, 231; *Mercury*, March 12, 1852; *Courier*, Jan. 25, 1854; P. Hagood to Marcellus Hammond, May 21, 1851, Hammond Papers, University of South Carolina; *SQR* 4 n.s. (July 1851): 69, 74; 2 n.s. (Sept. 1850): 69, 71, 82; 8 n. s. (Oct. 1853): 368.

26. Simms sought continually to place South Carolina and its Revolutionary heroes in an unimpeachable position. See *Simms Letters*, 5: 324; *Courier*, Aug. 17, 1854, Sept. 4, 1853; *SQR* 16 (Oct. 1849): 257-258. (My purpose is not to discuss Simms' views of history, but to point out how he constantly applied them, even in his magazines.)

27. Simms was proud of his academic friends and always sought learned articles from them. See *Simms Letters*, 3: 12-13, 84; *SQR* (July 1852), (Oct. 1853), (Oct. 1849), July 1849), (Jan. 1850, *passim*).

28. *SQR* 15 (Apr. 1849): 164-165, 120-130.

29. Ibid., 5 n. s. (Jan. 1852): 182-187, 192-195.

30. *The Partisan* (New York, 1853), x; *Views and Reviews* (1 Ser.), 67-68; *SQR* 6 n. s. (July 1852), 159-161, 203, 222, 227-228, 233.

31. *Mercury*, Aug. 12, 1852; *Simms Letters*, 3: 11, 160, 173; *SQR* 6 n. s. (July 1852), 235; 1 n. s. (Apr. 1850): 228-229; 2 n. s. (Nov. 1850): 513.

32. *SQR* 1 n. s. (Apr. 1850): 192-197.

33. *Mercury*, May 10 1853; *Simms Letters*, 3: 107; Hammond to Simms, Nov. 18, 1853, Hammond Papers, Library of Congress; *SQR* 3 n. s. (Apr. 1851): 569.

34. *SQR* 16 (Oct. 1849): 261.

35. Obviously, Simms wanted to avoid creating any jealousy between Hammond and Rhett. See *SQR* 4 n. s. (Oct. 1851), 273-274, 276; *Simms Letters*, 3: 133-134, 138, 107.

36. *SQR* 4 n. s. (July 1851): 112, 116, 107-110, 117; *Simms Letters*, 3: 126, 138.

37. *Simms Letters*, 3: 133, 97, 94, 160.

38. Hammond to Simms, March 8, 1850, Hammond Papers, Library of Congress; *Simms Letters*, 3: 44.

39. *SQR* 2 n. s. (Sept. 1850): 208-209, 210, 212, 213.

40. See previous chapter for discussion of South Carolina secessionist cooperationist controversy. *Mercury*, Apr. 3, 1849; Hammond Diary, Dec. 15, 1849, James Hamilton to Hammond, July 24, 1849, Hammond to Marcellus Hammond, July 30, 1849, Hammond Papers, University of South Carolina; *SQR* 15 (July 1849): 311, 275.

41. Louisa McCord was the wife of the wealthy planter, David J. McCord. *Mercury*, March 11, 1853; *Simms Letters*, 3: 133, 227; *SQR* 4 n. s. (Oct. 1851), 277-298, 300, 302, 305; 7 n. s. (Jan. 1853): 204-205.

42. *Simms Letters*, 3: 209, 574; *SQR* 2 n. s. (Nov. 1850), 527; 5 n. s. (Jan. 1852): 255; 4 n. s. (Oct. 1851): 350, 351, 300-315; 3 n. s. (Jan. 1851): 192, 193, 195, 225, 282, 283; 3 n. s. (Apr. 1851): 534; also see Osterweis, *Romanticism and Nationalism in the Old South*, pp. 120, 151.

43. *Mercury*, March 11, July 15, 1853; *SQR* 7 n. s. (Jan. 1853): 204; 8 n. s. (July 1853): 38-39, 46-49.

44. *Courier*, Sept. 30, 1853; *Simms Letters*, 3: 147; *SQR* 5 n. s. (Apr. 1852), 203; 2 n. s. (Sept. 1850): 198, 200, 204; 3 n. s. (Jan. 1851): 49-51, (Apr. 1851): 556; 6 n. s. (Oct. 1852): 535-536; see also Bohner, *John Pendleton Kennedy*, p. 138.

45. *Courier*, Feb. 28, 1854; *SQR*, 10 n. s. (July 1854): 260; 7 n. s. (Jan. 1853): 205; 3 n. s. (Jan. 1851): 133.

46. There were many complicated issues over printing and delivery which plagued Simms, but they are not important to this study. See *Mercury*, Dec. 30, 1853, Oct. 11, 1853; *Courier*, Sept. 25, 1852, Oct. 11, 1853, Apr. 14, 1854; Francis Lieber to William Porcher Miles, Dec. 10, 1854, Miles Papers; *Simms Letters*, 3: 12, 13, 21, 142, 132, 194, 208, 209, 210, 212; 4: 203; Simms to Hammond, Aug. 18, Nov. 24, 1852, Hammond Papers, Library of Congress.

47. *Mercury*, Jan 13, 31, 1855; *Courier*, Nov. 22, Dec. 21, Nov. 22, 1853, June 6, 1854; *Simms Letters*, 3: 289-290, 298, 328, 334, 355-356, 357, 362; Hammond to Simms, Aug. 28, Dec. 6, 1854, Hammond Papers, Library of Congress.

48. *The Golden Christmas*, fly leaf; *Mercury*, July 22, 1853; *Courier*, Sept. 25, 1852, July 13, Sept. 30, 1853, Feb. 9, March 1, June 5, 1854.

8 A Political Adviser to the Secession Movement

SMARTING FROM the Northern lecture tour and somewhat at a loss for literary endeavor after resigning as editor of the *Southern Quarterly Review*, Simms temporarily indulged his favorite neurosis, self-pity, and he returned to his plantation. He revised his novels for a new edition, wrote many political essays, and had little time for any new fiction. His fame began to spread as the South's intellectual leaders at last came to recognize the importance of his work and activities for the entire South. Many editorials were written and lectures given on Simms' place in Southern fiction and his contributions to South Carolina's history. Simms was in great demand as a public lecturer and, though seeming to grow increasingly tired, he spoke often on the familiar themes of the professional man's duty to his community, the common Southern heritage, the value of a Southern press, and the necessity for a suffering South to separate from Northern oppression. He was elected to the Montgomery Commercial Convention in May 1858. He was also again offered the presidency of South Carolina College in Columbia, which he declined because he could not afford the office. Subsequently he was nominated to fill the United States Senate seat of the deceased Josiah James Evans. As his fame spread throughout the South, Simms was plagued by personal illness and tragedy. He had constant headaches and stomach trouble and continual eye infections. His cotton crops failed, and when his Charleston residence burned early in

1860, he was forced to sell part of his library in order to feed his family.[1]

Yet some of Simms' happiest and most useful moments were spent in those last four years before secession, as fame brought swarms of admirers to his door and constant requests for literary and political advice. A coterie of young Charleston intellectuals often gathered to discuss writing and politics with him at his friend John Russell's bookstore. From the discussions emerged the idea of a new periodical to counteract Northern attacks on Southern society. When *Russell's Magazine* appeared in April 1857, Simms was its leading adviser, critic, and guiding spirit, always stressing the importance of directing and influencing the cultural development of the cotton states. In a lengthy article for *Russell's*, the poet Paul Hamilton Hayne summed up what Simms had come to mean for the South and its young writers, by saying that Simms had made Southerners proud of their heritage and confident in their future. Simms also contributed to *Russell's*, stressing in the "Literary Prospects of the South" the link between the importance of an indigenous literature and its aid in a sectional crisis. He looked forward to the sectional break, when the South would finally publish its own writers, and when Southern intellectuals would emerge as philosopher statesmen to help the South weather the storm of separation. In his poetry for *Russell's* and the Charleston newspapers, Simms emphasized love of native land and importance of roots. In his review columns he urged the South to recognize the importance of its intellectuals, and he reiterated his Carlylean call for the great man to rise up and lead the South.[2]

If he was important as an adviser to youth, his sense of duty and mission in his search for a great man finally resulted in the most important phase of his long public career. Always on the fringe of the political scene, Simms found a most interesting and rewarding avocation as personal counselor and speech writer to many of South Carolina's leading public figures. He worked with Miles, Hammond, Lawrence M. Keitt, the Rhetts, Orr, and his neighbor, David F. Jamison. Employing all his talents gained from years of public activity as a propagandist for his section, Simms influenced the cautious combination of practical and romantic behavior of many of the men who would create a united South and lead South Carolina to secession.[3]

Most important in his career as adviser was Simms' influence on the political career of the brilliant but perverse James Henry Hammond. He had worked untiringly for over a decade to return Hammond to public life. When Andrew Pickens Butler resigned from the Senate in 1857, Simms began a campaign to put Hammond's name before the state legislature in hopes of electing him to the vacant seat. Under Simms' influence, William J. Grayson wrote a lengthy article in *Russell's* demanding Hammond's return to public life. Simms forced Hammond to shake his lethargy and visit Columbia to talk to the legislators. Simms' years of propagandizing and cajolery were finally rewarded when the legislature elected Hammond to the Senate on November 30, 1857. Rhett's secessionist Charleston *Mercury* considered Hammond's election a triumph, and it called the new Senator a true "champion of the rights of the States." Simms was ecstatic. Knowing that Hammond gained a moderate image because of his fear that South Carolina might be forced to act alone, Simms laid plans to help formulate a policy which would unite Southern Congressmen in the defense of the South, without appearing so radical as to alienate the other Southern states. As Hammond's speech writer, historical researcher, editor, and chief source of political ideas, he helped to restore the great man's self-esteem and in turn to prepare the South for secession.[4]

Hammond was apprehensive about his new political position, confused at the lack of unity or policy among Southerners, and disgusted with the bickering and poor intellectual quality of South Carolina Congressmen in particular. Simms, aware of his friend's anxieties, wrote often to him and began to gather a coterie of loyal and intelligent followers for Hammond. Writing political advice to his friend William Porcher Miles, who had just been elected to the House of Representatives, Simms suggested that Miles cultivate Hammond's friendship and plan to serve the new Senator as liaison to the lower House. He cautioned Miles on the seriousness of current political issues, and he suggested that Miles work closely with Hammond. He wanted to make certain that Miles, a Charleston radical who would have some trouble with his constituents if he supported too moderate a policy toward the Union, fully understood Hammond's political position. He told Miles that Hammond supported Buchanan and the Democratic party only as long as the President did not sacrifice Southern interests to Northern democracy. He wanted Miles to remain calm but firm in espousing the Southern cause, and to participate cautiously in Congressional floor discussions. On the Kansas issue Simms advocated a more radical position for Miles, hoping that the young Congressman would impress his feelings of sectional loyalty upon Hammond.[5] In this way, Simms' own radical predilections could influence Hammond and, at the same time, temporize Miles.

In a long letter to Hammond, Simms outlined a plan of action concerning Congressional and sectional politics. Since the South was an agrarian society which lacked the opportunity to communicate and to disseminate ideas continually, Southerners were cautious conservatives who did not share the daring of the urban, commercial North. Long a sufferer at the lack of Southern sophistication, Simms knew that his people would rather accept the status quo than revolt against Northern aggression. But he also knew that many Southerners would follow the magnetism of a personal leader who spoke as a moderate while organizing the radical Southerners. He cautioned Hammond to influence his colleagues in Washington in hopes of organizing them into a solid front. Simms hoped that a united Southern Democratic faction in Congress, led by Hammond and Mississippi's Jefferson Davis, might serve as the catalyst to drive the Northern Democrats out of the party. Convinced that the Southern people would eventually support such persuasive leadership, Simms thought it imperative that Hammond calculate the degree of radicalism which would be acceptable to most Southerners. Hammond's fame was "very precious" to Simms, and the author wanted to make certain that his best friend would apply his resources to the cause of secession at the proper time.[6]

Knowing that Simms had recently written Miles on the subject, Hammond also enlisted Simms' advice on the upcoming debate over the Kansas statehood bill. He was uncertain as to how he should stand on the Kansas issue. Privately he confided to Simms that the South should secede if Kansas were not admitted as a slave state, but he personally found little economic or political value in the extension of slave territory. Hammond was convinced that there were too few slaves in the South to push colonization of a new territory, and he wanted Southerners first to develop their own 850,000 square miles of territory. He asked Simms to survey the strategic and political significance of the Western lands. Hammond expected Simms' report to verify his own views on the future of the Southern empire.[7]

In part contradicting his radical advice to Miles, Simms advised Hammond to take a moderate position based on a practical view of political priorities. Certain that the struggle over a pro-slavery constitution for Kansas was not the proper test for a slow-moving agricultural people, Simms urged Hammond not to think of the issue as a choice between Kansas and disunion. As an expansionist, Simms hoped for the solidification of the slave system throughout the Southwest, and he assumed that eventually all of Mexico would become part of the South. Aware that slavery might someday have no meaning for South Carolina, and having gone too far to turn back from his drive for a Southern Confederacy, Simms wanted to protect the South. Kansas, a territory which could never sustain a slave system, meant little to the South's future. Cautioning Hammond against taking a fire-eating position in his upcoming Senate speech, Simms advised his friend to praise the Union but to abandon his dream of a future unity between the sections. He maintained some hope that the North would purge itself of the abolitionists, and he wanted Hammond to point out that Northern leaders were obviously victims of mass opinion concerning the Kansas question. He advised Hammond to attack the new Republican party as a divisive force, and at the same time to admonish Northern Democrats for allowing Douglas to divide the party over the Kansas issue. In short, Simms emphasized moderation and sectional loyalty. He concluded with a promise to keep Hammond informed of his and other Southerners' views on Kansas, and he prepared to 'collect material for the upcoming speech.[8]

Choosing March 4 as the day for his speech, Hammond attacked Douglas' stand on Kansas by associating the Western politician with the anti-Lecompton Republican faction, thus hoping to destroy Douglas' political power in the South. Hammond, who took many ideas from his extensive correspondence with Simms, assumed a moderate position on Kansas statehood in order to entice conservative Southerners to consider their common interests. He claimed that Congress had no constitutional power to interfere with or amend a territorial legislature's provisional constitution, and he fixed upon the slave question as the true source of the Kansas debates. Hammond was actually lecturing his fellow Southerners on their common grounds for unity. He condemned the North for raising again the divisive question of slave extension, and he criticized Northerners for plundering and robbing the South of its rightful chance at material growth within the Union. Stating his view that "cotton was king," he cautioned the North that it needed the South. Since Northerners could not survive without Southern cotton, its politicians had to appease the South, Hammond said. Besides, the class society of the South, based on Negro slavery, provided a model of a cautious and conservative society in times of social chaos. By warning the North, Hammond was building bridges to other Southern states through his praise of the South's harmony of political and social institutions, in which the slave represented the "mud-sill" or controlled working class. The slave, who could not care for himself, was essential to the harmony of all classes. Hammond concluded by cautioning Douglas and other Northerners that any attempt to end slavery through forced contraction of the system would destroy the Union.[9]

Congressmen, leading South Carolina politicians and intellectuals, plus the influential Charleston *Courier* rallied to support Hammond's speech on Kansas. Some were confident that he had solidified his position in South Carolina by capturing both the radical and conservative factions. Others wrote that he had lumped Douglas with Seward and the "Black Republicans," thus checking the political appeal of the Illinois politician. The *Courier* agreed with Hammond's defense of slavery, saying that the North needed "the conservative balance wheel of the South, to save its political and social system from utter overthrow." In the opinion of the *Courier*, Hammond was "a worthy successor of Calhoun."[10] Pleased with the praise and attention which had been given to his speech, Hammond wanted his friend Simms' reaction, and he promised to send Simms a copy. More pleased than if he had made the speech himself, Simms found his praise for Hammond's able defense of slavery tame in comparison with most of the comments he had heard. Both men were too tired from their long battles to jump to any hopeful conclusions. But Simms felt a certain sense of pride in the proof that Hammond was indeed the South's natural leader, a man capable of great statesmanship. Simms believed that Hammond had "struck the right chord *for the South*," and he was delighted that his moderate advice had helped to further the cause of Southern independence.[11]

Since the speech had made Hammond famous throughout the South, the politically minded Simms sought to consolidate his friend's power in South Carolina in order to enhance Hammond's political bargaining position. If Hammond could control the state, Simms was certain that he could lead the South to secession. Fully aware of the proper image a politician had to create and the importance of controlling public opinion, Simms again pursued the plan of taking over the debt-ridden, fire-eating Charleston *Mercury* and turning it into a pro-Hammond organ of Southern nationalist propaganda. Previously Hammond had refused to manufacture opinion at home and had dissuaded Simms from purchasing the *Mercury*. Besides, he considered Simms a great man of letters, above the petty debates of politics, and too famous to dabble in political propaganda. But Hammond had misjudged his friend and, after months of discussion, he finally accepted the importance of controlling the *Mercury*'s volatile editorial page. Partly because Simms had convinced him that the *Mercury* without the Rhetts would be the most influential newspaper in the South, Hammond secretly agreed to support a pool of buyers with financial aid, but only if Simms consented to edit the paper.[12]

Although Simms had been the main exponent of the need for a Hammond-controlled political organ, when Hammond suggested that he actually edit the paper, the novelist backed down. While Simms was positive that such a moderate paper would help to create his long-sought Southern nationalism, he himself felt too old and sickly to undertake a new editorial task. He was much too interested in speech-writing, dabbling with local politics, and in influencing the work in *Russell's*

Magazine, to attempt to correct an editorial page which he believed had been badly run for over ten years. Promising Hammond and Miles that he would write editorials for the paper and would serve the new owners in an advisory capacity, Simms was relieved when the sale fell through and the *Mercury* continued under the Rhetts' control. Now Simms could continue to aid the Rhett family while he criticized their foolish radical tactics.[13] Perhaps, as the power behind the *Mercury*, he would have made it the outstanding Southern nationalist organ. But like his friend Hammond, Simms was indecisive at important moments in his life. He remained a carping, pessimistic politician, calling for apocalypse but refusing to take a positive step in the direction of secession.

Intrigue over the vacancy created by the death of Senator Josiah James Evans may also have made Simms cautious in any attempt to undermine the power of the Rhetts in South Carolina. He wanted the Senate seat himself, but he was not surprised when the legislature chose a more moderate man for the position. Besides, Hammond had begun to rely more on his advice, so there was little time to consider his own career.[14]

Hammond was particularly interested in Simms' views on the recent British aggression in the Gulf of Mexico. Simms wanted Hammond to tell other Southern Congressmen of the need to improve trade relations between Great Britain and the South. He observed that the South could not afford to fight Northern battles, especially when Northern Democrats were using trouble with England to unite the party and to destroy the growing sectional alliance. He was convinced that the national Democratic party was finally dying, and he asked Hammond to increase his efforts to build a Southern party to protect agriculture—not from England, but from the North. He concluded a long letter on foreign policy and domestic politics by encouraging Hammond to question the Northern party and to point out to his Southern colleagues the menace which Northern politicians represented for the South.[15]

Perhaps his closeness to the South Carolina radicals, his many talks with the Charleston politicians around Russell's bookstore, and his large correspondence and friendship with Congressmen Lawrence M. Keitt, Milledge L. Bonham, and Francis W. Pickens made Simms appear too detached from the realities of the compromises necessary to Washington politics. He praised Hammond's performance as a moderate statesman in Congress, but he was displeased that the Senator did not take a more active role in attacking the national Democrats. For his part, Hammond had discovered the realities of national politics, had helped to counter Douglas' power in the South, and had agitated for increased Southern control of the national Democrats. Although he often used Simms' own works to express his views in Congress, greatly respected his friend's political wisdom, and valued his speech-writing abilities, Hammond opposed the immediate need for a strictly sectional party, and he joined James L. Orr in continuing to control the national party in the South.[16] Both the author and the Senator, growing old and probably a bit cynical of the South's future, ultimately believed in secession, but Hammond had become the more moderate of the two.

Upon Hammond's return to his South Carolina plantation Redcliffe after a long session in Washington, Simms chided his friend for enjoying the capital's good food and wine and then complaining about an upset stomach. He praised Hammond's statesmanlike, moderate performance, and he was excited over the prospects of a completely united South Carolina, dedicated to moving the entire South to secession. He suggested that Hammond take no public part in local politics but remain in a position to dictate the party organization without incurring the wrath of the conservative and radical elements in the state. Simms was seriously displeased with Hammond's vote in favor of the Kansas statehood bill, and he encouraged the Senator to speak out on certain issues which disturbed many of the state's radical leaders. To that end he planned a public dinner at Beach Island for Hammond, to which many of the state's more powerful political figures would be invited and where Hammond would have the opportunity to defend his recent actions in Congress. Simms, who had just finished editing and partially re-writing a political speech for Keitt, would assist Hammond in writing a few moderate comments, in hopes of influencing the people of South Carolina.[17]

Severely in debt, depressed over the death of his father-in-law and his wife's and children's illnesses, Simms nevertheless consulted Hammond on his special political performance at

Beach Island. But he could not be present for the dinner. He was extremely chagrined, because he had wanted the opportunity to observe Hammond in action again, and he had felt that his presence would moderate the Senator's comments. Hoping Hammond would attack the Northern Democratic party, he advised his friend to help "seal the fate" of that party in the South. He warned Hammond to drink nothing. Remembering Keitt, who had delivered a befuddled oration at the Citadel while he was so drunk that he had to be carried to the podium, he wanted to make certain that Hammond was clear-headed and forceful.[18]

Perhaps it might have been better for Hammond if he had been drunk at Beach Island, because his actions might then have been explainable. On July 22, 1858, before approximately 1,500 invited guests, Hammond vociferously defended his actions in the previous Senate session. Although the speech was not printed and was certainly never meant for newspaper publication, accounts of the evening showed that Hammond had for too long been out of public office and had forgotten that a political figure had to be cautious in justifying his vote. He claimed to have voted for the Kansas bill because he considered Kansas unsuitable for slavery. Refusing to contemplate separate-state secession, he remarked in the presence of many immediate secessionists that a union of at least five Southern states should precede any talk of secession. He also attacked any idea of reviving the slave trade, because he feared that it would destroy the slave market in the Southeast.[19]

Many South Carolinians, including Hammond's political enemies in Columbia, resented what they considered an obviously pro-Union speech. At first Rhett merely mentioned the speech in the *Mercury*, but soon adverse reactions filled the pages of the newspaper. Attacking both the *Mercury* and the Richmond *Whig*, which misunderstood Hammond's willingness to secede, the *Courier* praised the Senator as a "conservative statesman," unwilling to destroy the Union immediately but certainly willing to go with South Carolina "whenever the emergency demands it."[20] Seeking to dissuade the younger Rhett from printing further attacks on Hammond, Simms visited the editor in Charleston. He told Rhett that Hammond was capable of defending himself against his enemies and that the Senator remained a secessionist. Hammond favored "carrying on the war constitutionally until the people themselves were ripe for revolution." Besides, the Senator hoped for a confrontation with the Northern Democrats in 1860, and Simms suggested that the *Mercury* rally behind Hammond's plan of moderate radicalism. Cautioning Rhett that Kansas was no issue for South Carolina, Simms assured the newspaperman that most of Hammond's speech had been reported inadequately. He promised that Hammond would soon clarify his Beach Island oration.[21]

Before he wrote his speech for an address at Barnwell Court House on October 29, 1858, Hammond wanted Simms' views on what to say and how to answer his critics. Simms replied that Hammond should not retaliate against his enemies in the newspapers, but save everything for the speech, which should be carefully prepared.[22] Simms, who was also commissioned to read and to edit the speech in advance, and to comment on the state's reaction to it, urged Hammond not only to express his own opinions but also to reflect the opinion of his constituents. Although he was working with his editors and planning a trip to New York, Simms also edited the speech for publication in the *Mercury*. In the course of many conversations and letters, the two old politicos began to formulate a speech which would hopefully please all Carolinians. Simms suggested that Hammond urge the state to support a move for a cooperationist South, composed of the cotton states. Hammond believed that two Republican Presidencies should precede secession, whereas Simms advised him to state categorically that the election of any "Black Republican President" would necessitate secession. Yet he urged Hammond to avoid unnecessary agitation. He reminded Hammond that his speech was for the entire South and should therefore be designed to bring the rest of the South closer to South Carolina.[23] Happy in his advisory capacity, the novelist departed for New York. But he was soon crushed by the deaths of his two young sons, Sydney and Beverly Hammond Simms. Although heartbroken at the loss, his interest in Hammond's upcoming speech continued, and he again advised the Senator "to correct the vulgar report of your speech," to alter his moderate position, and to advocate united Southern secession.[24]

Suffering from Simms' tragedy and constantly sick to his stomach, Hammond traveled to the courthouse to make what should have been the most important speech of his political life. If he had followed Simms' advice, this speech could have gained him the leadership of the secession movement. Although his oration reflected much of Simms' thought, the Senator was unable to deliver a forceful address. Again defending his vote on the English bill because Kansas was unimportant to the South, Hammond suggested that the South develop its own resources before agitating for expansion. Finding the reopening of the slave trade controversy a camouflage of serious internal economic problems, he urged that the South abandon its attempt to extend slavery and therefore any hopes of restoring the political equilibrium between North and South, and instead to seek to unite against the North. Through an economic policy of mixed agriculture and manufacturing, and opposition to the tariff, the South was politically safe within the Union. Besides, as Simms had so often told him, an overwhelming percentage of Southerners favored the Union. Therefore, South Carolinians had no recourse but to remain in the Union until the South could be united. Advising his fellow Carolinians against any attachment to the national party system, he explained that the North would forever be politically divided and that the South had to form its own political faction in Congress. To achieve unity Hammond reiterated his and Simms' views on Southern abolitionists, and he called for the entire South to purge its borders of antislavery supporters. In conclusion, Hammond vowed to follow his section's popular opinion, and he asserted his faithfulness to his section within or without the Union.[25]

At once Hammond's enemies began to accuse him of moderation. The *Mercury* was mildly opposed to his view of the South's strength in the Union, and the Rhetts accused him of believing in Northern justice. Trescot told Miles that Hammond had been foolish to discuss the slave trade, but he admired Hammond's political honesty. However, the usually astute Trescot misjudged the Senator and claimed that Hammond was too loyal to the national Democratic party. On the other hand, many Northerners found Hammond's speech too radical and disliked his continual protection of slavery, but some also praised his courageous moderate stand.[26] But none of his critics could match Hammond's self-criticism. Although proud of his attack on Seward, Hammond told Miles that no public figure was free to speak his mind in the South while reporters were present. Claiming that illness had kept him from truly expressing his wishes, Hammond was furious and yet frightened that the *Mercury* could call him an unprincipled compromiser. Although ostensibly warning Miles against speaking out on public issues, and reiterating his loyalty to the South, Hammond closed his correspondence with a plea for understanding. He knew that most Southerners opposed secession in 1858 and that Miles must openly work for Southern unity.[27]

But it remained for Simms to give the final praise to the realism of Hammond's speech and to help the Senator regain his will to serve the South. When Hammond solicited Simms' opinion of the speech, the writer replied that Hammond had spoken as a true statesman, a man obviously to be reckoned with on the national scene, perhaps even as a candidate for the Presidency. Like the *Mercury*, which later apologized for attacking Hammond, Simms realized that the Senator was correct in assuming that the South was not then united, and that it would be inexpedient to propose secession at that time. He found that Hammond, far from becoming a Unionist, was really attacking Douglas and calling for dissolution of the national party system.[28]

Both men were exhausted from their public service to the South, and both realized that they were slowly accomplishing the division of the Union. Politically they knew that the Republicans would soon destroy the Northern Democrats. They only wondered whether the South would be prepared to act when that event occurred. Besides, their own state had taken a moderate step in electing James Chesnut to the Senate. Perhaps some of the thanks was due to them. At least Simms would have a strong effect on the political behavior of both Chesnut and Hammond during the next two years. Like Hammond, Chesnut realized the importance of Simms' conservative but secessionist voice in the coming crisis.[29]

Although Simms made a faint attempt to return to writing fiction early in 1859, his political contacts left him little time for any serious writing of his own. He realized his political obligations and exercised his influence to moderate the South Carolina "hotheads," such as the younger Rhett and his radical *Mercury*, in order to avoid driving the rest of the South out of the growing sectional alignment. Besides, he was certain that the Republicans would capture the Northern vote from the Democrats and elect their candidate in 1860. He knew that a Republican victory in 1860 would permanently fragment the Democratic party and would help to create a strictly sectional party, perhaps with Hammond as its leader. Simms felt that Calhoun's dream of a purely sectional alignment in political parties was imminent. Therefore, he envisioned himself the moderating force in South Carolina and exacted from Rhett a promise of moderation. He also assured Rhett of Hammond's loyalty to radicalism, and he asked the young editor to begin a campaign to support Hammond as the Southern Democratic candidate for the Presidency.[30]

Echoing Simms' views, Hammond wanted to restrain the radicals in South Carolina, because he did not want the state to appear to be the leader of the secessionist movement.[31] But both men knew that the Rhetts were by no means as serious a threat to the South as was Orr's insistence upon supporting Douglas and the national Democrats in the upcoming Charleston convention. Orr would support secession, but he was too pessimistic to believe that the South was ready to act. Therefore Simms and Hammond sought to neutralize Orr's position in South Carolina, while at the same time conciliating the radicals. They played a dangerous and thankless political game, relying on their many friends and allies to calm the state and to deprive Orr of any support for Douglas in South Carolina. That they in part succeeded was obvious from the events of 1860. Despite severe headaches and terrible cramps in his legs, Simms had spent much time aiding Hammond, because he was convinced that the next election would decide the fate of the Union.[32]

Not only politicians deprived Simms of the time to write fiction, but also other writers who sought his advice. In the late 1850s Simms found his advisory capacity extending beyond South Carolina to include writers throughout the South. He answered the many letters from young poets, novelists, and historians directed to his large storehouse of literary experience and knowledge of the South's romantic past. He advised John Esten Cooke to investigate old letters and papers in order to improve his factual understanding of the South's place in American fiction. He felt that by being accurate in his poems, Cooke could represent the South favorably to Northerners. He offered research materials and accepted the request to read William J. Rivers' new manuscript. Cautioning Rivers to remain independent, never lower his standards, and to accept no patronage from those who would change his writing style, Simms advised him to work harder and to take more time to create.[33] Though at times ill and fast becoming a complaining old man, Simms was anxious to see the results of his years of effort as a literary consultant. If helping to further the young talents who breathed nationalism into their writing would aid his section, he would gladly give them much of his time.

While he advised politicians, wrote critical commentary and offered encouragement to fellow men of letters, and defended Southern fiction in the Charleston *Mercury*, Simms managed somehow to publish a long novel on South Carolina's colonial period, *The Cassique of Kiawah*. Simms was praised as the best American novelist since the death of Cooper, and his new work received local acclaim far superior to the novel's merit. The *Courier* went so far as to call it a work of genius and even reprinted the entire dedication in poetic form. The dedication, addressed to William Porcher Miles, expressed Simms' deep and abiding pessimism about the future of the South. It symbolically depicted the loss of his two young sons as a curse upon his home and family, and at the same time it revealed the political significance of the novel. Simms lamented the unworthiness of his life and vowed to pay tribute to his political and intellectual friend, while he hoped to leave his prose works as a tribute to his deceased sons.[34]

The Cassique of Kiawah in its own way reflected the breakup of a family, which perhaps was necessary in order to make a healthier new family out of the remnants of the old. Simms at first wanted to write another Revolutionary War novel, but he decided instead to return to an earlier South Carolina, when it was still possible to save the family (or keep the South in the Union). Historically speaking, Simms had given up on the Union by the end of the Revolutionary War. Therefore in setting his historical romance along the banks of the Edisto River in 1684, when the colony was less than thirty years old, Simms seemed to be pushing back to the source of the South's separate life. Giving perhaps his most detailed historical treatment of the state, and capturing the brutal language of civilized Englishmen who attempted to settle the land, he centered the romance around the defeat of the Cherokee Indians at the battle of Kiawah and the permanent settlement of the little colony at Charleston. It was a period marked by Indian uprisings, the real threat of pirate and French and Spanish raids, and the political war between the Goose Creek (or anti-proprietary) and proprietary factions. Simms also devoted much attention to the spoiled slave as loyal family servant.

The novel was replete with the typical details of a colonial romance, insignificant in themselves. But the petty civil divisions caused by outside British influence (Simms allowed the leading character to call for another Civil War in England in order to free the colony), which led to bitter partisan struggle, allowed Simms to become present-minded in his analysis of the permanent settlement of South Carolina. Realizing that Governor Robert Quary was incompetent and weak, literally incapable of governing the infant colony, Simms chided the South Carolina of his own day: ". . . but competence to office was no more requisite in those days than in ours." For Simms, the one advantage of the colonial officeholder was that an excellent leader such as Thomas Smith, the anti-proprietary governor, could remain in office for life. Once a staunch believer in rotation in office, the ex-Jacksonian had turned to a belief in a rigid caste and class system. Simms was proud of the influx of Scotch-Irish settlers into Charleston, men who "aimed at something (and this is a right ambition) of social position for themselves and their descendants."[35] In the 1850s Simms found himself in the position of defending the stability of an established power of the descendants of those "noble commoners."

These new leaders destroyed the Indian menace to Charleston, deprived the outside proprietors of their power in the colony, and vowed to remain in the colony in order to make it independent. Simms continued to berate the proprietary sup-

porters for remaining loyal to England. He considered them a
society "lacking the courage to assert an independent and well-
founded standard of judgment for itself." Comparing the past
to 1859, he said, "We have our intrinsic resources, material
and mental, if we only knew how, and had the courage to apply
them." It was finally the young hero Harry who, equating
England with the North, vowed never again to return to
England, but rather to remain in the new colony of Carolina.
Once one claimed the value of the free new world, it became his
destiny, conservative or not, to free the new world from the
restrictions of the old.[36] At least in fiction, Simms had justified the end of the Union, and he optimistically called for its
destruction in order to save the future of the South.

But Simms' optimism was tempered, as was demonstrated
in his revision of the *History of South Carolina* in order to
make it more relevant to the 1850s. He had returned to his
history with the realization that he was chronicling a transi-
tional period—one in which the South was "just entering on the
first chaotic phase"—and the future of its secessionist policy
was doubtful. He had rewritten the history because he felt that
by re-creating his own state's important position in the South's
past he could place South Carolina at the forefront of the coming revolution.[37] A despondent Simms told John Esten
Cooke that he knew that Southerners would never do his work
justice. But Simms seemed to regard loyalty to his section as
more important for an artist than personal acclaim. In these
last few years of his active career, he finally realized the importance of his own words.[38]

To his old friend Miles he confided the value of his new
history. Not only did the book provide the Southern student
with a helpful guide to his section's past, but it was also instrumental to the state's political leaders. He suggested that
Miles and other South Carolinians keep a copy of his history in
Washington. He hoped to give Southern Congressmen political
ammunition from the South's past in order to attack the present
Northern enemy. Especially since the present condition of the
country demanded a general reconsideration of the South's
position, Simms wanted his political readers to appreciate the
historical responsibilities of South Carolina in the coming
struggle. One lesson above all he wanted to teach from his "im-

perfect story of the past." He cautioned the politician to "cling to the soil of his birth in the day of its difficulty, with the resolution of the son who stands above the grave of a mother and protects it from violation."[39] For Simms, "unanimity among our citizens will always give them unconquerable strength," since the views of the state's majority, in all questions of public expediency or policy, would be the course of patriotism his history wished to convey.[40] Gone were the days when the young writer chose to sacrifice his career rather than to submit to a test oath which would inhibit his freedom of speech. A South Carolina of one political voice had finally been achieved.

He further instructed the politicians of the South in an analysis of Calhoun's career, claiming that the great man had become the symbol of Southern statesmanship. Calhoun's public life chronicled the South's growing resistance to Northern encroachment upon its rights. Simms said that Calhoun had anticipated the outcome of sectional controversy and that he had predicted and worked for the ruin of the prevailing political system. His advocacy of a nationalistic South which could ward off the aggression of the larger Northern states had endeared the "cast iron" man to Simms and other antebellum Southern intellectuals. Until the war began, Simms continued to raise the specter of the martyred statesman, neglected in his own time and frustrated in his true ambitions. He had discovered a useful piece of propaganda from the immediate past, and he resolved never to rest his pen until Calhoun's requests had been fulfilled.[41]

But the revised *History of South Carolina* also contained concrete suggestions for achieving independence. Again attacking Southern persistence in maintaining an agricultural society, he insisted upon the need for the South to rely on industry. Unless the new nation realized the importance of economic diversification, it would be at the mercy of all of Europe and the United States, Simms declared. He cautioned that an agricultural section bred sparseness at a time when the South desperately required a growing, healthy population. Also, agriculture was unfavorable to education, because "communities purely agricultural can never exhibit the same degree of intellectual activity with communities commercial or manufacturing." No longer was there any place for romanticizing the beauty of the pastoral South or for reveling in the quaintness of a pre-capitalist economic splendor. Simms had learned his historical lessons much too well. Any selfish reasons he might have had for changing the South to an urban civilization, which at times became confused with his attachment to the soil, were subverted to the reality of economic self-sufficiency. Believing secession was imminent, he hoped that Northern manufacturers would never again feed and clothe the South. He closed his last work of history with a warning to the South from its own romantic and carefree past. He hoped that his chronicle would not only stir the patriotic emotions of narrow politicians, but would guide the South's leaders to face the economic and political realities of the present.[42]

The *Courier* had predicted that Simms' history would prove "to be a valuable addition to the historical literature of the country." Paul Hamilton Hayne reviewed the history for *Russell's Magazine*, and concentrated on Simms' treatment of the nullification controversy. Hayne warned that Congress was still intent upon making the state a vassal of the North just as in nullification days. After having read the history, Hayne, like Simms, knew that secession was near. In conclusion, Hayne called Simms' book not only a splendid example of Southern unity but a detailed and relevant chronicle of the South's grievances within the Union. Other friends hoped that Simms would turn to more "profound researches," perhaps even to write of the state's early patriots. Any man who so cherished his own state's past, claimed the *Courier*, ought to write the biographies of John Rutledge, Christopher Gadsden, and Henry Laurens.[43]

Hammond wanted Simms to come to Washington, where his historical talents would be useful in the impending political struggles. He asked the writer to serve as adviser to Southern Congressmen and to receive the praise due him in his old age. Miles, Keitt, and Hammond thought it appropriate that Simms, while visiting the capital, should give a speech on George Washington at the unveiling of an equestrian statue of the great Southerner. But Simms declined. He was suffering from physical and mental exhaustion and did not believe that he could make the journey in such hectic times. Besides, he was busy writing long reviews and political columns in the *Mercury*. He was also finding himself politically occupied as adviser to and reconciler of opposing political views in South Carolina.[44]

Simms had finally persuaded himself of the inevitability of secession. Frightened at what he knew would be an irreversible decision, bewildered at the potential consequences of such an act, yet no longer pessimistic, Simms faced the last year of the Union with a renewed hope for positive action on the part of the entire South. He knew that South Carolina and its politicians would have to lead the South toward secession, and he was positive that the breakup of the national Democratic party would mean the end of the accursed Union. As a man of letters and one of the spokesmen for the state's radicals, Simms planned to continue his role as adviser, researcher, and writer for radical political leaders, while at the same time he worked to moderate the radical press and the immediate secessionists who could destroy South Carolina's position of leadership in the rest of the South. He realized that his state should appear to follow the South to secession, while it secretly provided the leadership and impetus for united Southern action against the election of a Radical Republican President. Simms' influence on Miles, Keitt, Hammond, the Rhetts, and even the moderate Orr was incalculable. He molded their rhetoric and helped to dictate their actions in those last hectic months which seemed so chaotic but in reality were the result of years of planned state action.[45]

After he had persuaded Hammond to return to Washington despite the Senator's feigned illnesses, Simms felt certain that his old friend would continue his moderate but persuasive pattern of organizing Southern opposition to the national Democratic party. But he was not convinced that his scholarly but impetuous young friend Miles would be able to maintain a moderate appearance while inwardly working for the state's radicals. Miles, who had begun to carry a weapon during Congressional sessions, had become increasingly sensitive to the dilatory behavior of his fellow Southerners. Privy to Christopher G. Memminger's secret negotiations with Virginia's leaders, Miles seemed constantly bothered by Memminger's requests for petty advice and was infuriated by his apparent failure to secure Virginia's definite commitment to follow the attempt of South Carolina's radicals to block Douglas' nomination.[46] To tone down Miles' radicalism, Simms wrote to him often, praising his behavior in Congress and assuring him of his growing political importance in South Carolina. He advised Miles to avoid writing about or discussing the upcoming Democratic convention in Charleston, and he convinced him that "the probabilities are that it will break up in a row—that there will be found certain irrepressible conflict there which no soft sawdering will reconcile." Therefore, Simms cautioned Miles against antagonizing more moderate Southerners before the time to strike.[47]

But by modifying Miles' public position, Simms subjected his friend to the Rhett faction's accusation that he was betraying his fellow radicals in Charleston. This charge became all the more dangerous when the city's more moderate politicians, who were Douglas supporters, began a campaign to replace Miles in Congress. Hammond had previously written Simms that Orr was also working to remove Miles from his seat in order to turn Charleston toward Douglas. Knowing that so much depended on the defeat of Douglas at the Democratic convention in Charleston, Simms tried to convince the Rhett faction to support Miles and to defend him from radical smears in the Charleston *Mercury*. The elder Rhett was won over and soon believed Miles a patriotic Southerner, if not an immediate secessionist. Rhett also promised to support Miles for re-election. Simms assured Miles that he would be re-elected, and he attempted to restore Miles' confidence by telling him that David F. Jamison, a powerful low-country radical and close political ally of Simms, had supported his recent speeches in Congress.[48] Through his active work for Miles, Simms contributed to the anti-Douglas feeling in Charleston.

Despite Simms' behind-the-scenes activities, the state seemed unprepared to disrupt the national Democratic party, since moderates were elected to the national convention. Many of the state's leaders either were apathetic to national politics or followed Orr in believing that Douglas was the best national candidate for the South.[49] Alabama, however, was instructed to follow that former South Carolina radical, William Lowndes Yancey, who vehemently opposed Douglas and planned to

challenge the weak fugitive slave plank in the Cincinnati platform. Since . Douglas was certain that the two-thirds vote
necessary to nominate him could not be secured, he hoped to
gain moderate Southern strength through first debating the
platform. There began a debate over the constitutionality of
protecting slavery in the territories. When it became obvious to
Yancey and his followers that the party would not endorse the
protection of slavery in the territories, they left the convention
and formed their own Southern bloc. The South Carolina
delegation, initially pledged to Douglas, followed Yancey, and
the Mississippi, Louisiana, Florida, Texas, and Arkansas
delegations also withdrew. The convention disbanded without
nominating a candidate. It voted to meet again in Baltimore,
where Douglas was certain to be nominated in the absence of
the Southern delegations.[50]

The walkout unified secessionist feeling in South
Carolina. At last it was obvious that the national Democratic
party would do nothing to protect slavery. Moderate Southern
states also realized that the ultra-radical South Carolinians
were merely followers of the radical lower South. Calm resignation had settled over the state and it was now time for the
radical elements to persuade the politicians and the people to
accept a Southern convention which would nominate a
Southern Presidential candidate.[51] Miles revealed that there
was no longer any hope for the South in the Union, and Simms
praised his statement, claiming that Southern unity had finally
been achieved. Simms declared that the popular will of a new
nationalism was reflected in the convention walkout, and he
urged political leaders to direct the momentum of national
feeling. He believed that if they acted quickly and called for a
Southern convention, they could achieve the permanent nationalism a third-party candidate would give the South.[52]

Richmond was chosen as the place for the Southern convention, and late in May, South Carolina held a convention in
Columbia to elect delegates to the Richmond convention.
Ostensibly the Richmond convention was called in hopes of
reuniting the national party, but many Southerners saw an opportunity to nominate their own candidate and to write their
own party platform. Since most of South Carolina's delegates
chose to support a united South, Rhett's attempt to push for im-

mediate secession was denied. Still, most of the South Carolina delegation felt that it was only a matter of time until the entire South seceded.[53]

As a reviewer and political correspondent for the *Mercury*, and as a public figure planning for future state strategy, Simms hoped that the Richmond convention would nominate a strong third-party candidate, permanently divide the Democratic party, and throw the election into the House of Representatives, thus assuring the election of a Southerner. When John C. Breckinridge and Joseph Lane were nominated for President and Vice President respectively, Simms was sure that they would carry the entire South. Calming the impatient Miles, Simms wrote that "we have done all for the present in bringing the Cotton States to act together, and in absorbing so many of the Slave States." As correspondent for the *Mercury*, Simms interviewed his friend Jamison and received a detailed account of the Richmond convention. Simms was certain that all Southerners, even Orr, now had to abandon the national party, "by the inevitable pressure of irrepressible causes and conflicts." However, he still refused openly to advocate immediate secession. Besides, he knew that a successful cooperationist South would eventually produce secession.[54]

Despite increasing debts and the loss of his Charleston house and many of his family possessions by fire, Simms took no time to feel sorry for himself.[55] His hopes of secession were too near, and he had to use his journalistic talents and his keen political mind in the struggle to expedite that event. He accused reformers of causing civil war and predicted that Seward would probably control the next President. Sarcastically, he asked what the fence-sitters Wise and Hunter of Virginia would do. He cautioned his friends on the *Mercury* to forget Douglas and to use the paper to attack the newly nominated Republican, Abraham Lincoln. By concentrating its forces on Lincoln, the *Mercury* could further emphasize the differences between North and South and could prepare the way for Lincoln's election, thus forcing the South to secede. With this strategy in mind he outlined a platform for Miles' use in Congress, concerning South Carolina's actions in the upcoming election. Under no circumstances should South Carolina appear to lead the South, he counseled. Long aware of the rest of the South's jealousy of South Carolina's aristocratic and radical leadership, he again advised Miles to persuade other Southerners of Lincoln's danger to the South, without appearing to push for immediate secession.[56]

As he gave political advice, Simms also maintained a continuous barrage of anti-Northern propaganda through his articles for the *Mercury*. Praising Carlyle's honesty and conscience in calling for the overthrow of "the false government, the false hero," he was not generous to Northern historical propagandists. He accused *The Century* magazine of political bigotry and bias against the South, and he pointed out that "abolitionism has completely taken possession of the Northern mind."[57] Following Hammond's dictum that cotton was king, Simms wrote that cotton had created a culture too precious to lose to fanaticism. Finally, Simms speculated on the effect of the loss of slavery to the South. He again raised the specter of abolitionist intervention, and he wondered how the North could countenance the actions of John Brown. He fixed on Congressman Salmon P. Chase and Wendell Phillips as outstanding examples of zealots who would not rest until slavery had been abolished. He warned Southerners that the "irrepressible conflict must come," and he called for the use of arms to defend slavery.[58]

In a long review of Thomas Prentice Kettell's *Southern Wealth and Northern Profits*, Simms finally argued the economic and political necessity of immediate secession. If the South would "shake off connection with the Union," he said, it would "rise to national independence and prosperity unexampled in history." He said that since the Northern majority in Congress robbed an agricultural minority of its resources, the South had to protect its economic future by leaving the Union. As a student of history he examined the bitter struggle to unify Italy, where the "systematic aggression by the trading capital city . . . dense in population, upon the scattered agricultural tribes" had ruined the rights of private systems and had destroyed a valuable agricultural culture. Pointing also to past events in the United States, he saw a pattern of increasing Northern greed, even gluttony. Again referring to his cultural argument, he pictured the excesses of Northern material culture; its luxury, pride, and prosperity increasingly sneered at Southern literature and art. Simms advocated a Southern confederacy for mutual protection and again blamed the South's condition on weak, corrupt political parties. The nation-savers who had gathered at Charleston and traitorously removed to Baltimore were "hucstering politicians," who used the nation for their own profit. Simms thought that it was time for the people of the South to direct its politicians to lead the South out of the Union. Simms closed his polemical article with praise for Kettell and a vicious attack on Hinton Rowan Helper. He advised Northerners to read Kettell in order to understand the necessity for Southern secession.[59]

Other events, which Simms would help to expedite, propelled South Carolina toward secession. Anticipating the upcoming elections of the legislature, Hammond cautiously told Simms that he would follow the legislature's lead. Simms had helped to prepare Hammond for disunion. Satisfied that South Carolina was ready to secede, alone if necessary, he too anticipated the election of a radical legislature. Held in mid-October, the results showed that almost the entire legislature was secessionist. In the session to choose electors for Breckinridge, Governor William Henry Gist, an up-country radical, asked the legislators to remain in session in order to take positive action in the event Lincoln was elected. He asked the legislators to prepare to call for a convention and was "constrained to say, that the only alternative left, . . . is the secession of South Carolina from the Federal Union." He promised that the long-desired cooperation of Southern states was imminent, and he assured the legislature that the entire South would immediately follow South Carolina into disunion. Relieved after years of effort, Simms was convinced that the moment Lincoln's election was certain, the legislature would vote to hold a state convention. To friends he finally counseled an all-out move toward secession, because he felt sure that the South's leading politicians supported Governor Gist's proposals.[60]

Along with other leading politicians, Simms founded a mysterious organization known as the "1860 Association." Its purposes were to ascertain the intentions of other Southern states and to circulate inflammatory secessionist propaganda. Simms prepared pamphlets for circulation throughout the

South, and he participated in discussions on the best means of arming the state. In Washington, Hammond was briefed on this radical organization and perhaps even suggested the organization of a militia known as the Minute Men. Simms also kept Keitt and Miles informed about the new leadership. Milledge Bonham, ex-governor and fire-eater, was solicited for the names and addresses of his political acquaintances for purposes of building a cadre of loyal secessionists. Simms and others hoped that "by placing in the hands of the *youth* and *genius* of the South thousands of these incendiary pamphlets," they would be prepared for quick action as soon as they knew the results of the Presidential election. The Association furthered the cause of immediate secession, and, as Simms told James Lawson, "Unionism is dead and Conservative Politicians dare not open their mouths." Yet there was a certain calm about Simms and the Association as, through the Committee of Safety and Vigilance, they carefully adhered to the law while they organized troops and support throughout the South.[61]

With the wells so poisoned, it had become only a matter of time before the election of Lincoln would force the delegates to decide just when the state would secede. On November 13, by a unanimous vote in both houses, the South Carolina legislature called a convention to meet on December 17.[62] Hoping to be a member of the convention, Simms busily organized friends in Barnwell to support immediate secession. Although the radicals were defeated in their attempts to dominate the elections for delegates to the convention, there was unanimity in South Carolina for the necessity for action. A conservative victory meant only that the state was eager to present a cautious yet forceful image to the rest of the South. Indicative of the mood of the state were Hammond's and Chesnut's resignations from the Senate. The action of Hammond, a hero of the moderates, completely disrupted their camp and created the impression that secession was imminent.[63]

Extremely agitated and at the same time relieved, Simms continued to write for the *Mercury* and to glory in the "new" South. His many poems, often poor, hurried pieces of doggerel, reflected both his mood and the mood of the state. He urged optimism, denying that the future held disaster. It was "the time for our rescue, or never," as he called on voices from the

dead to spur his followers. Realizing that the aggression would
never stop, he at first believed that there would be no war, but
he soon welcomed the catharsis of battle. In one poem Simms
sought to resurrect South Carolina's leadership during the
Revolution, in hopes of again having the state follow its
destiny. He lamented the quality of Northern periodicals, and
he encouraged Southerners to patronize their own writers. He
seemed pleased that the South would at last have to support
DeBow's Review and the *Southern Literary Messenger*, because they spoke for the South.[64]

To close friends in the North, Simms wrote of his love for
the South and the necessity of action. His ties with editors,
publishers, and literary friends had been strained to the limit,
and slowly he began to sever correspondence and connections
with his once-close Northern associates. He wrote James
Lawson that the Union was dead. He asked his friends to settle
his accounts and to pay all outstanding debts for his articles.
He suggested that Lawson take charge of his copyrights, fearing that his books would be pirated after secession. In his opinion, New York City had become a refuge for abolitionists, and
he no longer felt comfortable there.[65]

In the short time remaining before the convention met,
Simms wrote a long letter to his Northern friend and colleague,
John Jacob Bockee, explaining South Carolina's grievances
against the Union. Bitterly he accused his friends of trying to
save the Union because they had "fattened" on and needed the
South. Safety required the minority section to "cut asunder the
bonds that give you such a fearful power over us." He asked
Bockee why no Northern intellectuals had sympathized with
the South after John Brown's raid. Apparently the entire North
had become abolitionist. If slavery had caused friends to
separate, the South nevertheless could not exist without it,
Simms insisted. Since the South could never overcome the
united majority of Northern Democrats and Republican power,
plus the disloyalty of its old friends, Simms felt that it had no
choice but to secede in a united body. He cautioned Bockee
against weeping for the Union, since the country stood a better
chance of survival as two nations.[66]

Clear in conscience and proud of his own role, Simms sur-
veyed the work of the convention. His friend Jamison was its

president, and both men expected a unanimous vote for secession. It seemed that South Carolina had long ago made up its mind, assured of Southern support and loyalty.[67] The convention met in Columbia on December 17, but because of a smallpox epidemic it moved to Charleston. Voting seemed to be a formality, as organization for action was the prevailing topic. On December 20, a unanimous vote was given for secession. There was no debate, no discussion. The state convention of South Carolina made a plea for other Southern states to join it in a separate Confederacy, and declared South Carolina an independent commonwealth. Although Simms was not a delegate, his views were well represented by those members who rhetorically compared the North to Great Britain and reiterated the necessity of a Southern Union.[68]

The people of South Carolina were ecstatic. Citizens danced in the streets of staid Charleston, lit bonfires, and partied throughout the night. Writing in the *Mercury*, Simms praised the uniformity which vindicated conservative liberty over "arrogant and tyrannous oppressions." "South Carolina," he said, "has resumed her entire sovereign powers, and, unshackled, has become one of the nations of the earth." Finally, he exclaimed, "a mighty voice of great thoughts and great emotions spoke from the mighty throat of one people as a unit."[69] Back in Woodlands and vicariously reliving the activities in Charleston, he probably missed a very short review of his *Areytos* in the *Mercury*. But Rhett had captured the versatility of Simms. "The South," said Rhett, "owes a large debt to this, her voluminous and sectional writer," who was prepared "to lay down the pen for the sword."[70]

On December 21, 1860, the secession convention wrote an ordinance for a new oath of public office.[71] The oath called for complete allegiance to the state, and Simms, who had vehemently opposed the Test Oath of 1834, actively supported this added infringement upon civil liberties. The sensitive man of letters had traveled a long and tortuous route to 1860. He had influenced his fellow Southerners, but they also influenced him. As the South became an increasingly closed society, Simms, the artist in politics, had become the man for whom Calhoun had searched in 1850. From the one-time advocate of open debate, he came to support Calhoun's insistence upon

uniformity of opinion and political behavior in the South. His
writing and political actions helped to create that climate of
opinion, and Simms came to believe his own propaganda.
South Carolina and most of the South had achieved a Southern
consensus, a general agreement on the necessity for united action and a refusal to countenance opposition to its beliefs. In
helping to create and to perpetuate that consensus, Simms had
realized the artist's value for Southern society. But the result of
that consensus was civil war. His task was over; the rest of his
life, always devoted to his beloved South, would be one of
poverty and frustration.

NOTES

1. It is impossible to make a quantitative judgment as to Simms' influence as a political adviser. An analysis of the public speeches and political activities of South Carolina's leaders reflects Simms' literary phraseology, his philosophy of history, and his political views regarding national parties, Southern society, and the state's role in the course to secession. But these views were also expressed by political figures with whom Simms had absolutely no contact. It is also probably true that Simms envisioned his advisory role as being more significant than it actually was. For praise of Simms and his rewards, see *Courier*, March 5, Oct. 7, 1857, May 5, Oct. 19, Oct. 23, 1858, Feb. 21, 1860; *Mercury*, July 10, 1857, July 2, 1858; *Simms Letters*, 3: 502, 505, 4: 50, 53-54, 58, 64, 71, 75-76, 78, 82. To trace Simms' lecture tours, 1857-1860, see *Simms Letters*, 3: 484, 489-490, 491, 500-502; *Courier*, Jan. 20, Oct. 7, 10, 1857, Feb. 25, 1860; *Mercury*, Jan. 20, March 16, 1857; Simms to Lawson, March 31, 1857, Simms to Levert, March 15, 1857, Charles Carroll Simms Papers.

2. *Simms Letters*, 3: 513, 520, 4: 11; *Courier*, March 10, Feb. 17, Oct. 17, 1857; *Mercury*, Apr. 27, Nov. 2, 1857; *Russell's Magazine* 2 (Nov. 1857): 153, 154-155, 159-160; (Dec. 1857): 242; 1 (Apr. 1857): introduction; 3 (June 1858): 193-206; Simms to Joseph Carels, Jan. 25, 1858, Charles Carroll Simms Papers. See also Kate Harbes Becker, *Paul Hamilton Hayne: Life and Letters* (Belmost, N. C., 1951), pp. 16, 6-7; Madeleine B. Stern, "John Russell: 'Lord John' of Charleston," *NCHR* 26 (July 1949): 286, 292.

3. For Simms' interest in the concept of leadership, see *Courier*, Apr. 1, 1858; *Mercury*, Feb. 10, June 16, 1858; "Heroes and Hero-Worship," *Russell's Magazine*, 3 (Apr. 1858): 35; "Arcadia," 3 (Sept. 1858): 507; *Simms Letters*, 3: 506-507; Hammond to Col. John Cunningham, June 26, 1857, Hammond to Simms, Aug. 13, 1857, Hammond Papers, Library of Congress.

4. *Mercury*, July 14, Oct. 5, Dec. 1, 1857; *Russell's Magazine* 1 (Apr. 1857): 80; Hammond to Editors of Charleston *Mercury*, Oct. 2, 1857, Hammond Diary, May 6, Sept. 29, Dec. 9, 1857, Hammond Papers, University of South Carolina; Simms to Hammond, Nov. 10, Dec. 12, 1857, Hammond to Simms, Dec. 19, 30, 1857, Hammond Papers, Library of Congress; Francis W. Pickens to Beaufort T. Watts, Oct. 24, 1857, Hammond to Watts, Dec. 15, 1857, MSS, Beaufort Taylor Watts Papers, South Caroliniana Library, University of South Carolina; Pickens to G. N. Trudeau, Pickens Papers, Duke University; James Hamilton to Whitemarsh B. Seabrook, Oct. 9, 1857, MSS, James Hamilton Papers, South Caroliniana Library, University of South Carolina.

5. *Simms Letters* 3: 518; 4: 3, 4, 10, 11, 33, 34; Hammond to Harry Hammond, Jan. 14, 1858, F. W. Capers to Hammond, Feb. 12, 1858, Hammond Papers, University of South Carolina; Trescot to Miles, Feb. 7, 1858, Miles Papers; see also Roy Franklin Nichols, *Disruption of American Democracy*, pp. 159-180.

6. *Simms Letters*, 4: 16-17, 18, 19, 20, 22, 30.

7. Ibid., 4: 35; Hammond to Simms, Jan. 20, 1858, Hammond Papers, Library of Congress; also see Merritt, *James Henry Hammond* pp. 116-117.

8. *Simms Letters*, 4: 16, 22, 23-29, 32; Hammond to Harry Hammond, Apr. 11, 1858, Hammond Papers, University of South Carolina; Hammond to Simms, Jan. 28, 1858, Hammond Papers, Library of Congress; also see Chauncey S. Boucher, *South Carolina and the South on the Eve of Secession, 1852 to 1860* (St. Louis, 1919), pp. 102-104; Roy Franklin Nichols, "The Kansas-Nebraska Act: A Century of Historiography," *MVHR* 43 (Sept. 1956): 187-212. The most thorough study of the subject is still Allan Nevins, *Ordeal of the Union* 4 vols. (New York, 1947-1950), 2: 250-304.

9. *Appendix to the Congressional Globe*, 35th Cong., 1 Sess., Senate, pp. 68-72; "Are Working Men Slaves?" undated MSS in Hammond Papers, Library of Congress. (I have elaborated

on Hammond's comments to illustrate how similar his views were to Simms'.)

10. *Courier*, March 9, 1858; O. P. Fitzsimmons to Hammond, March 17, 1858, H. R. Cook to Hammond, March 17, 1858, Hammond Papers, University of South Carolina; John C. Cochran to Miles, March 31, 1858, W. H. Trescot to Miles, May 2, 1858, James H. Taylor to Miles, Apr. 8, 1858, Miles Papers. In 1860, many Southerners were still praising Hammond's speech; see "Troup" (I. W. Hayne), *To the People of the South: Senator Hammond and the Tribune* (Charleston, 1860), pp. 3, 5, 6, 7.

11. *Russell's Magazine* 3 (Apr. 1858): 96; *Simms Letters* 4: 41, 44; Hammond to Simms, March 5, May 3, 1858, Hammond Papers, Library of Congress.

12. I. W. Hayne to W. P. Miles, Apr. 17, 1858, Samuel W. Tupper to Miles, Apr. 19, 1858, I. W. Hayne to Hammond, Apr. 21, 1858, Miles Papers; *Simms Letters* 4: 56, 58; Hammond to Simms, Feb. 7, March 22, 24, 1858.

13. *Simms Letters*, 4: 46-47, 48-51; Hammond to Simms, Apr. 5, 1858, Hammond Papers, Library of Congress; also see White, *Robert Barnwell Rhett*, pp. 145-146.

14. *Mercury*, July 28, 1858; *Courier*, Oct. 19, 1858; *Simms Letters*, 4: 75-76, 82; Hammond to Simms, May 21, 1858, Hammond Papers, Library of Congress.

15. *Simms Letters*, 4: 65-66; Hammond to Simms, June 20, 1858, Hammond Papers, Library of Congress; see Merritt, *James Henry Hammond* p. 121; Philip Shriver Klein, *President James Buchanan, a Biography* (University Park, Pa., 1962), pp. 318-320.

16. Simms to Hammond, June 26, July 10, 16, 1858, Hammond Papers, Library of Congress.

17. *Simms Letters*, 4: 65-72, 77.

18. Ibid., pp. 79-80.

19. *Courier*, July 23, 1858; Simms to Hammond, June 11, 1858, Hammond to Simms, Aug. 13, 1858, Hammond Papers, Library of Congress; also see Boucher, *South Carolina and the South*, p. 122; Merritt, *James Henry Hammond*, pp. 122-124; Ronald Takaki, "The Movement to Reopen the African Slave Trade in South Carolina," *SCHM* 66 (Jan. 1965): 51-52, 47-48.

20. *Courier*, Aug. 5, 1858; *Mercury*, July 26, Aug. 9, 1858; Milledge Bonham to Brother [?], Aug. 14, 1858, MSS, Milledge Bonham Papers, South Caroliniana Library, University of South Carolina.

21. *Simms Letters*, 4: 84-86, 94-95.

22. *Courier*, Sept. 4, 1858; Hammond to Marcellus Hammond, Oct. 22, 1858, Hammond Papers, University of South Carolina.

23. *Simms Letters*, 4: 88-90.

24. William Gilmore Simms, *The Cassique of Kiawah* (New York, 1859), dedication page; *Simms Letters*, 4: 87, 93-95; W. P. Miles to A. P. Aldrich, Oct. 27, 1858, Miles Papers.

25. Why Hammond refused to give a forceful address is inexplicable. That some scholars have claimed Hammond's speech reflected Unionist sentiment shows an absence of thoughtful textual analysis. See James Henry Hammond, *Speech of . . . delivered at Barnwell Court House, October 29th, 1858* (Charleston, 1858), pp. 3-5, 7, 8-9, 10, 11, 14-15, 16; also see Merritt, *James Henry Hammond*, pp. 124-126; Laura A. White, "The National Democrats in South Carolina, 1852-1860," *South Atlantic Quarterly* 28 (1929): 380; Charles W. Ramsdell, "The Natural Limits of Slavery Expansion," *MVHR* 16 (Sept. 1929): 151-171; Nichols, *Disruption of American Democracy*, p. 326.

26. *Mercury*, Nov. 2, 1858; *Courier*, Jan. 24, 1859; Trescot

to Miles, Feb. 8, 1859, Miles Papers; Hammond Diary, Apr. 16, 1861, Major Benjamin Alvord to Marcellus Hammond, Jan. 3, 1858 (misdated; should be 1859), Hammond Papers, University of South Carolina; *The Regina Coeli, Correspondence between the Hon. James H. Hammond and John H. B. Latrobe, Esq.* (Baltimore, 1858), pp. 4-8, 36-37.

27. Hammond to Miles, Nov. 5, 17, 23, 1858, Miles Papers.

28. No doubt Simms had a great deal to do with bringing the Rhetts around to his view on Hammond's position. See *Mercury*, Nov. 2, 1858, Feb. 11, 1859; Simms to Hammond, Nov. 22, 1858; Hammond Papers, Library of Congress; *Simms Letters*, 4: 97.

29. Hammond to Simms, Dec. 15, 1858, Hammond Papers, Library of Congress; also see Merritt, *James Henry Hammond*, p. 128; Boucher, *South Carolina and the South*, pp. 122-124; White, "National Democrats in South Carolina," p. 380.

30. Hammond Scrapbook, 1858-1859, March 26, 1859, Hammond to Simms, Jan. 1, 1859, Simms to Hammond, Jan. 10, March 2, 1859, Hammond Papers, Library of Congress; *Mercury*, Apr. 12, 1859; *Courier*, Apr. 8, 1859; I. W. Hayne to W. P. Miles, March 10, 1859, Miles Papers; Miles to Trescot, Feb. 8, 1859, MSS, William Porcher Miles Papers, South Caroliniana Library, University of South Carolina; *Simms Letters*, 4: 118-119; Francis W. Pickens to M. L. Bonham, Bonham Papers.

31. Hammond to Simms, July 30, 1859, Simms to Hammond, Aug. 24, 1859, Hammond Papers, Library of Congress; Wallace, *Political Life and Services of Robert Barnwell Rhett*, pp. 5, 45-47.

32. Simms to Hammond, Sept. 18, 1859, James L. Orr to Hammond, Sept. 17, 1859, Hammond Papers, Library of Congress; *Simms Letters*, 4: 176; also see D. H. Hamilton to Miles, Dec. 9, 1859, Miles Papers, University of North Carolina. Extremely valuable are the Milledge L. Bonham Papers; see W. E. Martin to Bonham, Dec. 27, 1859.

33. *Mercury*, May 21, July 16, Aug. 4, Oct. 1, 1859; *Courier*, June 14, 1859; Hammond to Simms, Feb. 26, 1859, Simms to Hammond, Aug. 24, 1859, Hammond Papers, Library of Congress; *Simms Letters*, 4: 156, 165, 168; *SLM* 28 (May 1859): 370; *Russell's Magazine* 5 (Aug. 1859): 392-393; 6 (Nov. 1859): 76-79, 175; see also Simms to William J. Rivers, June 13, Sept. 12, 1859, Charles Carroll Simms Papers; David Morley McKeithan, ed., *A Collection of Hayne Letters* (Austin, Texas, 1944), pp. 85-86.

34. *Cassique of Kiawah*, dedication, p. 7; *Courier*, May 17, 1859; *Mercury*, June 14, 1859.

35. *Cassique of Kiawah*, pp. 14, 24, 92-94, 192, 242, 291, 307, 432-433, 438, 455, 587, 600; for the historical setting see M. Eugene Sirmans, *Colonial South Carolina; a Political History, 1663-1763* (Chapel Hill, 1966), especially chap. 3.

36. *Cassique of Kiawah*, pp. 114, 111, 108, 134, 428, 429, 597.

37. *Courier*, July 14, Sept. 13, 1859.

38. *Simms Letters*, 4: 181-182, 186; John Russell to Simms, Oct. 14, 1860, Charles Carroll Simms Papers.

39. Simms, *History of South Carolina* (all subsequent references are to the 1860 edition), pp. 6, 7, 391; Gabriel Manigault, *The Signs of the Times* (New York, n.d.), p. 9.

40. *History of S. C.*, p. 391. (In the *Mercury*, Aug. 10, 1858, Simms praised Bancroft for his fairness to all sections in the Revolution. By 1860 even Bancroft's objective tone was offensive to Simms.)

41. Ibid., pp. 430-431; Manigault, *The Signs of the Times*, p. 58.

42. *History of S. C.*, p. 436.

43. *Courier*, July 14, Sept. 13, 1859; *Russell's Magazine* 6 (Jan. 1860): 375-376; (March 1860): 557.

44. Hammond to Simms, Jan. 14, 1860, Hammond Papers, Library of Congress; *Simms Letters*, 4: 185-188; Simms to Lawson, Feb. 18, 1860, Charles Carroll Simms Papers; *Mercury*, Jan. 17, 20, Feb. 25, May 25, 28, June 26, 1860; see also Ollinger Crenshaw, "The Speakership Contest of 1859-1860," *MVHR* 29 (Dec. 1942): 337.

45. In this manner Simms' own political views and the sentiments of his writings well reflected the prevailing cautious secessionist view in South Carolina.

46. *Courier*, Feb. 18, 1860; *Mercury*, Feb. 7, 1860; C. Fitzsimmons to Hammond, Feb. 24, 1860; Hammond to Dr. H. Block, Jan. 22, 1860, Hammond Papers, University of South Carolina; Hammond to Beaufort T. Watts, Dec. 6, 1859, Watts Papers; Lewis M. Hatch to W. P. Miles, Dec. 6, 1859, D. H. Hamilton to Miles, Dec. 9, 1859, Jan. 23, 1860, Christopher G. Memminger to Miles, Dec. 27, 1859, Jan. 3, 9, 30, 1860, Gov. William Gist to Miles, Dec. 20, 1859, Miles Papers, University of North Carolina.

47. *Simms Letters*, 4: 193-194, 204; Dwight L. Dumond, ed., *Southern Editorials on Secession* (New York, 1931), pp. 67-69.

48. *Simms Letters*, 4: 193, 194, 204, 210, 211; Hammond to Simms, Apr. 3, 8, 1860, Hammond Papers, Library of Congress; Robert Barnwell Rhett, Jr. to Miles, Apr. 17, 1860, Miles Papers, University of North Carolina.

49. Trescot to Miles, Feb. 22, 1860, Miles Papers, University of North Carolina; see Lillian A. Kibler, "Unionist Sentiment in South Carolina in 1860," *JSH* 9 (Aug. 1938): 349; Edward G. Mason, "A Visit to South Carolina in 1860," *Atlantic Monthly* 53 (Feb. 1884): 247.

50. *Courier*, Apr. 21, 1860; *Mercury*, Jan. 14, 1860; R. B. Rhett to Miles, March 28, 1860, D. H. Hamilton to Miles, Apr. 4, 1860, Miles Papers, University of North Carolina; Spann Hammond to Hammond, Apr. 21, 1860, Hammond Papers, University of South Carolina; *The Official Proceedings of the Democratic National Convention, Held in 1860, at Charleston*

and Baltimore (Cleveland, 1860), pp. 41, 56; see also Austin L. Venable, "The Conflict between the Douglas and Yancey Forces in the Charleston Convention," *JSH* 8 (May 1942): 226, 234, 237; J. Jeffrey Auer, ed., *Antislavery and Disunion, 1858-1861; Studies in the Rhetoric of Compromise and Conflict* (New York, 1963), pp. 175-178; John Cochrane, "The Charleston Convention," *Magazine of American History* 14 (July-Dec. 1885): 148-153.

51. See *Mercury*, May 1, 21, June 6, 1860; *Courier*, May 2, 1860.

52. *Simms Letters*, 4: 221; also see Ollinger Crenshaw, *The Slave States in the Presidential Election of 1860* (New York, 1945), pp. 198-227.

53. *Proceedings of the State Democratic Convention, May 30-31, 1860* (Charleston, 1860), pp. 4-6, 16, 17, 23-24, 31-33, 40-42, 49, 55-59, 75-76, 84-85, 87; also see Trescot to Miles, May 8, 12, 1860, Henry D. Lesesne to Miles, May 12, 1860, D. H. Hamilton to Miles, May 29, 1860, Miles Papers, University of North Carolina; Gov. Gist to Watts, May 6, 1860, Watts Papers; Ashmore to Orr, May 23, 1860, Orr-Patterson Papers; Hammond letter to *Courier*, May 15, 1860, in Scrapbook, 1858-1859, Hammond Papers, Library of Congress.

54. *Mercury*, June 30, 1860; *Simms Letters* 4: 221-226, 227-228, 232; Hammond to Simms, July 10, 1860, Hammond Papers, Library of Congress.

55. *Simms Letters*, 4: 215, 219.

56. Ibid., 4: 231-234; Hammond to John Cunningham, Aug. 1, 1860, Hammond Papers, Library of Congress; *Mercury*, Apr. 11, 1860.

57. *Mercury*, May 7, June 22, 27, 1860. (Simms' review columns in the *Mercury* are examples of the growing excitement in South Carolina.)

58. *Mercury*, May 23, 1860. For discussion of these fears, see Steven A. Channing, *Crisis of Fear* (New York, 1970).

59. *Simms Letters*, 4: 214; *Mercury*, June 20, 1860.

60. See John McGeehee to Hammond, Oct. 5, 1860, Miles to Hammond, Aug. 15, 1860, Hammond to I. W. Hayne, Sept. 19, 1860, Hammond to Simms, Sept. 23, Oct. 23, 1860, Simms to Hammond, Oct. 16, 1860, Hammond Papers, Library of Congress; *Simms Letters*, 4: 245, 249-250, 258; *Message 1, Executive Dept., Columbia, S. C., Nov. 5, 1860*, MSS, W. H. Gist Papers, South Caroliniana Library, University of South Carolina; also see Charles Edward Cauthen, "South Carolina's Decision to Lead the Secessionist Movement," *NCHR* 18 (Oct. 1941): 362, 365.

61. *Simms Letters*, 4: 268; Townshend to Bonham, Oct. 16, 1860, W. M. Tennent to Bonham, Oct. 10, 1860, Bonham Papers; Lawrence M. Keitt to Miles, Oct. 30, 1860, Miles Papers, University of North Carolina; C. Fitzsimmons to Hammond, Oct. 19, 1860, Hammond Papers, University of South Carolina.

62. *Mercury*, Nov. 10, 1860; *Simms Letters*, 4: 263; Cauthen, "South Carolina's Decision," p. 372.

63. *Simms Letters*, 4: 261, 265, 281-282; *Mercury*, Oct. 16, Nov. 21, 30, 1860; *Courier*, Nov. 7, 1860; Benjamin Alvord to Marcellus Hammond, Nov. 23, 1860, C. Fitzsimmons to Hammond, Oct. 19, Nov. 29, 1860, Hammond Diary, pp. 163-172, Hammond Papers, University of South Carolina; Hammond to Bonham, Oct. 3, 1860, Bonham Papers; Watts to Hammond, Dec. 1, 1860, Watts Papers; Hammond to Simms, Nov. 12, 1860, Simms to Hammond, Dec. 5, 1860, Hammond to Marcellus Hammond, Nov. 12, 1860, Hammond Papers, Library of Congress; Simms to Lawson, Dec. 5, 1860, Charles Carroll Simms Papers; see also F. J. Moses, "How South Carolina Seceded, by the Private Secretary of Gov. Pickens of South Carolina," *The Nickell Magazine* (Dec. 1897), 349. (There is still much confusion on Hammond's reasons for resigning from the

Senate, mostly caused by later entries in his diary. I hope
in a future study of Hammond to shed further light on this
matter.)

64. *Mercury*, Sept. 19, Nov. 8, 21, Dec. 19, 1860; *Courier*,
Sept. 27, 1860.

65. *Simms Letters*, 4: 249, 250, 252, 260, 280.

66. Ibid., 4: 287, 288, 291, 293, 296, 297-298, 300-302,
304; the *Mercury* printed Simms' letter in full on Jan. 17,
1861, perhaps to further stir action in South Carolina. See also
Nichols, *Disruption of American Democracy*, Pt. V.

67. *Courier*, Nov. 6, 26, 27, Dec. 13, 1860; Ashmore to
Miles, Nov. 15, 1860, Miles Papers, University of North
Carolina; M. C. Butler to Bonham, Dec. 11, 1860, Gist to Bonham, Dec. 6, 1860, Pickens to Bonham, Dec. 5, 1860, and
most damaging, E. S. Shuter to Bonham, Dec. 13, 1860 (Shuter
was already preparing to celebrate South Carolina's secession),
Bonham Papers.

68. *Simms Letters*, 4: 308-311; Miles to Bonham, Dec. 19,
1860, Bonham Papers; *Journal of the Public Proceedings of
the People of South Carolina, Held in 1860-61. Together with
the Ordinance Adopted* (Charleston, 1860), pp. 5, 8-12, 55-56
(hereafter cited as *Convention Journal, 1860-61*); *The Address
of the People of South Carolina, Assembled in Convention, to
the People of the Slaveholding States of the United States*
(Charleston, 1860), pp. 3-16; see also Wooster, "An Analysis
of the Membership of the Secession Conventions of the Lower
South," pp. 362-368; T. Harry Williams, *Romance and
Realism in Southern Politics* (Athens, Ga., 1961), p. 16.

69. *Mercury*, Dec. 21, 1860; *Courier*, Dec. 21, 1860.

70. *Mercury*, Dec. 22, 1860.

71. *Convention Journal, 1860-61*, p. 59.

Epilogue: The Last Years

ALTHOUGH SIMMS' long-sought goal of Southern nationalism was achieved, his intellectual and political odyssey was not completed. There was a new Confederacy to preserve and perpetuate, and failing that, the South would have to accommodate to the new industrial world. His last poverty-stricken years were trying. Closest friends, North and South, either died or grew too senile to be of service and comfort. Still active as writer and editor, he published little of lasting literary value, but much of social and political use to the new South. Until he died, Simms remained the intellectual as public man, utilizing his literary and political talents to rebuild the South, retaining much of the past but also assisting in forging a new hope for his section within the Union.

Simms was enthusiastic over secession, and he wrote often to Miles and Jamison of the need to prepare for war. Confident the South could defend itself, he devised plans for protecting Charleston and its offshore fortifications and for capturing Fort Sumter. In collaboration with the fire-eating Rhett family, Simms wrote detailed articles which explained the need to control Fort Sumter. The fort had become a matter of pride, and Simms' *Mercury* articles contributed to the agitation for attacking the fort and beginning the war. Certain that the South could dictate peace terms if it took the offensive, he used the

Mercury to urge the Confederate Congress to establish a permanent central government and to prepare for immediate war.[1]

But Simms soon grew bored with military planning, and frustrated over his own lack of recognition. He resumed his writing of political literature, and he urged young writers to record the war's drama. His wartime fiction, composed of poems for the *Mercury* and the *Southern Literary Messenger*, and a short story, "Paddy McGann," for the Richmond-based *Southern Illustrated News*, could not measure up to his prodigious output of pre-war days. "Paddy McGann" sang the praises of the victory at Vicksburg, and the simple poems called for courage in the face of the constant Northern shelling of Charleston. Simms used the spire of St. Michael's church as the symbol of Confederate desire to continue the war; as long as it stood, the Confederacy would last. Besides using literature as inspiration, Simms helped to establish a publishing house in Richmond. He also planned a library for the Confederacy which would house the biographies, letters, and manuscripts of the South's leading political and literary figures. But as paper grew scarce and people found little opportunity to read, Simms sensed that few cared about a tired and apparently useless old man and his work.[2]

He was not entirely correct. When Woodlands burned early in 1862, leaving the family without shelter, friends in Columbia and Charleston raised $3,600 to help rebuild Simms' home and library. They even claimed that, had it not been for the strain of war, the whole state would have joined in the tribute to "your great public worth." His friends considered the money only a "moderate installment of the large debt which the State has so long owed." Simms humbly replied that he was now confident that he had not "labored in vain" for the South's affection and esteem. Stating that he would continue to merit their confidence by devoting his talents to the Confederate cause, he vowed to rebuild Woodlands.[3]

Although he was rewarded with high acclaim and even appointed to the prestigious Board of Visitors of the Columbia Military Academy, Simms seemed unable to stand the pressures of wartime privation and the fears that his son "Gilly" would die in battle. In September 1863, his wife died. She had been a simple woman who had borne many children, tolerated her husband's overbearing personality and mercurial mind, and outwardly played a small part in his life. But Simms missed her strength and comfort. As he grieved, he began to reflect on his wasted life. He wrote little, neglected his precious correspondence, and even refused to keep up with political events. His neighbor and close friend, Alfred Proctor Aldrich, found him morose, often forgetting the drift of an argument or repeating himself. Simms grew impatient and snapped at friends who did not immediately agree with him. He wrote Hammond of his dissatisfaction with Jefferson Davis, predicted widespread famine, and was certain that the Confederate government would tax the people to death. His instability after losing his wife and his fears of impending military defeat often drove him to lament his years of service to an ungrateful homeland.[4]

But for too many years Simms had been conditioned to support his section. Before long, during a long visit with Hammond, he again argued politics and military strategy. He persuaded John Russell to locate a set of Horace Walpole's letters and writings for Hammond, and he encouraged his friend to record his lifetime of political observations. Although Simms was certain that Grant and Sherman would soon invade South Carolina, he tried to calm Hammond's growing fears of defeat. He soothed Hammond after the death of the Senator's mother, and he encouraged Hammond to take a more active role in public affairs. Simms persuaded Hammond to give corn to the government, and he convinced him not to oppose the Confederate Impressment Act. Like Hammond, he knew that many of the local government officials were corrupt, but the army had to be fed. He cautioned Hammond that true Southerners must sacrifice their selfish economic interests on behalf of the cause. That was how Simms had always lived and how he expected Hammond to live.[5]

Remaining actively involved in local affairs was all the two old secessionists could do. They were too enfeebled to serve in the army. Mostly they watched old friends, such as David F. Jamison, die of infirmities and disappointment.[6] When Hammond finally died late in 1864 after years of chronic if not psychosomatic illness, Simms lost his closest friend. Hammond had been Simms' subsidizer during lean years and

one of his few confidants. Simms was completely discouraged
over the loss of such a valued and able friend, yet he consoled
Hammond's family and gave them hope for a victorious South.
In an obituary for the *Mercury*, he paid tribute to Hammond's
genius and attempted to inspire the present generation to continue the conflict which Hammond had helped to cause. Simms
also took charge of Hammond's unpublished writings, and prepared one of the panels for Hammond's vault. His poem, a
eulogy to the dead hero, contained all of Simms' own frustrations and reflected his search for leadership. Above all, he used
Hammond's death as an occasion to revitalize South Carolinians by urging them on to more heroic efforts.[7]

Even Simms knew that Hammond's death, like his
resignation from the Senate, spelled a turning point in Southern
affairs. Hearing of Sherman's march, he prepared for the inva-
sion of South Carolina. While he was visiting in Columbia,
stragglers from Sherman's army burned Woodlands as they
pillaged their way through the heart of the low country. His
library, an invaluable collection of thirty years, went up in
flames. Worst of all, Sherman's army, probably by accident,
burned the beautiful capital city of Columbia. Most of the city
was destroyed and over half its population robbed of their personal possessions.[8]

As the surrender of the Confederate army seemed imminent, Governor A. G. Magrath commissioned Simms to
write a pamphlet describing the burning of Columbia. It was
first published in booklet form and later in installments in the
Columbia *Daily Phoenix*. *The Sack and Destruction of Columbia* graphically portrayed the heroic defense of the city and the
terrible destruction caused by Sherman's army. In his pamphlet
Simms sought to immortalize the South's struggles. He wanted
"to make the melancholy record of our wretchedness as complete as possible." Claiming that Sherman was irresponsible,
Simms was certain that the general had intended to burn
Charleston as well, but the horrors of Columbia had stopped
him. The account was no ordinary analysis of a military defeat.
Simms wanted future generations to remember Sherman as the
hated Yankee who helped to unite the South, even in defeat.[9]

To many, surrender meant final disillusion. To Simms, defeat meant that the South must resume its place in the Union

while preserving its sectional image. During the war he had felt useless and inactive; after the war he again became active in politics, and he was appointed to a select Committee of Twenty-One to study the best means of South Carolina's returning to the Union. His Barnwell neighbors wanted to elect him to the state constitutional convention, but he declined because of his many debts and ill health. But despite his familial obligations, he promised to serve if elected to the state legislature.[10]

Simms resumed one of his favorite occupations as editor of the Columbia *Phoenix*, a tri-weekly newspaper designed to inform South Carolinians of the actions of the new pro-Northern government. Although it was difficult to find a working press, the proper type, and sufficient paper, in the short time Simms was associated with the *Phoenix* he made it a political organ to help revive Columbia from its ashes. Calling for united effort to rebuild the city, Simms said there was no place for despondency in a new South "superior even to the past." Simms attacked his former friend, Governor Benjamin F. Perry, for his pro-Northern sentiments and his inability to pay the salaries of state legislators. Although the government seemed destitute and the people seemed demoralized over defeat, Simms urged moderation and respect for the new legal system. He called for more constables to arrest pillagers in the city, and he asked citizens to prepare for the future. When Simms was forced to give up the newspaper late in 1865, he was confident that he had accomplished much toward restoring the city as a viable community.[11]

While he managed to overcome the sickness of self-pity which plagued many South Carolinians, his own plight seemed to worsen. Those were no times for a man of letters. He rarely wrote fiction, since no publisher could afford to pay for his work. To make ends meet, he had to sell most of his personal belongings and books. He traveled to New York to visit old friends, from whom he received surprisingly warm receptions. He became a New York correspondent for the *Courier*, solicited writers to chronicle the lost cause, and above all searched for a way to make a living through his writing. Often bitter and morose, Simms still pursued his avowed mission of resurrecting Southern letters.[12]

But Simms' despondency over the poor state of letters in the nation seldom lasted for long. When he returned from New York, he moved in with his daughter Chevillette Roach in Charleston and began a joint editorship with Henry Timrod of the *South Carolinian*. Although Simms did most of the work, there was little pay, and he had other projects on his mind.[13] During the war he had collected poems published in Confederate newspapers and magazines, and in his spare time at the *South Carolinian* office he put them into an anthology called *War Poetry of the South*. Although the mediocre poetry sold poorly, it proved to be one of the finest collections of its type. Like his newspaper work, his editing had specific political significance. Simms collected the poems because they exemplified the unity which could be achieved through re-creating the national feeling of the Confederacy. He wanted to make certain that the South would never forget its sacrifices.[14]

To this end, Simms proposed to return to writing history. His library was almost gone, and he had been forced to sell his valuable collection of Revolutionary manuscripts to the Long Island Historical Society. Still, he asked close friends for Congressional publications, contemplated a work on Texas' relations with Mexico, and actually started biographies of George Washington and James Henry Hammond. But aside from important review articles of historical works for the Charleston *Courier*, he published only an introduction to *The Army Correspondence of Colonel John Laurens*, a heroic casualty of the Revolutionary War. Again Simms searched for a symbolic hero, and again he used history to make statements about the horrors of Reconstruction in his own time. Comparing the British occupation of Charleston to Northern occupation during Reconstruction, he praised Laurens as a man who never knew when he was beaten. Simms called Laurens "the Bayard of America", and he again called for South Carolinians to be worthy of their ancestors.[15]

More important as examples of historical propaganda than the *Army Correspondence* were the many book reviews which Simms published in the Charleston *Courier* during the last years of his life. Predictably furious at the puritanical anti-Southern attitudes of George Bancroft, once an admired friend, Simms was also quite critical of Southern historians. Reviewing

Cornelia Spencer's *The Last Ninety Days of the War in North Carolina*, he accused the author of making worthless allusions to colonial times. Simms himself believed there was no use to look back eighty years while the "memory of five or six years is almost enough for the best and bravest of us all." In his review of George T. Curtis' *Life of Webster* he explored the importance of Calhoun to the postwar South, and in an evaluation of William H. Trescot's excellent study of J. Johnston Pettigrew, Simms heaped venom on the headstrong tendencies of his own age.[16]

Except for those digressions, Simms concentrated almost entirely upon the Civil War and its causes. Reviewing a life of Jefferson Davis, he diplomatically reserved judgment on the Confederate President until the years had mellowed the resentments. Nevertheless Simms exploited the propagandistic advantages of the martyr to the lost cause and attacked Reconstruction as a barbarous plot by Northern politicians to profit financially from the destitute South. As in the past, he fixed on one man to serve as a symbol for the future. In his column "The Book Table," Simms wrote a lengthy study commemorating the death of Stonewall Jackson. He wanted the entire South to celebrate that day and to make certain that "Rome must know the value of her own."[17]

Most important of all, Simms revealed much about himself in his book reviews on the coming of the Civil War. He wanted the South to state its opinion as to the causes of the war and the causes of the Confederacy's defeat as well. Yet he found Edward F. Pollard's history of the war inaccurate and disfigured by spite and anger. An impartial study, he was convinced, would vindicate the South and epitomize the lost cause. But in describing the coming of the war, Simms was less sanguine. He, who had once believed that the war was inevitable, was convinced that if the North had observed the constitutional rights of the South, there would have been no war. Reviewing John Esten Cooke's *Wearing the Grey*, Simms disclosed his own weakness: "We have failed to establish the cause, but we must not fail to give a true account of it," he claimed. His job was to prove to the South's youth that their fathers were not traitors but honest patriots, as he sought to counteract the Northern school books forced upon South

Carolinians by a radical legislature.[18] No doubt Simms' historical essays helped Southerners to regain confidence. But his unwillingness to face his previous views of the need for war and to chart his own historical role in a study of its causation revealed either his deep shame or his helplessness in observing the consequences of what he had helped to instigate.

Although historical propaganda occupied much of Simms' time, he also reviewed many works of Southern writers, encouraged young authors, wrote some fiction, and constantly promoted the publication of new magazines "in order that *the South shall have an organ*" for literary pursuits. He helped organize a Southern University Publishing Company in order to present facts about the South, wrote for little-known magazines such as the *New Eclectic Magazine*, and promoted the prestigious *Southern Review*. He wanted magazines in "all true Southern homes, and families; that the sons and daughters, to whom the future hopes and destinies of the South, will need to be confided, may be possessed of the necessary argument, on all the subjects which are precious to us now, in the day of our denial." Simms also wrote articles, often without pay, for the *Old Guard*. For him, this was the finest magazine in the South, and the most tenacious defender of the rights of the states. But it was the Charleston-based *Nineteenth Century* which held a special place for Simms, since he was responsible for its formation and its interest in South Carolina culture.[19] Periodical literature seemed important to him only in terms of its political contributions to the protection of Southern rights in a Northern-controlled society.

Simms produced three novels published serially following the war. One of them, *Voltmeier*, displayed some insight into Simms' own thoughts in his last years. Set in the hill country along the North Carolina border, *Voltmeier* on the surface was a mere adventure story, borrowing heavily from the themes of the border romances. The novel seemed to be a cathartic, giving Simms the opportunity to air his grievances against petty politicians and to attack the foolish attempts of the corrupt Reconstruction legislature at democratic government. In writing a tale about a smuggler and counterfeiter, Simms bared his own inner torments and attempted to work out his personal guilt and atonement for the South's defeat. In this respect Leonard

Voltmeier was a guilt-ridden Faust, certainly an image Simms created for himself. For Voltmeier, once a strong man, capable of any maneuver, brilliant and powerful, able to hold sway over many lives, was at last uncovered, forced to submit and fettered by his enemies. Simms saved this strange criminal by allowing him a heroic death, at last destroying his enemies and finding peace.[20]

But if this were all, *Voltmeier* would emerge only as an interesting tale, intensely personal, and entirely devoid of the politics of renewed hope in a new South. However, *Voltmeier*, like many of Simms' novels, was a *Bildungsroman*. The sub-character Wallace Fergus, Voltmeier's poor young cousin from South Carolina, who decided to visit Voltmeier in hopes of making his fortune, fell in love with Voltmeier's daughter Mignon. The most important character, therefore, was Fergus, who learned much from Voltmeier and came to reflect the hope of a new South. Fergus was taught that mankind and civilization would never progress, that society must come to understand itself. Voltmeier educated Fergus in the law, and the young man set up a thriving practice, only to be jailed for passing Voltmeier's counterfeit money. Voltmeier confessed, the young man was freed, married Mignon, and went to Europe with his bride, obviously to purge himself of the past and begin anew. When they returned to North Carolina, Fergus had had time to reflect on Voltmeier's fated life. He had learned that there was no such thing as a free and independent will, that man was "fettered by the circumstances and agencies of others." Fergus' education came in this realization; he was saddened but wise to the world and ready to face his own fate. Returned to his law practice, no doubt the young man would become a leading public servant, a man dedicated to the development of his section. Symbolically, Simms ended on the great hope of the New South. Voltmeier could see himself reborn in his own children and grandchildren, who were the true future of the New South.[21]

Using history and the novel as propaganda for a new South was not Simms' only method of aiding his section. Through his review column in the *Courier* and in many articles and speeches, the old man extolled the virtues of a new economic structure for the South. After a visit to the Florida sugar plantation of David Yulee, ex-senator and loyal Confederate, Simms called again for agricultural diversification. He wanted young businessmen to concern themselves with trade and commerce, and like Yulee, to learn the importance of building a sheep and cattle empire in the deep South. Back in South Carolina, in his famous column "Along the Highways and Byways" he praised the cotton manufacturing industry, which thrived under the management of William Gregg, Jr., son of Simms' old friend. Simms felt that it was time for all the people of the state to understand the value of mechanics and mechanical labor. The abundance of fuel and water power meant production of the state's own raw materials. He was proud of Orangeburg, which was destroyed by Sherman, rising from the ashes to become a manufacturing city. The College in Columbia was flourishing. It would turn out much-needed professional people—"patriotism, brains, and energy," as Simms expressed it—to create a prosperous state which would never again be subservient to Northern industry.[22] As in the antebellum days when Simms, romantically attached to the plantation, had realistically called for economic diversification, Simms now used his journalistic skills to promote a new and economically independent South Carolina.

Keen student of Southern society that he was, Simms wrote of the profound social revolution which was coming to his section. He called for a breakup of the large counties, since they were too unwieldy. The centers of population were too remote and isolated, and an affluent state needed increased population density and more county seats to foster centers of education and culture. Certain that the Negro would emigrate North, he advocated foreign immigration to South Carolina as a new source of skilled labor. He believed that the freedman could not work without supervision, and he argued that ex-slaves hindered the South's industrial growth. Simms, once the proud exponent of a slave system which he had felt was essential to Southern culture and society, wanted to exclude the black from the new and more sophisticated South.[23] If his views seem brutal and hypocritical in retrospect, one must remember that Simms' loyalty blinded him to anything but finding some means of achieving a financially independent South.

A realist about Southern society, a student of economics,

Simms also had the grace to combine materialism with a sense of beauty. Although he was tired, constantly sick to his stomach, and running high fevers throughout the last few months of his life, he accepted the opportunity to address the Charleston Floricultural and Horticultural Society in May 1870. His lecture entitled "The Sense of the Beautiful" exemplified his ability to combine economic reason with a romantic sense of mission. Filled with hope for the future, the speech enunciated the importance of beauty, finding it mostly in the work of the artist, whether writer, horticulturist, or student of Southern life. To rise above the crassness of the animal, Simms admonished his fellow Charlestonians to look at the beauty of life, both in nature and in society. A lifetime of trying to understand his own needs and duties had left him with a message of understanding for all Southerners. Sick, close to death, in constant pain, he could still deliver an address on the need for all Southerners to retain an aesthetic sense, that they might transcend their personal miseries and disasters to create a new world for themselves. While the South was bitterly involved in restoring its destroyed homes and businesses, Simms turned its mind to a contemplation of values. Giving the South a sense of mission, he also offered a style of life to his people.[24]

But this lecture was to be Simms' last statement. On June 11, 1870, he died in Charleston, the city which had taken so much from him and given so little in return. In death his name became a byword for heroism and dedication. He was praised from all quarters of the South, and his friends saw his life as one "suspended and merged into the imperceptible character of the artist." Some said he had been too much the politician, allowing his art to be subservient to South Carolina's struggle for independence. Simms would have been pleased, as his friends found subtle irony in his voice being heard from beyond the grave in the July issue of the *Nineteenth Century*. Better than the tolling of St. Michael's or the epitaph of a man who left his best work undone was that piece on freedom of speech. He viciously attacked Northern control over Southern presses and admonished his fellow writers for succumbing to threats. He damned the "wretches who rule us," and he was certain that the South would prevail. Realistically, he asked his fellow authors to defend the South, as he had done, by banding together. Yet his romantic conclusions best captured his own life, as he told Southerners that "the solution of the whole problem [Reconstruction] lies really in a catastrophe, more or less remote, which is yet inevitable."[25] Dedicated and myopic to the end, he died as he had lived, in a romantic haze of his own propaganda of self-deception.

To summarize Simms' career would be unnecessary. His actions revealed his life's work. His life could not be fully described as the life of a literary figure. But this should not diminish Simms' place in the intellectual and political history of the antebellum South. Having devoted a lifetime to the politics of literary propaganda in his obsession to create a united South, he became a symbol of Southern nationalism. He left a tradition of dedication to his state unsurpassed in the American experience. His plight was the tragedy of seeking to educate the South through personal devotion to a cause which was lost from the beginning. A sensitive, brilliant man of letters, he sacrificed his art willfully to an active public career. His best work of art was his own public life. Simms chose public life, and he fulfilled his public mission with an artist's flair and grace. Rarely has one man given so much, and so reflected his times, for so little reward.

NOTES

1. *Simms Letters*, 4: 315, 318-328, 329, 344, 345, 355-356, 365, 370-391; *Mercury*, Oct. 2, Dec. 13, 18, 21, 27, 1860, Feb. 4, March 2, 14, 16, Apr. 13, May 2, July 18, 1861; Caroline Glover to Caroline Gilman, Jan. 11, 1861, MSS, Caroline Gilman Papers, South Carolina Historical Society, Charleston. (Trent, *Simms*, pp. 261-262, claims that Simms had some influence on military policy. From a perusal of both William P. Miles' and David F. Jamison's correspondence there is no evidence of this influence. Nevertheless, Simms did convey a certain sense of urgency to his friends.)

2. *Simms Letters*, 4: 397-398; *Mercury*, Aug. 5, Dec. 10, 1863; SLM 34 (Feb.-March 1862): 101-105; Simms to William J. Rivers, May 31, 1862, Charles Carroll Simms Papers. See also Trent, *Simms*, pp. 272, 275-276, 278; Eaton, *Waning of the Old South Civilization*, pp. 94-98.

3. *The Daily South Carolinian*, July 10, 1862.

4. Simms to Hammond, Feb. 1, 1864, A. P. Aldrich to Hammond, May 3, 1864, Hammond Papers, Library of Congress; *Simms Letters*, 4: 437-439.

5. *Simms Letters*, 4: 457-459, 465; Hammond to Simms, Feb. 21, Apr. 15, June 12, Aug. 24, 1864, Hammond Papers, Library of Congress.

6. *Mercury*, Dec. 8, 1864; Hammond to Simms, Sept. 1, 1864, Hammond Papers, Library of Congress; *Simms Letters*, 4: 462; Trent, *Simms*, p. 279.

7. *Mercury*, Nov. 28, 1864; *Simms Letters*, 4: 471; tucked away in Hammond's Scrapbook of 1858 is a Simms poem "O Tempora! O Mores!" dedicated to Hammond's memory, Hammond Papers, Library of Congress. Also see Simms to Catherine E. Hammond, Oct. 25, 1869, Dec. 27, 1869, Feb. 3, 1870, Hammond Papers, Library of Congress.

8. *Simms Letters*, 4: 487, 484-486; also see Caroline Gilman to Eliza Gilman, Gilman Papers.

9. Columbia *Daily Phoenix*, Apr. 12, 1865; A. S. Salley, ed., *The Sack and Destruction of the City of Columbia*, by William Gilmore Simms (Atlanta, 1937), pp. 25, 29, 31, 39, 86-87, 82-83; see Trent, *Simms*, p. 283.

10. *Simms Letters*, 4: 500, 516; *Daily Phoenix*, June 15, 1865; see Jay B. Hubbell, ed., "Five Letters from George Henry Boker to William Gilmore Simms," *The Pennsylvania Magazine of History and Biography* 63 (1939): 66-67.

11. *Daily Phoenix*, March 21, May 4, 5, 1865; *Simms Letters*, 4: 510, 560.

12. *Courier*, Nov. 16, 1866; Simms to O. J. Victor, Dec. 17, 1865, letter from Simms (addressee unknown), Sept. 26, 1867, Simms to E. J. Mathews, Dec. 26, 1865, Charles Carroll Simms Papers; *Simms Letters*, 4: 620; 5: 17, 36, 38, 101, 125, 126, 275, 331; also see Edward Sculley Bradley, *George Henry Boker, Poet and Patriot* (Philadelphia, 1927), pp. 245-246.

13. Simms to Emily T. Goodwin, Dec. 25, 1868, Charles Carroll Simms Papers. Unfortunately there is no modern study of Reconstruction in South Carolina. See Neill W. Macaulay, Jr., "South Carolina Reconstruction Historiography," *SCHM*, 65 (Jan. 1964): 20-32. The best study of the period is still Francis Butler Simkins and Robert H. Woody, *South Carolina during Reconstruction* (Chapel Hill, 1932), see p. 18.

14. William Gilmore Simms, ed., *War Poetry of the South* (New York, 1867), viii; see also MSS article "Theory of Poetry," Henry Timrod Papers, South Caroliniana Library, University of South Carolina.

15. William Gilmore Simms, ed., *The Army Correspondence of Colonel John Laurens* (New York, 1867), pp. 9, 11, 13, 25, 27, 38-40, 48-49; Oliphant, "Historical Artist," p. 27; *Simms Letters*, 4: 572, 628; 5: 45, 121, 205, 251-252.

16. *Mercury*, Dec. 3, 1866; *Courier*, July 30, 1860, Feb. 8, Apr. 13, 1870.

17. *Courier*, May 10, 1866, Apr. 14, 1868.

18. Ibid., Nov. 13, 1866, Apr. 19, 1870; *Mercury*, Dec. 14, 1866.

19. *Simms Letters*, 5: 125-127, 153, 283, 285-286; *Courier*, June 4, 1867, Dec. 6, 1867, Jan. 28, 1868, June 1, July 3, 1869, March 29, 1870; *Mercury*, Dec. 12, 1866; Simkins and Woody, *S. C. During Reconstruction*, p. 355.

20. *Simms Letters*, 5: 139, 166; William Gilmore Simms, *Voltmeier*, unpublished MSS, Charles Carroll Simms Papers. I am grateful to Mrs. Oliphant and the late Donald Davidson for sharing their insight into the value of *Voltmeier* with me. See *Voltmeier*, pp. 46, 241, 454, 497, 507, 643, 682, 690. Trent, *Simms*, p. 312, mistakenly calls the novel merely a mountain romance.

21. *Voltmeier*, pp. 11, 17, 27, 241, 322, 327, 383, 475, 537, 601, 624, 669, 695-696.

22. *Simms Letters*, 5: 306-307, 308; *Courier*, "Flights to Florida," Feb. 27, March 5, 8, 14, 20, 1867; also see Jan. 27, June 7, 11, 12, 24, 25, 27, 1867.

23. *Courier*, Jan. 11, 16, 23, 28, 1867. (These articles are from Simms' "Highways and Byways" column.)

24. *Courier*, May 4, 1870, contains the text and review of "The Sense of the Beautiful." See *Simms Letters*, 5: 313, 316.

25. *The Nineteenth Century*, III, 2 (July 1870), 186-187, 184-185, III, 5 (Oct., 1870), 425-428; also see William Cullen Bryant, *Little Journeys to the Homes of American Authors* (New York, 1896), pp. 151-155; Charleston *News and Courier*, June 11, 1879; *The Unveiling of the Bronze Bust of William Gilmore Simms at White Point Garden* (Charleston, 1879).

Bibliography

I. MANUSCRIPTS

A. At Duke University, Durham, N. C.:
    Francis W. Pickens Papers
B. At the Institute of Early American History, Colonial Williamsburg Society, Williamsburg, Virginia:
    Nathaniel Beverly Tucker Papers
C. At the Library of Congress, Washington, D. C.:
    Franklin Harper Elmore Papers
    James Henry Hammond Papers
D. At the New York Public Library, New York City, N. Y.:
    Evert Augustus Duyckinck Papers
E. At the South Carolina Historical Society, Fire Proof Building, Charleston, S. C.:
    Caroline Gilman Papers
F. At the South Caroliniana Library, University of South Carolina, Columbia, S. C.:
    Milledge Bonham Papers
    Pierce Mason Butler Papers
    John C. Calhoun Papers [Many of these papers are on loan from other university archives.]
    James Chesnut, Jr., Papers
    Thomas Cooper Papers
    William H. Gist Papers
    James Hamilton Papers
    James Henry Hammond Papers

Paul Hamilton Hayne Papers
Paul Hamilton Hayne. *Politics of South Carolina.*
Samuel C. Jackson Papers
Ellison Summerfield Keitt Papers
Hugh Swinton Legaré Papers
Francis Lieber Papers
David James McCord Papers
George McDuffie Papers
Christopher Gustavus Memminger Papers
William Porcher Miles Papers
James L. Orr Papers
George Parks Papers
Benjamin F. Perry Papers
Francis W. Pickens Papers
Joel R. Poinsett Papers
Benjamin F. Porter Scrapbook, 1849-1850
William C. Preston Papers
Robert Barnwell Rhett Papers
Rutledge Family Papers
Charles Carroll Simms Papers
Edwin P. Starr Papers
Waddy Thompson Papers
Henry Timrod Papers
Beaufort Taylor Watts Papers
G. At the Southern Historical Collection, University of North
Carolina, Chapel Hill, N. C.:
Franklin Harper Elmore Papers
William Porcher Miles Papers
Orr-Patterson Papers
Benjamin F. Perry Journal, 1823-1863
Robert Barnwell Rhett Papers
Waddy Thompson Papers
Williams-Chesnut-Manning Papers

II. PUBLISHED DIARIES, CORRESPONDENCE,
SPEECHES, AND REMINISCENCES

Benton, Thomas Hart. *Thirty Years' View.* New York: D.
Appleton & Co., 1856.

Boker, George Henry. "Five Letters from George Henry Boker to William Gilmore Simms," edited by Jay B. Hubbell, *The Pennsylvania Magazine of History and Biography* 63 (1939).

Bryant, William Cullen. *Letters of a Traveler; or, Notes of Things Seen in America and Europe.* New York: G. P. Putnam, 1850.

Calhoun, John C. "Correspondence Addressed to John C. Calhoun, 1837-1849," edited by Chauncey S. Boucher and Robert P. Brooks, American Historical Association *Annual Report, 1929.* Washington: American Historical Association, 1930.

————. "Correspondence of John C. Calhoun," edited by J. Franklin Jameson, American Historical Association *Annual Report, 1899.* Washington: American Historical Association, 1900.

————. *The Works of John C. Calhoun,* edited by Richard K. Crallé. 6 vols. New York: D. Appleton & Co., 1851-1870.

A Compilation of the Messages and Papers of the Presidents, 1789-1902, Edited by James D. Richardson. 20 vols. Washington: Government Printing Office, 1903.

DeBow, James D. B. *The Political Annals of South Carolina,* by a citizen. Charleston: Office of Southern Quarterly Review, 1845.

Dissolution of the Union; Serious Reflections for the Citizens of South Carolina. By a friend of Union and Liberty. Charleston: W. Estill, 1832.

"Documents, Letters on Nullification in South Carolina, 1830-1834," edited by J. Franklin Jameson, *American Historical Review* 6 (July 1901).

Drayton, William Henry. *An Oration Delivered in the First Presbyterian Church, Charleston, on Monday, July 4, 1831, by the Honorable William Henry Drayton, to Which is Annexed, an Account of the Celebration of the 55th Anniversary of American Independence, by the Union and State Rights Party.* Charleston: W. S. Blain and J. S. Burges, 1831.

Elmore, Franklin Harper. *The Defense of the Bank of the State of South Carolina.* Columbia: Palmetto-State Banner, 1849.

Grayson, William J. "The Autobiography of William John Grayson," edited by Samuel Gaillard Stoney, *South Carolina Historical Magazine* 49-50 (1949-1950).

————. *Letter to His Excellency Whitemarsh B. Seabrook, Governor of the State of South-Carolina, on the Dissolution of the Union.* Charleston: A. E. Miller, 1850.

Hammond, James Henry. *An Address Delivered before the South-Carolina Institute, at Its First Annual Fair.* Charleston: Walker & James, 1849.

————. *Oration on the Life, Character, and Services of John C. Calhoun, delivered in Charleston, November 21, 1850, at the Request of the City Council.* Charleston: Walker & James, 1850.

————. *The Regina Coeli. Correspondence between the Honorable James H. Hammond and John H. B. Latrobe, Esq.* Baltimore: J. D. Toy, 1858.

————. *Selections from the Letters and Speeches of the Honorable James Henry Hammond of South Carolina.* New York: J. F. Trow & Co., 1866.

————. *Speech of James Henry Hammond at Barnwell Court House, October 29th, 1858.* Charleston: Walker & James, 1858.

Hayne, Paul Hamilton. "William Gilmore Simms," *Appleton's Journal of Popular Literature, Science, and Art,* July 30, 1870.

————. *A Collection of Hayne Letters,* edited by David Morley McKeithan. Austin: Univ. of Texas Press, 1944.

Hundley, Daniel R. *Social Relations in Our Southern States.* New York: H. B. Price, 1860.

Legaré, Hugh Swinton. *Writings of Hugh Swinton Legaré, consisting of a Diary of Brussells and Journal of the Rhine; Extracts from his Private and Diplomatic Correspondence; Orations and Speeches; and Contributions to the New York and Southern Reviews. Prefaced by a Memoir of His Life.* Edited by his sister. Charleston: D. Appleton & Co., 1845-1846.

Manigault, Gabriel. *The Signs of the Times.* New York (n. p.) n. d.

Martineau, Harriet. *Retrospect of Western Travel.* New York: Harper & Bros., 1838.

Moses, F. J. "How South Carolina Seceded, by the Private Secretary of Governor Pickens of South Carolina," *The Nickell Magazine*, December 1897.

Perry, Benjamin Franklin. *Reminiscences of Public Men, with Speeches and Addresses.* Greenville, S. C.: Shannon & Co., 1889.

———. *Speech of Honorable B. F. Perry, of Greenville District, delivered in the House of Representatives of South Carolina on the 11th December, 1850,* . . . . Charleston: J. B. Nixon, 1851.

Pinckney, Henry Laurens. *Oration on the Fourth of July, 1833.* Charleston, 1833.

Polk, James Knox. *The Diary of James K. Polk,* edited by Milo Milton Quaife. 4 vols. Chicago: A. C. McClurg & Co., 1910.

Porcher, Frederick Adolphus. "The Memoirs of Frederick Adolphus Porcher," edited by Samuel Gaillard Stoney, *South Carolina Historical Magazine* 47 (1946).

Rhett, Robert Barnwell. *Oration of the Honorable R. Barnwell Rhett, before the Legislature of South Carolina, November 28, 1850.* Columbia: A. S. Johnston, 1850.

Selby, Julian A. *Memorabilia and Anecdotal Reminiscences of Columbia, South Carolina.* Columbia: R. L. Bryan Co., 1905.

Simms, William Gilmore. *The Letters of William Gilmore Simms,* edited by Mary C. Simms Oliphant, Alfred Taylor Odell, and T. C. Duncan Eaves. 5 vols. Columbia: Univ. of South Carolina Press, 1952-1956.

Smith, William. *Speech at Spartanburg, South Carolina, August 1, 1831.* Columbia: Office of the Hive, 1832.

Taylor, Bayard, and Hayne, Paul Hamilton. *The Correspondence of Bayard Taylor and Paul Hamilton Hayne,* edited by Charles Duffy. Baton Rouge: Louisiana State Univ. Press, 1945.

Trescot, William H. *The Position and Course of the South.* Charleston: Walker & James, 1850.

Trollope, Frances. *Domestic Manners of the Americans.* 2 vols. London: Whittaker, Treacher & Co., 1832.

"Troup" (Isaac W. Hayne), *To the People of the South. Senator Hammond and the Tribune.* Charleston (n. p.), 1860.

III.   PUBLIC DOCUMENTS

The Address of the People of South Carolina, Assembled in Convention, to the People of the Slaveholding States of the United States. Charleston: Evans & Cogswell, 1860.

Appendix to the Congressional Globe; Thirty-fourth Congress, First Session. Washington: Government Printing Office, 1856.

The Charleston Directory, and Annual Register, for 1837 and 1838, edited by Daniel J. Dowling. Charleston: D. J. Dowling, 1837.

Condensed Proceedings of the Southern Convention, held at Nashville, Tennessee, June, 1850. Jackson, Miss.: Fall & Marshall, 1850.

The Congressional Globe; First Session of the Thirty-fifth Congress; Special Session of the Senate. Washington: Government Printing Office, 1858.

Extract of Minutes of the Charleston Chamber of Commerce. Charleston: By the Chamber, 1845.

Journal of the House of Representatives of South Carolina, 1844-1846. Columbia: State Printer, 1846.

Journal of the Public Proceedings of the Convention of the People of South Carolina, held 1860-'61. Together with the Ordinances Adopted. Charleston: Evans & Cogswell, 1860.

Journal of the State Convention of South Carolina; together with the Resolution and Ordinance. Columbia: Johnston & Cavis, 1852.

List of Tax Payers of Charleston for 1859. Charleston: Evans & Cogswell, 1860.

The Official Proceedings of the Democratic National Convention, held in 1860, at Charleston and Baltimore. Cleveland: Nevin's Print, 1860.

Proceedings of the Convention of 1832, in *State Papers on Nullification*. Boston: Beals, Homer, 1834.

Proceedings of the Democratic State Convention of South Carolina . . . 5th and 6th of May, 1856, ... Columbia: R. W. Gibbes, 1856.

Proceedings of the Great Southern Co-operation and Anti-Secession Meeting held in Charleston, September 23, 1851. Charleston: Walker & James, 1851.

Proceedings of the National Democratic Convention, May 30-31, 1860. Southern Guardian Steam-Power Press, 1860.

The Reports and Resolutions of the General Assembly of the State of South Carolina, 1847. Columbia: State Printer, 1847.

The Resolutions and Addresses, Adopted by the Southern Convention, held at Nashville, Tennessee, June 3d to 12th Inclusive, in the Year 1850. Nashville: H. M. Watterson, 1850.

Southern Editorials on Secession, edited by Dwight Lowell Dumond. New York: The Century Co., 1931.

State Documents on Federal Relations: The States and the United States. Vol. IV: *The Tariff and Nullification, 1820-1833*, edited by Herman V. Ames. Philadelphia: Univ. of Pennsylvania, 1902.

The Statutes at Large of South Carolina, 1682-1866. 13 vols. Columbia: State Printer, 1836-1875.

IV. NEWSPAPERS

Charleston *City Gazette and Commercial Daily Advertiser*. 1824-1833.

Charleston *Daily Courier*. 1828-1870.

Charleston *Evening News*. Odd copies, 1844-1856.

Charleston *Mercury*. 1828-1860.

Charleston *Southern Patriot*. Various copies, 1841-1848.

Columbia *Daily Phoenix*. 1865.

Columbia *South Carolinian*. Editorials and legislative reports, 1844-1846.

Columbia *Times*. Various issues, 1830-1831.

Greenville *Southern Patriot*. Odd copies, especially 1851-1855.

Greenville *Mountaineer*. Odd copies.

Palo Alto. August to November, 1848, entire.

Sumter *Black River Watchman*. Odd copies, 1850-1860.

V. MAGAZINES

The Album. Charleston, 1825.

The American Whig Review. New York, 1849-1850.

Appleton's Journal of Literature, Science, and Art. 1870.

The Cosmopolitan: An Occasional. Charleston, 1833.

DeBow's Review. New Orleans and Charleston, 1846-1860.

Godey's Lady's Book. Philadelphia, 1841.

Harper's New Monthly Magazine. New York, 1857.

The Magnolia, or Southern Monthly. Savannah and Charleston, 1840-1843.

Niles' National Register. Washington.

The Nineteenth Century. Charleston, 1869-1870.

The Orion. Atlanta and Charleston, 1842-1844.

The Pleiades and Southern Literary Gazette. Charleston, 1829.

The Rural Carolinian. Charleston, 1870.

Russell's Magazine. Charleston, 1857-1860.

Self-Instructor. Charleston, 1854.

Snowden's Ladies Companion. Charleston [?], 1841.

The Southern Literary Gazette. Charleston, 1828-1829.

Southern Literary Journal. Charleston, 1835-1839.

Southern Literary Messenger. Richmond, 1834-1864.

The Southern Quarterly Review. Charleston, 1847-1854.

Southern Review. Charleston, 1828-1832.

The Southern Rose. Charleston, 1832-1839.

The Southern and Western Monthly Magazine and Review, or Simms's Magazine. Charleston, 1845-1846.

VI.   WORKS BY SIMMS

Aryetos: or, Songs of the South. Charleston: John Russell, 1846, 1860.

The Army Correspondence of Colonel John Laurens, edited by William Gilmore Simms. New York: Bradford Club, 1867.

Atalantis: A Story of the Sea. New York: J & J Harper, 1832.

Beauchampe. 2 vols. Philadelphia: Lea & Blanchard, 1840 (later revised in one volume as *Charlemont.* New York: Redfield, 1856).

Border Beagles. 2 vols. Philadelphia: Carey & Hart, 1840.

The Book of My Lady. Philadelphia: Key & Biddle, 1833.

Carl Werner. 2 vols. New York: George Adlard, 1838.

The Cassique of Kiawah. New York: Redfield, 1859.

Castle Dismal. New York: Burgess, Stringer & Co., 1844.

The Charleston Book: A Miscellany in Prose and Verse. Charleston: Samuel Hart, 1845.

Charleston and Her Satirists. Charleston: James S. Burgess, 1848.

The City of the Silent: A Poem. Charleston: Walker & James, 1850.

Confession. 2 vols. Philadelphia: Lea & Blanchard, 1841.

Count Julian. New York: William Taylor, 1845.

The Damsel of Darien. 2 vols. Philadelphia: Lea & Blanchard, 1839.

"*Domestic Manners of the Americans,* by Mrs. Trollope," *The American Quarterly Review* 7 (1832): 109-133.

Donna Florida. Charleston: Burgess & James, 1843.

Early Lays. Charleston: A. E. Miller, 1827.

Egeria. Philadelphia: E. H. Butler & Co., 1853.

Eutaw. New York: Redfield, 1856.

Father Abbott. Charleston: Miller & Browne, 1849.

Flirtation at the Moultrie House. Charleston: Edward C. Councell, 1850.

The Forayers. New York: Redfield, 1855.

The Geography of South Carolina. Charleston: Babcock & Co., 1843.

The Golden Christmas; A Chronicle of St. John's Berkeley. Charleston: Walker, Richards & Co., 1852.

Grouped Thoughts and Scattered Fancies. Richmond: Wm. MacFarlane, 1845.

Guy Rivers. New York: Harper & Brothers, 1834, New York: Redfield, 1855.

Helen Halsey. New York: Burgess, Stringer & Co., 1845.

The History of South Carolina. Charleston: Babcock & Co., 1840, 1860.

Inauguration of the Spartanburg Female College, on the 22nd August, 1855, . . . Spartanburg: By the Trustees, 1855.

Katherine Walton. Philadelphia: A. Hart, 1851.

The Kinsmen. 2 vols. Philadelphia: Redfield, 1841 (later retitled *The Scout*, New York, 1854).

Lays of the Palmetto: A Tribute to the South Carolina Regiment, in the War with Mexico. Charleston: John Russell, 1848.

The Life of Captain John Smith, the Founder of Virginia. Philadelphia: Geo. F. Cooledge & Co., 1846.

The Life of the Chevalier Bayard. New York: Harper & Bros., 1847.

The Life of Francis Marion. Boston: G. F. Cooledge & Bro., 1856.

The Life of Nathanael Greene, Major-General in the Army of the Revolution. New York: George F. Cooledge & Brother, 1849.

The Lily and the Totem. New York: Baker & Scribner, 1850.

Lyrical and Other Poems. Charleston: Ellis & Neufville, 1827.

Marie de Berniere. Philadelphia: Lippincott, Grambo & Co., 1853.

Martin Faber. New York: Harper & Bros., 1833. 2 vols., 1837.

Mellichampe. 2 vols. New York: Harper & Bros., 1836.

Michael Bonham. Richmond: John R. Thompson, 1852.

"Miss Martineau on Slavery," *Southern Literary Messenger* 3 (1837): 641-657.

Monody on the Death of General Charles Cotesworth Pinckney. Charleston: Gray & Ellis, 1825.

"The Morals of Slavery," in *The Pro-Slavery Argument*. Charleston: Walker, Richards & Co., 1852.

Norman Maurice; or, the Man of the People. Richmond: John R. Thompson, 1851.

The Partisan. 2 vols. New York: Harper & Bros., 1835.

Pelayo. 2 vols. New York: Harper & Bros., 1838.

Poems, Descriptive, Dramatic, Legendary, and Contemplative. 2 vols. New York: Redfield, 1853.

The Power of Cotton. New York: Chatterton & Brother, 1856.

The Prima Donna. Philadelphia: L. A. Godey, 1844.

The Remains of Maynard Davis Richardson, with a Memoir of His Life. Charleston: O. A. Roorbach, 1833.

Richard Hurdis. 2 vols. Philadelphia: Carey & Hart, 1838.

The Sack and Destruction of the City of Columbia, edited by A. S. Salley. Atlanta: Oglethorpe Univ. Press, 1937.

Self-Development. Milledgeville, Ga.: Thalian Society, 1847.

The Sense of the Beautiful. Charleston: Walker, Evans & Cogswell, 1870.

The Social Principle: The True Source of National Permanence. Tuscaloosa, Ala.: Erosophic Society of the Univ. of Alabama, 1843.

The Sources of American Independence. Aiken, S. C.: The Council, 1844.

Southern Passages and Pictures. New York: Geo. Adlard, 1839.

Southward Ho! New York: Redfield, 1854.

A Supplement to the Plays of William Shakespeare. New York: Geo. F. Cooledge & Bro., 1848.

The Sword and the Distaff. Charleston: Walker, Richards & Co., 1852 (later retitled *Woodcraft*).

The Tri-Color; or, the Three Days of Blood in Paris. London: Wigfall & Davis, 1830.

Vasconselos. New York: Redfield, 1853.

Views and Reviews in American Literature, History, and Fiction. First Series, edited by C. Hugh Holman. Cambridge, Mass: Harvard Univ. Press, 1962. Second Series. New York: Wiley & Putnam, 1846.

The Vision of Cortes, Cain, and Other Poems. Charleston: J. S. Burges, 1829.

Voltmeier. From an unpublished MSS, South Caroliniana Library.

War Poetry of the South, edited by William Gilmore Simms. New York: Charles B. Richardson, 1867.

The Wigwam and the Cabin. New York: Wiley & Putnam, 1845.

The Yemassee. 2 vols. New York: Harper & Bros., 1835.

VII.   SECONDARY WORKS: HISTORY

Andrews, Columbus. *Administrative County Government in South Carolina.* Chapel Hill: Univ. of North Carolina Press, 1933.

Auer, J. Jeffrey, ed. *Antislavery and Disunion, 1858-1861; Studies in the Rhetoric of Compromise and Conflict.* New York: Harper & Row, 1963.

Bancroft, Frederic. *Calhoun and the South Carolina Nullification Movement.* Baltimore: Johns Hopkins Univ. Press, 1928.

Boucher, Chauncey Samuel. *The Nullification Controversy in South Carolina.* Chicago: Univ. of Chicago Press, 1916.

––––––. *The Secession and Co-operation Movements in South Carolina, 1848 to 1852.* (Washington University Studies, vol. 5, no. 2.) St. Louis: Washington Univ., 1918.

––––––. *Sectionalism, Representation, and the Electoral Question.* (Washington University Studies, vol. 4, pt. 2, no. 1.) St. Louis: Washington Univ., 1916.

––––––. *South Carolina and the South on the Eve of Secession, 1852 to 1860.* (Washington University Studies, vol. 6, no. 2.) St. Louis: Washington Univ., 1919.

Bridge, John S. C. *A History of France from the Death of Louis XI.* 5 vols. Oxford: Clarendon Press, 1921-1936.

Callcott, George H. *History in the United States 1800-1860.* Baltimore: Johns Hopkins Univ. Press, 1970.

Cardozo, Jacob N. *Reminiscences of Charleston*. Charleston: J. Walker, 1866.

Carpenter, Jesse T. *The South as a Conscious Minority, 1789-1861*. New York: New York Univ. Press, 1930.

Clark, W. A. *History of Banking Institutions Organized in South Carolina Prior to 1860*. Columbia: The State Company, 1922.

Cole, Arthur Charles. *The Irrespressible Conflict, 1850-1865*. New York: MacMillan, 1934.

———. *The Whig Party in the South*. Gloucester, Mass.: Peter Smith, 1962.

Cotterill, Robert S. *The Old South: The Geographic, Economic, Social, Political, and Cultural Expansion, Institutions, and Nationalism of the Ante-bellum South*. Glendale, Calif.: Arthur H. Clark, 1936.

Craven, Avery Odelle. *Civil War in the Making, 1815-1860*. Baton Rouge: Louisiana State Univ. Press, 1959.

———. *The Coming of the Civil War*. New York: Charles Scribner's Sons, 1942.

———. *The Growth of Southern Nationalism, 1848-1861*. Baton Rouge: Louisiana State Univ. Press, 1953.

———. *The Repressible Conflict, 1830-1861*. Baton Rouge: Louisiana State Univ. Press, 1939.

Crenshaw, Ollinger. *The Slave States and the Presidential Election of 1860*. Baltimore: Johns Hopkins Univ. Press, 1945.

Dickinson, G. Lowes. *The Greek View of Life*. New York: Doubleday, Page & Co., 1925.

Dodd, William E. *The Cotton Kingdom: A Chronicle of the Old South*. New Haven: Yale Univ. Press, 1919.

Du Bois, W. E. B. *The Suppression of the African Slave Trade in the United States of America*. New York: Longmans, Green, & Co., 1896.

Dumond, Dwight Lowell. *The Secession Movement, 1860-1861*. New York: MacMillan, 1931.

Easterby, James H. *History of the College of Charleston*. Charleston [n. p.], 1935.

———, ed. *The South Carolina Rice Plantation*. Chicago: Univ. of Chicago Press, 1945.

Frederickson, George M. *The Black Image in the White Mind*. New York: Harper & Row, 1971.

Freehling, William H. *Prelude to Civil War; the Nullification Controversy in South Carolina, 1816-1836*. New York, Harper & Row, 1966.

Gaines, Francis Pendleton. *The Southern Plantation: A Study in the Development and the Accuracy of a Tradition*. New York: Columbia Univ. Press, 1924.

Genovese, Eugene D. *The Political Economy of Slavery*. New York: Pantheon, 1966.

———. *The World the Slaveholders Made*. New York: Pantheon, 1969.

Green, Fletcher M. *Constitutional Development in the South Atlantic States*. Chapel Hill: Univ. of North Carolina Press, 1930.

Hammond, Bray. *Banks and Politics in America from the Revolution to the Civil War*. Princeton: Princeton Univ. Press, 1957.

Hesseltine, William Best. *The South in American History*. New York: Prentice-Hall, 1951.

Houston, David Franklin. *A Critical Study of Nullification in South Carolina*. New York: Longmans, Greene, & Co., 1908.

Howe, Daniel W. *Political History of Secession, to the Beginning of the American Civil War*. New York: G. P. Putnam's Sons, 1914.

Ingle, Edward. *Southern Sidelights: A Picture of Social and Economic Life in the South a Generation before the War*. New York: T. V. Crowell & Co., 1896.

Irving, John B. *The South Carolina Jockey Club*. Charleston: Russell & Jones, 1857.

Jenkins, William Sumner. *Pro-Slavery Thought in the Old South*. Chapel Hill: Univ. of North Carolina Press, 1935.

Johnson, Gerald W. *The Secession of the Southern States*. New York: G. P. Putnam's Sons, 1933.

King, William L. *The Newspaper Press of Charleston, South Carolina*. Charleston: E. Perry, 1882.

Kraus, Michael. *A History of American History*. New York: Farrar & Rinehart, 1937.

Link, Arthur and Patrick, Rembert (eds.). *Writing Southern History*. Baton Rouge: Louisiana State Univ. Press, 1966.

Lloyd, Arthur Young. *The Slavery Controversy, 1831-1860*. Chapel Hill: Univ. of North Carolina Press, 1939.

Lofton, John M. *Insurrection in South Carolina: The Turbulent World of Denmark Vesey*. Yellow Springs, O.: Antioch Press, 1964.

Luxon, Norval Neil. *Niles' Weekly Register, News Magazine of the Nineteenth Century*. Baton Rouge: Louisiana State Univ. Press, 1947.

McGrane, Reginald C. *The Panic of 1837; Some Financial Problems of the Jacksonian Era*. Chicago: Univ. of Chicago Press, 1924.

Macy, Jesse. *Political Parties in the United States, 1846-1861*. New York: MacMillan, 1917.

Morgan, Edmund S. *The Birth of the Republic, 1763-89*. Chicago: Univ. of Chicago Press, 1956.

Nevins, Allan. *Ordeal of the Union*. 4 vols. New York: Charles Scribners' Sons, 1947-1950.

Nichols, Roy Franklin. *The Disruption of American Democracy*. New York: MacMillan, 1948.

Overdyke, William Darrell. *The Know-Nothing Party in the South*. Baton Rouge: Louisiana State Univ. Press, 1950.

Ratchford, Benjamin U. *American State Debts*. Durham: Duke Univ. Press, 1941.

Ravenel, Mrs. St. Julien. *Charleston, the Place and the People*. New York: MacMillan, 1907.

Rhett, Robert Goodwyn. *Charleston, an Epic of Carolina*. Richmond: Garrett & Massie, 1940.

Russel, Robert Royal. *Economic Aspects of Southern Sectionalism, 1840-1861*. Urbana, Ill.: Univ. of Illinois Press, 1924.

Schaper, William August. "Sectionalism and Representation in South Carolina," American Historical Association *Annual Report, 1900*, Vol. I. Washington: American Historical Association, 1901.

Schultz, Harold S. *Nationalism and Sectionalism in South Carolina, 1852-1860*. Durham: Duke Univ. Press, 1950.

Simkins, Francis Butler and Woody, Robert H. *South*

Carolina during Reconstruction. Chapel Hill: Univ. of North Carolina Press, 1932.

Simms, Henry Harrison. *Emotion at High Tide, Abolition as a Controversial Factor, 1830-1845*. Richmond (privately printed), 1960.

Sirmans, M. Eugene. *Colonial South Carolina; a Political History*. Chapel Hill: Univ. of North Carolina Press, 1966.

Smith, Alfred Glaze. *Economic Readjustment of an Old Cotton State, South Carolina, 1820-1860*. Columbia: Univ. of South Carolina Press, 1958.

Smith, Justin Harvey. *The Annexation of Texas*. New York: The Baker & Taylor Co., 1911.

Snowden, Yates. *History of South Carolina*. 5 vols. Chicago: Lewis Publishing Co., 1920.

The South in the Building of the Nation. 13 vols. Richmond: Southern Historical Publication Society, 1909-1913.

Stanwood, Edward. *American Tariff Controversies in the Nineteenth Century*. 2 vols. Boston: Houghton Mifflin Co., 1903.

Sydnor, Charles Sackett. *The Development of Southern Sectionalism, 1819-1848*. Baton Rouge: Louisiana State Univ. Press, 1948.

Taussig, Frank William. *The Tariff History of the United States*. New York: G. P. Putnam's Sons, 1931.

Taylor, George Rogers. *The Transportation Revolution*. New York: Harper & Row, 1951.

Taylor, Rosser Howard. *Ante-bellum South Carolina: A Social and Cultural History*. Chapel Hill: Univ. of North Carolina Press, 1942.

Thompson, Edgar T., ed. *Perspectives on the South: Agenda for Research*. Durham: Duke Univ. Press, 1967.

Tindall, George B., ed. *The Pursuit of Southern History*. Baton Rouge: Louisiana State Univ. Press, 1966.

Turner, Frederick Jackson. *The United States, 1830-1850: The Nation and Its Sections*. New York: Henry Holt, 1935.

Van Deusen, John George. *Economic Basis of Disunion in South Carolina*. New York: Columbia Univ. Press, 1928.

Wallace, David Duncan. *South Carolina: A Short History*,

1520-1948. Chapel Hill: Univ. of North Carolina Press, 1951.

————. *History of South Carolina*. 4 vols. New York: The American Historical Society, 1934.

Wender, Herbert. *The Southern Commercial Conventions*. (The Johns Hopkins University Studies in Historical and Political Science, vol. 48, no. 4.) Baltimore: Johns Hopkins Univ. Press, 1930.

Wolfe, John Harold. *Jeffersonian Democracy in South Carolina*. (The James Sprunt Studies in History and Political Science, vol. 24, no. 1.) Chapel Hill: Univ. of North Carolina Press, 1940.

Wooster, Ralph A. *The Secession Conventions of the South*. Princeton: Princeton Univ. Press, 1962.

VIII. SECONDARY WORKS:

INTELLECTUAL AND LITERARY

Arieli, Yehoshua. *Individualism and Nationalism in American Ideology*. Baltimore: Penguin Books, 1966.

Bassett, John Spencer. *The Middle Group of American Historians*. New York: MacMillan, 1917.

Bigland, Eileen. *The Indomitable Mrs. Trollope*. New York: Lippincott, 1954.

Boorstin, Daniel J. *The Americans: The National Experience*. New York: Vintage, 1966.

Brooks, Van Wyck. *The World of Washington Irving*. New York: E. P. Dutton & Co., 1944.

Cash, Wilbur J. *The Mind of the South*. New York: A. A. Knopf, 1941.

Cowie, Alexander. *The Rise of the American Novel*. New York: American Book Co., 1948.

Curti, Merle. *The Growth of American Thought*. New York: Harper & Bros., 1943.

Eaton, Clement. *The Freedom of Thought-Struggle in the Old South*. New York: Harper & Row, 1964.

————. *The Growth of Southern Civilization, 1790-1860*. New York: Harper & Row, 1961.

————. *The Mind of the Old South*. Baton Rouge: Louisiana State Univ. Press, 1964.

————. *The Waning of the Old South Civilization, 1860's-1880's*. Athens, Ga.: Univ. of Georgia Press, 1968.

Ekirch, Arthur A., Jr. *The Idea of Progress in America, 1815-1860*. New York: Columbia Univ. Press, 1944.

Elkins, Stanley M. Slavery: *A Problem in American Institutional and Intellectual Life*. New York: Universal Library, 1963.

Erskine, John. *Leading American Novelists*. New York: H. Holt & Co., 1910.

Hoole, William Stanley. *The Ante-bellum Charleston Theatre*. Tuscaloosa, Ala.: Univ. of Alabama Press, 1946.

Houghton, Walter E. *The Victorian Frame of Mind*. New Haven: Yale Univ. Press, 1964.

Hubbell, Jay B. "Literary Nationalism in the Old South," in *American Studies in Honor of William Kenneth Boyd*, edited by David Kelly Jackson. Durham: Duke Univ. Press, 1940.

————. *The South in American Literature, 1607-1900*. Durham: Duke Univ. Press, 1954.

Jackson, David Kelly, ed. *American Studies in Honor of William Kenneth Boyd*. Durham: Duke Univ. Press, 1940.

Jameson, J. Franklin. *The History of Historical Writing in America*. New York: Greenwood Press, 1969.

Kaul, A. N. *The American Vision*. New Haven: Yale Univ. Press, 1969.

Leisy, Ernest E. *The American Historical Novel*. Norman, Okla.: Univ. of Oklahoma Press, 1950.

Levin, David. *History as Romantic Art*. New York: Harcourt, Brace, & World, Inc., 1963.

Link, Samuel Albert. *Pioneers of Southern Literature*. Nashville: Barbee & Smith, 1896.

Matthiessen, F. O. *American Renaissance*. New York: Oxford Univ. Press, 1941.

McDowell, Tremaine. "The Negro in the Southern Mind Prior to 1850," in Seymour L. Gross and John E. Hardy (eds.), *Images of the Negro in American Literature*. Chicago: Univ. of Chicago Press, 1968.

McIlwaine, Shields R. *The Southern Poor-White—from Lubberland to Tobacco Road*. Norman, Okla.: Univ. of Oklahoma Press, 1939.

Meyers, Marvin. *The Jacksonian Persuasion*. New York: Vintage, 1960.

Miller, Perry. *The Raven and the Whale*. New York: Harcourt, Brace & World, Inc., 1956.

Minor, Benjamin Blake. *The Southern Literary Messenger, 1834-1864*. New York: The Neale Publishing Co., 1905.

Moore, Arthur K. *The Frontier Mind*. New York: McGraw-Hill, 1963.

Moses, Montrose J. *The Literature of the South*. New York: T. V. Crowell & Co., 1910.

Mott, Frank Luther. *A History of American Magazines*. 4 vols. Cambridge, Mass.: Harvard Univ. Press, 1930-1957.

Osterweis, Rollin G. *Romanticism and Nationalism in the Old South*. New Haven: Yale Univ. Press, 1949.

Parrington, Vernon Louis. *Main Currents in American Thought*. 2 vols. New York: Harcourt, Brace & Co., 1927.

Parks, Edd Winfield. *Segments of Southern Thought*. Athens, Ga.: Univ. of Georgia Press, 1938.

Phillips, Ulrich Bonnell. "Literary Movement for Secession," in *Studies in Southern History and Politics*. New York: Columbia Univ. Press, 1914.

Pope-Hennessy, Una. *Three English Women in America*. London: E. Benn Ltd., 1929.

Rutherford, Mildred Lewis. *The South in History and Literature, a Hand-Book of Southern Authors from the Settlement of Jamestown, 1607, to Living Writers*. Athens, Ga.: Univ. of Georgia Press, 1906.

Schenk, H. G. *The Mind of the European Romantics*. New York: Anchor Books, 1969.

Sellers, Charles G., ed. *The Southerner as American*. Chapel Hill: Univ. of North Carolina Press, 1960.

Skotheim, Robert Allen. *American Intellectual Histories and Historians*. Princeton: Princeton Univ. Press, 1966.

Smith, Bernard. *Forces in American Criticism; a Study in the History of American Literary Thought*. New York: Harcourt, Brace & Co., 1939.

Smith, Henry Nash. *Virgin Land: The American West as Symbol and Myth*. New York: Vintage Books, 1957.

Spencer, Benjamin T. *The Quest for Nationality; an American Literary Campaign*. Syracuse, N. Y.: Syracuse Univ. Press, 1957.

Spiller, Robert Edward and Others. *Literary History of the United States*. 4 vols. New York: MacMillan, 1955-1963.

Stafford, John. *The Literary Criticism of "Young America"; a Study in the Relationship of Politics and Literature 1837-1850*. Berkeley, Calif.: Univ. of California Press, 1952.

Stanton, Frank. *The Leopard's Spots*. Chicago: Univ. of Chicago Press, 1960.

Stephenson, Wendell Holmes. *The South Lives in History*. Baton Rouge: Louisiana State Univ. Press, 1955.

Taylor, William R. *Cavalier and Yankee*. New York: George Braziller, 1961.

Van Doren, Carl. *The American Novel*. New York: MacMillan, 1921.

Van Tassell, David. *Reading America's Past*. Chicago: Univ. of Chicago Press, 1960.

Ward, John William. *Andrew Jackson: Symbol for an Age*. New York: Oxford Univ. Press, 1955.

————. *Red, White, and Blue: Men, Books, and Ideas in American Culture*. New York: Oxford Univ. Press, 1969.

Wauchope, George A. *Writers of South Carolina*. Columbia: The State Co., 1910.

————. "Literary South Carolina," *Bulletin No. 133 of the University of South Carolina*, December 1, 1923.

Williams, T. Harry. *Romance and Realism in Southern Politics*. Athens, Ga.: Univ. of Georgia Press, 1961.

Wish, Harvey. *The American Historian*. New York: Oxford Univ. Press, 1960.

IX.   SECONDARY WORKS: BIOGRAPHY

Allen, John D. "Philip Pendleton Cooke: Virginia
Gentleman, Lawyer, Hunter, and Poet," in *American Stud-
ies in Honor of William Kenneth Boyd*, edited by David
Kelly Jackson. Durham: Duke Univ. Press, 1940.

Ambler, Charles Henry. *Thomas Ritchie; a Study in Virginia
Politics*. Richmond: Bell Book & Stationary Co., 1913.

Arvin, Newton. *Herman Melville*. New York: Sloan, 1950.

Bayless, Joy. *Rufus Wilmot Griswold*. Nashville: Vanderbilt
Univ. Press, 1943.

Becker, Kate Harbes. *Paul Hamilton Hayne: Life and Letters*. Belmont, N. C.: Outline Co., 1951.

Bigelow, John. *William Cullen Bryant*. Boston: Houghton,
Mifflin & Co., 1890.

*Biographical Directory of the American Congress, 1774-
1927*. Washington: Government Printing Office, 1928.

Bohner, Charles. *John Pendleton Kennedy*. Baltimore:
Johns Hopkins Univ. Press, 1967.

Bradley, Edward Sculley. *George Henry Boker, Poet and
Patriot*. Philadelphia: Univ. of Pennsylvania Press, 1927.

Capers, Gerald M. *John C. Calhoun, Opportunist: a Reappraisal*. Gainesville, Fla.: Univ. of Florida Press, 1960.

Capers, Henry D. *The Life and Times of Christopher
Gustavus Memminger*. Richmond: Everett Waddey Co.,
1893.

Carson, James Petigru. *Life, Letters and Speeches of James
Louis Petigru, the Union Man of South Carolina*. Washington: W. H. Lowdermilk & Co., 1920.

Chitwood, Oliver P. *John Tyler, Champion of the Old
South*. New York: D. Appleton-Century Co., 1939.

Coit, Margaret L. *John C. Calhoun, an American Portrait*.
Boston: Houghton, Mifflin, 1950.

Coulter, E. Merton. *John Jacobus Flourney, Champion of
the Common Man in the Antebellum South*. Savannah:
Georgia Historical Society, 1942.

Craven, Avery Odelle. *Edmund Ruffin, Southerner: A Study
in Secession*. New York: D. Appleton & Co. 1932.

Current, Richard N. *John C. Calhoun*. New York: Washington Square Press, 1963.

Dahl, Curtis. *Robert Montgomery Bird*. New York: Twayne Publishers, Inc., 1963.

Dyer, Brainerd. *Zachary Taylor*. Baton Rouge: Louisiana State Univ. Press, 1946.

Freidel, Frank. *Francis Lieber, Nineteenth Century Liberal*. Baton Rouge: Louisiana State Univ. Press, 1947.

Fuess, Claude Moore. *Daniel Webster*. 2 vols. Boston: Little Brown, & Co., 1930.

Going, Charles Buxton. *David Wilmot, Free-Soiler*. New York: D. Appleton & Co., 1924.

Grayson, William J. *James Louis Petigru, a Biographical Sketch*. New York: Harper & Bros., 1866.

Green, E. L. *George McDuffie*. Columbia: The State Co., 1936.

Grossman, James. *James Fenimore Cooper*. Stanford, Calif.: Stanford Univ. Press, 1949.

Hamilton, Holman. *Zachary Taylor*. 2 vols. Indianapolis: Bobbs-Merrill, 1941-1951.

Hayne, Paul Hamilton. *Lives of Robert Young Hayne and Hugh Swinton Legaré*. Charleston: [Privately Printed], 1878.

Hedges, William L. *Washington Irving: An American Study, 1802-1832*. Baltimore: Johns Hopkins Univ. Press, 1965.

Hoover, Merle M. *Park Benjamin*. New York: Columbia Univ. Press, 1948.

Hunt, Gaillard. *John C. Calhoun*. Philadelphia: G. W. Jacobs & Co., 1908.

Jervey, Theodore D. *Robert Y. Hayne and His Times*. New York: MacMillan, 1909.

Kibler, Lillian Adele. *Benjamin F. Perry, South Carolina Unionist*. Durham: Duke Univ. Press, 1946.

Klein, Philip Shriver. *President James Buchanan, a Biography*. University Park, Pa.: Pennsylvania State Univ. Press, 1962.

Lerner, Gerda. *The Grimké Sisters from South Carolina, Rebels against Slavery*. Boston: Houghton, Mifflin, 1967.

Malone, Dumas. *The Public Life of Thomas Cooper, 1759-1839*. New Haven: Yale Univ. Press, 1926.

McCormac, Eugene I. *James K. Polk, a Political Biography*. Berkeley, Calif.: Univ. of California Press, 1922.

Meigs, William M. *The Life of John Caldwell Calhoun*. 2 vols. New York: Neale Publishing Co., 1917.

Merritt, Elizabeth. *James Henry Hammond*. Baltimore: Johns Hopkins Univ. Press, 1923.

Nye, Russell Blaine. *George Bancroft, Brahmin Rebel*. New York: A. A. Knopf, 1944.

Osgood, Samuel. *Evert Augustus Duyckinck, His Life, Writings and Influence*. Boston: D. Clapp & Son, 1879.

Parks, Edd Winfield. *William Gilmore Simms as Literary Critic*. Athens, Ga.: Univ. of Georgia Press, 1961.

Pease, Otis A. *Parkman's History: The Historian as Literary Artist*. New Haven: Yale Univ. Press, 1953.

Quinn, Arthur Hobson. *Edgar Allen Poe*. New York: Appleton-Century-Crofts, 1941.

Rhea, Linda. *Hugh Swinton Legaré, a Charleston Intellectual*. Chapel Hill: Univ. of North Carolina Press, 1934.

Ridgely, Joseph V. *John Pendleton Kennedy*. New York: Twayne Publishers, Inc., 1966.

————. *William Gilmore Simms*. New York: Twayne Publishers, Inc., 1962.

Rippy, J. Fred. *Joel R. Poinsett, Versatile American*. Durham: Duke Univ. Press, 1935.

Stewart, Randell. *Nathaniel Hawthorne: A Biography*. New Haven: Yale Univ. Press, 1948.

Stillé, Charles J. *The Life and Services of Joel R. Poinsett*. Philadelphia: (Reprint from Pa. Magazine of History and Biography), 1888.

Styron, Arthur. *The Cast-Iron Man, John C. Calhoun and American Democracy*. New York: Longmans, Rreen & Co., 1935.

Trent, William Peterford. *William Gilmore Simms*. Boston: Houghton, Mifflin   Co., 1892.

Wagenknecht, Edward Charles. *Henry Wadsworth Longfellow: A Portrait of an American Humanist*. New York: Oxford Univ. Press, 1966.

Wallace, Daniel. *Political Life and Services of the Honorable Robert Barnwell Rhett; Also His Speech at Grahamville, South Carolina, July 4, 1859*. Cahaba, Ala. [n. p.], 1859.

Waples, Dorothy. *The Whig Myth of James Fenimore Cooper*. New Haven: Yale Univ. Press, 1938.

White, Laura A. *Robert Barnwell Rhett: Father of Secession*. New York: American Historical Association, 1931.

Williams, Stanley T. *Life of Washington Irving*. 2 vols. New York: Oxford Univ. Press, 1935.

Wiltse, Charles M. *John C. Calhoun*. 3 vols. Indianapolis: Bobbs Merrill, 1944-1951.

Wish, Harvey. *George Fitzhugh, Propagandist of the Old South*. Baton Rouge: Louisiana State Univ. Press, 1943.

X.   SECONDARY WORKS: ARTICLES

Ames, Herman V. "John C. Calhoun and the Secession Movement of 1850," *American Antiquarian Society* (1918).

Applewhite, Joseph Davis. "Some Aspects of Society in Rural South Carolina in 1850," *North Carolina Historical Review* 29 (1952): 39-63.

Bean, W. G. "Anti-Jeffersonianism in the Ante-Bellum South," *North Carolina Historical Review* 12 (1935): 103-124.

Boucher, Chauncey Samuel. "The Annexation of Texas and the Bluffton Movement in South Carolina," *Mississippi Valley Historical Review* 6 (1919): 3-33.

————. "*In Re* That Aggressive Slavocracy," *Mississippi Valley Historical Review* 8 (1921): 13-79.

————. "Representation and the Electoral Question in Antebellum South Carolina," *Proceedings of the Mississippi Valley Historical Association for 1915-1916* 9 (1917): 110-125.

Buck, Paul Herman. "The Poor Whites of the Ante-bellum South," *American Historical Review* 21 (1925): 41-54.

Capers, Gerald M. "A Reconsideration of John C. Calhoun's Transition from Nationalism to Nullification," *Journal of Southern History* 14 (1948): 34-48.

Cauthen, Charles Edward. "South Carolina's Decision to Lead the Secession Movement," *North Carolina Historical Review* 18 (1941): 360-372.

Cochrane, John. "The Charleston Convention," *Magazine of American History* 14 (1885): 148-153.

Conger, John L. "South Carolina and the Early Tariffs," *Mississippi Valley Historical Review* 5 (1919): 415-433.

Craven, Avery Odelle. "The Turner Theories and the South," *Journal of Southern History* 5 (1939): 291-314.

Crenshaw, Ollinger. "The Speakership Contest of 1859-1860," *Mississippi Valley Historical Review* 29 (1942): 323-338.

Crowell, John. "A Reminiscence of Dr. Simms," *The Rural Carolinian* 2 (1870): 62.

Dillard, A. W. "William Gilmore Simms and Augustus Baldwin Longstreet," *Nineteenth Century* 3 (1870): 425-430.

Donald, David. "The Proslavery Argument Reconsidered," *Journal of Southern History* 37 (1971): 3-18.

Ellen, John C., Jr. "Political Newspapers of the South Carolina Up Country, 1850-1859: A Compendium," *South Carolina Historical Magazine* 63 (1962): 86, 158.

Fitzsimmons, Matthew A. "Calhoun's Bid for the Presidency, 1841-1844," *Mississippi Valley Historical Review*, 38 (1951): 39-60.

Foran, William A. "Southern Legend: Climate or Climate of Opinion," *The Proceedings of the South Carolina Historical Association, 1956*, 6-22.

Foster, Herbert D. "Webster's Seventh of March Speech and the Secession Movement, 1850," *American Historical Review* 27 (1922): 245-270.

Freehling, William H. "Spoilsmen and Interests in the Thought and Career of John C. Calhoun," *Journal of American History* 52 (1965): 25-42.

Fuller, John D. P. "The Slavery Question and the Movement to Acquire Mexico," *Mississippi Valley Historical Review* 21 (1934): 31-48.

Govan, Thomas P. "Was Plantation Slavery Profitable?" *Journal of Southern History* 8 (1942): 513-555.

Guilds, John C., Jr. "Bryant in the South: A New Letter to Simms," *Georgia Historical Quarterly* 37 (1953).

———. "Simms's First Magazine, *The Album*," *Studies in Bibliography, Papers of the Bibliographical Society of the University of Virginia* 8 (1956).

———. "Simms's Views on National and Sectional

Literature, 1825-1845," *North Carolina Historical Review* 34 (1957): 393-405.

————. "William Gilmore Simms and the Cosmopolitan," *Georgia Historical Quarterly* 41 (1957): 31-41.

Hayne, Paul Hamilton. "Ante-Bellum Charleston," *The Southern Bivouac* 1 (1885): 257-268, 327, 336.

Higham, John. "The Changing Loyalties of William Gilmore Simms," *Journal of Southern History* 9 (1943): 210-223.

Holman, C. Hugh. "The Influence of Scott and Cooper on Simms," *American Literature* 23 (1951): 203-218.

————. "Simms and the British Dramatists," *Publications of the Modern Language Association* 65 (1950): 346-359.

————. "The Status of Simms," *American Quarterly* 10 (1958): 181-185.

————. "William Gilmore Simms' Picture of the Revolution as a Civil Conflict," *Journal of Southern History* 15 (1949): 442-462.

Hoole, William S. "A Note on Simms's Visits to the Southwest," *American Literature* 6 (1934): 334-336.

————. "William Gilmore Simms's Career as Editor," *Georgia Historical Quarterly* 29 (1935): 47-54.

Jarrell, Hampton M. "Simms's Visit to the Southwest," *American Literature* 5 (1933): 29-35.

Kibler, Lillian A. "Unionist Sentiment in South Carolina in 1860," *Journal of Southern History* 9 (1938): 346-366.

Lander, Ernest M., Jr. "The Calhoun-Preston Feud, 1836-1842," *South Carolina Historical Magazine* 59 (1958): 24-37.

————. "Dr. Thomas Cooper's Views in Retirement," *South Carolina Historical Magazine* 54 (1953): 173-181.

Lord, C. W. "Young Lewis Wigfall: South Carolina Politician and Duelist," *South Carolina Historical Magazine* 59 (1958): 96-112.

Macaulay, Neill W., Jr. "South Carolina Reconstruction Historiography," *South Carolina Historical Magazine* 65 (1964): 20-32.

Malone, Dumas. "Thomas Cooper and the State Rights Movement in South Carolina, 1823-1830," *North Carolina Historical Review* 3 (1926): 184-197.

Mason, Edward G. "A Visit to South Carolina in 1860,"
    Atlantic Monthly, 53 (1884): 241-250.
Morris, J. Allen. "The Stories of William Gilmore Simms,"
    American Literature 14 (1942): 32ff.
Nichols, Roy Franklin. "The Kansas-Nebraska Act: A Cen-
    tury of Historiography," *Mississippi Valley Historical Re-
    view* 63 (1956): 187-212.
Oliphant, Mrs. A. D. "William Gilmore Simms—Historical
    Artist," *Report of the Secretary and Treasurer for 1942,
    University of South Caroliniana Society* (Columbia,
    1943), pp. 1-19.
Owsley, Frank L. "The Fundamental Cause of the Civil
    War: Egocentric Sectionalism," *Journal of Southern
    History* 7 (1941): 3-18.
Page, Elizabeth F. "The Romance of Southern Journalism,"
    The Taylor-Trotwood Magazine 11 (1910): 140-148.
Perkins, Howard C. "A Neglected Phase of the Movement
    for Southern Unity, 1847-1852," *Journal of Southern
    History* 12 (1946): 153-203.
Ramsdell, Charles W. "The Natural Limits of Slavery Ex-
    pansion," *Mississippi Valley Historical Review* 16
    (1929): 151-171.
Randall, James G. "The Blundering Generation," *Mississip-
    pi Valley Historical Review* 27 (1940): 3-28.
Raybeck, Joseph G. "The Presidential Aspirations of John
    C. Calhoun, 1844-1848," *Journal of Southern History* 14
    (1948): 331-356.
Ryan, Frank W. "The Opinions of Editor William Gilmore
    Simms of the *Southern Quarterly Review*, 1849-1854,"
    *The Proceedings of the South Carolina Historical Asso-
    ciation*, 1959, pp. 25-35.
Sioussat, St. George L. "Tennessee, the Compromise of
    1850, and the Nashville Convention," *Mississippi Valley
    Historical Review* 2 (1915): 313-347.
Spencer, Benjamin T. "A National Literature, 1837-1855,"
    American Literature 8 (1936).
Stephenson, Nathaniel W. "Southern Nationalism in South
    Carolina, in 1851," *American Historical Review* 36
    (1931): 314-335.
Stephenson, Wendell Holmes. "William P. Trent as a

Historian of the South," *Journal of Southern History* 15 (1949): 285-299.

Stern, Madeleine B. "John Russell: 'Lord John' of Charleston," *North Carolina Historical Review* 26 (1949): 285-299.

Stewart, Randell. "Hawthorne's Contributions to the Salem *Advertiser*," *American Literature* 5 (1933): 327-341.

Stoney, Samuel Gaillard. Review of *The South in American Literature, South Carolina Historical Magazine* 56 (1955): 123.

Takaki, Ronald. "The Movement to Reopen the African Slave Trade in South Carolina," *South Carolina Historical Magazine* 66 (1965): 38-54.

Tandy, Jeannette Reed. "Pro-Slavery Propaganda in American Fiction in the Fifties," *South Atlantic Quarterly* 21 (1922): 41-50, 170-178.

Taylor, Rosser Howard. "The Gentry of Antebellum South Carolina," *North Carolina Historical Review* 17 (1940): 114-131.

Thatcher, Harold W. "Calhoun and Federal Reinforcement of State Laws," *American Political Science Review* 36 (1942): 873-880.

Tucker, Robert C. "James Henry Hammond and the Southern Convention," *The Proceedings of the South Carolina Historical Association, 1960*, pp. 4-14.

Venable, Austin L. "The Conflict between the Douglas and Yancey Forces in the Charleston Convention," *Journal of Southern History* 8 (1942): 226-241.

Voigt, Gilbert P. "The 'Periclean Age' of Beaufort," *South Carolina Historical Magazine* 58 (1957): 218-223.

Wade, Richard C. "The Vesey Plot: A Reconsideration," *Journal of Southern History* 30 (1964): 143-161.

Weir, Robert M. "The Harmony We Were Famous For: An Interpretation of Pre-Revolutionary South Carolina Politics," *William and Mary Quarterly*, Third Series 26 (1969): 473-501.

Welsh, John R. "William Gilmore Simms, Critic of the South," *Journal of Southern History* 26 (1960): 201-214.

Welter, Rush. "The History of Ideas in America: An Essay

in Redefinition," *Journal of American History* 51 (1965): 599-614.

Whaley, Grace W. "A Note on Simms's Novels," *American Literature* 2 (1930): 173-174.

White, Laura A. "The National Democrats in South Carolina, 1852-1860," *South Atlantic Quarterly* 28 (1929): 370-389.

Wiltse, Charles M. "A Critical Southerner: John C. Calhoun on the Revolution of 1848," *Journal of Southern History* 15 (1949): 299-310.

Wooster, Ralph A. "An Analysis of the Membership of Secession Conventions in the Lower South," *Journal of Southern History* 24 (1958): 360-368.

————. "Membership of the South Carolina Secession Convention," *South Carolina Historical Magazine* 55 (1954): 185-196.

Young, Anna W. "William Gilmore Simms," *Electra: A Magazine of Pure Literature* 3 (1885): 421-423.

XI. DISSERTATIONS AND THESES

Barre, Elizabeth F. "A Study of the Indian in William Gilmore Simms's Novels and Short Stories." Unpublished Master's thesis, Department of English, University of South Carolina, 1941.

Bass, Robert Duncan, ed. "The Autobiography of William J. Grayson." Unpublished Ph.D. dissertation, Department of English, University of South Carolina, 1933.

Belser, William G., Jr. "William Gilmore Simms, Maecenas of the Old South." Unpublished Master's thesis, Department of English, University of South Carolina, 1933.

Herbert, Edward T. "William Gilmore Simms as Editor and Critic." Unpublished Ph.D. dissertation, Department of English, University of Wisconsin, 1958.

Jarrell, Hampton McNeely. "William Gilmore Simms, Realistic Romancer." Unpublished Ph.D. dissertation, Department of English, Duke University, 1932.

Ryan, Frank Winkler, Jr. "The *Southern Quarterly Review,*

1842-1857: A Study in Thought and Opinion in the Old South." Unpublished Ph.D. dissertation, Department of English, University of North Carolina, 1955.

Stirton, Thomas. "Party Disruption and the Rise of the Slavery Extension Controversy, 1840-1846." Unpublished Ph.D. dissertation, Department of History, University of Chicago, 1956.

Straka, Gerald Milton. "The Influence of Thomas Carlyle on the Old South, 1848-1865," Unpublished Master's thesis, Department of History, University of Virginia, 1953.

Tucker, Robert C. "James Henry Hammond, South Carolinian." Unpublished Ph.D. dissertation, Department of History, University of North Carolina, 1958.

Welsh, John R. "The Mind of William Gilmore Simms." Unpublished Ph.D. dissertation, Department of English, Vanderbilt University, 1951.

XII.   BIBLIOGRAPHICAL AIDS

Easterby, James Harold. *Guide to the Study and Reading of South Carolina History*. Columbia: Historical Commission of South Carolina, 1949-1950.

Salley, Alexander Samuel. *Catalogue of the Salley Collection of the Works of William Gilmore Simms*. Columbia: State Co., 1943.

Turnbull, Robert James. *Bibliography of South Carolina, 1563-1950*. Charlottesville, Va.: Univ. of Virginia Press, 1956.

Wegelin, Oscar. *A Bibliography of the Separate Writings of William Gilmore Simms of South Carolina, 1806-1870*. Hattiesburg, Miss.: The Book Farm, 1941.

Index